Penguin Books
THE PENGUIN BOOK
OF AUSTRALIAN AUTOBIOGRAPHY

✦ ✦ ✦ ✦

John and Dorothy Colmer have taught English at the
University of Adelaide where John Colmer was until
recently the Jury Professor of English Language and
Literature. They have individually written on a wide
range of subjects and co-edited four previous
anthologies.

Penguin Books Australia Ltd,
487 Maroondah Highway, P.O. Box 257
Ringwood, Victoria 3134, Australia
Penguin Books Ltd,
Harmondsworth, Middlesex, England
Penguin Books,
40 West 23rd Street, New York, N.Y. 10010, U.S.A.
Penguin Books (Canada) Limited,
2801 John Street, Markham, Ontario, Canada L3R 1B4
Penguin Books (N.Z.) Ltd,
182–190 Wairau Road, Auckland 10, New Zealand

First published by Penguin Books Australia, 1987

Introduction and Selection Copyright © John and Dorothy Colmer, 1987

Typeset in Goudy Old Style by Abb-typesetting Pty Ltd,
Collingwood, Victoria
Made and printed in Australia by
The Book Printer, Maryborough, Victoria 3465

CIP

The Penguin book of Australian autobiography.

Includes index.
ISBN 0 14 007513 5.

1. Australia – Biography. I. Colmer, John, 1921–   .
II. Colmer, Dorothy.

920'.094

THE
PENGUIN BOOK
OF AUSTRALIAN
AUTOBIOGRAPHY

Introduced and Edited by
John and Dorothy Colmer

◆ ◆ ◆ ◆

PENGUIN BOOKS

CONTENTS

♦ ♦ ♦ ♦

INTRODUCTION

*To have been young, and then to grow older, and finally
to die is a very mediocre form of human existence; this
belongs to every animal. But the unification of the
different stages of life . . . is the task set for human beings.*

                                        (Kierkegaard)

Autobiography is both a form of literary striptease and an archaeology of the self. As the art of confession, revelation and self-discovery, it has its roots in religion, as St Augustine's *Confessions* reminds us. Even today it retains a confessional strain. Whether the invention of the Venetian mirror produced the Renaissance self-portrait or a new concern with the self produced the mirror is still a matter of debate. But certainly from the Romantic period onwards writers such as Rousseau, Wordsworth and De Quincey created some of their best works in the form of self-portraits. It proved the ideal form for exploring the Romantic preoccupation with the self, the supreme importance of childhood experience (Wordsworth's 'The Child is Father of the Man') and the acute tensions felt between the individual and society in a mechanised age. It also proved an expansive and hospitable form in which to achieve unity of being in an increasingly fragmented world. To many twentieth-century writers, however, this Romantic search for a permanent core of being within a process of constant changes seems an illusion. Thus, Roland Barthes deliberately frustrates the reader's attempts to create a unity from the fragments of his past life. And Patrick White uses a form of literary cubism in *Flaws in the Glass* to create multiple and often contradictory images of the self.

In autobiography the writer and the subject are formally the same, even when the past self appears a complete stranger and the sense of fragmentation is overwhelming. 'The voice of the writer and the person described are experienced by the reader as a living unity', remarks A. O. J. Cockshut.[1] Yet behind such a unity lies a dynamic and dialectical relationship, as Dorothy Hewett makes clear in 'Autobiographically Speaking'. In atomic physics, Heisenberg discovered the indeterminacy principle, the principle that scientific objectivity can never be achieved, because the instruments of atomic measurement, in the very process of measuring, change that which is to be measured. In autobiography there is a double indeterminacy principle at work. Firstly, the observer who is a measurer of his past self changes the object in the very process of observation and recreation. And, secondly, the transformation of the past self changes the nature of the observer, who is never the same at the end of the work as at the moment of writing the first page. Hal Porter is a striking example. The romantic Werther-like young man wandering on the Williamstown pier at the beginning of *The Paper Chase* is very different from the young man the reader left at the end of *The Watcher on the Cast-Iron Balcony*, and his attitude towards the death of his mother is very different. The process of recreating his past self has transformed his present writing self.

The impulse to write the story of one's life is particularly strong in new and rapidly changing countries. 'This story is all about myself,' Miles Franklin states at the opening of *My Brilliant Career?* Her ensuing address to her 'dear fellow Australians' makes it clear that she has

---

1 A. O. J. Cockshut, *The Art of Autobiography in 19th and 20th Century England*, Yale University Press, New Haven and London, 1984, p. 216.

a truth to tell about her country as well as herself. Over fifty years later, in *Country and Calling*, the distinguished historian Sir Keith Hancock tells his readers that he proposes to record his education – 'giving that word the meaning that Henry Adams gave it – a man's endeavour to discover himself in relation to his native land and his work and his idea of history.' Donald Horne actually incorporates the word 'education' into the title of his autobiography, *The Education of Young Donald*, calling it an example of 'sociography' rather than autobiography, because 'the central character is presented as a social animal.' Many of the extracts in this anthology illustrate the fact that in Australia the impulse to record a hitherto unrecorded world, to chart rapid social changes and to discover the truth about national identity has been as strong as the impulse to discover the self, and, moreover, is inseparable from it.

The personal element is slight in the earliest attempts to describe the new country. These are the explorers' journals. But the situation is very different in the highly sensational convict memoirs. In these, the writer is his own hero. The memoirs are almost indistinguishable from picaresque novels; they are rogues' tales full of trickery, daring adventure and boastful triumphs over the forces of law and order. The *Memoirs of James Hardy Vaux* appeared as early as 1819. For the author the work served to demonstrate his superior powers and the injustice of his punishment, while for his readers it offered an exciting narrative of crime and a vivid picture of life in the penal colony. Vaux, Cash and Mortlock, although far from reliable witnesses, present a very different picture of the penal system from Marcus Clarke's in *His Natural Life*. They reveal the various opportunities for self-advancement that existed within that system. They delight in their powers to exploit and outwit a repressive society. Although they possess the monstrous egotism that Stendhal thought necessary for all autobiography, they lack the equally necessary powers of self-analysis and self-knowledge.

Now that the first-hand accounts of ordinary folk have attained a new importance in reconstructing the past we are unlikely to ignore the sociological value of convict memoirs or of such autobiographical sketches as those of Rolf Boldrewood, whose *Old Melbourne Memories* (1884) contrasts the Melbourne of the early 1840s with the rich and bustling city of the 1880s. Boldrewood also records his youthful excitement as a new settler taking up his first run, Squattlesea Mere. 'My run!

My own station! How fine a sound it had, and how fine a thing it was that I should have the sole occupancy – almost ownership – of about 50,000 acres.' These words bring alive a whole phase of Australian social history.

In his classic study, Roy Pascal draws a clear distinction between memoir and autobiography, the first concerned mainly with other people and outward events, the second with the history of the self.[2] But it would be both pedantic and irrational to observe such a distinction in this anthology, since the two modes are often inseparable in Australia. From the convict memoirs of Vaux and others to *The Education of Young Donald*, what Horne describes as the 'attempt to show what social history can be like when told through *people*', has been a recurrent element. But books of amusing anecdotes like Kym Bonython's *Ladies' Legs and Lemonade*, the factual memoirs of the great and famous, and ghosted autobiographies of the stars of the sporting and show biz worlds have no place in this anthology, since they normally lack both literary distinction and that peculiar inwardness of truth that is the mark of authentic autobiography.

Roy Pascal also distinguishes between 'straight' autobiography and autobiographical fiction, but to exclude the latter in the following extracts would be to deny the reader the pleasure of seeing how such writers as Miles Franklin, Henry Handel Richardson, George Johnston and David Malouf express the exciting process of self-discovery in the form of fiction. It would also exclude the other pleasure of comparing 'straight' and fictional accounts, as one can by comparing Franklin's *My Brilliant Career?* and *Childhood at Brindabella*, Richardson's *The Getting of Wisdom* and *Myself When Young*, and Malouf's *Johnno* and *12 Edmondstone Street*.

2 Roy Pascal, *Design and Truth in Autobiography*, Routledge & Kegan Paul, London, 1960, pp. 3–9. The following titles indicate the fresh interest taken in this genre: Richard N. Coe, *When the Grass Was Taller: Autobiography and the Experience of Childhood*, Yale University Press, New Haven & London, 1984; James Olney (ed.) *Autobiography: Essays Theoretical and Critical*, Princeton University Press, N.J., 1980. John Pilling, *Autobiography and Imagination: Studies in Self-Scrutiny*, Routledge & Kegan Paul, 1981; William C. Spengemann, *The Forms of Autobiography: Episodes in the History of a Literary Genre*, Yale University Press, New Haven and London, 1980.

Deconstructive criticism has made us more aware that all our constructions of reality – historical, scientific or imaginative – are fictive. They are imaginative constructs. Viewed thus Hal Porter's autobiography *The Watcher on the Cast-Iron Balcony* is as much a piece of fictive discourse as George Johnston's famous autobiographical novel *My Brother Jack*. Nevertheless, useful distinctions can be made. The novelist, unlike the autobiographer, is free to invent situations and characters, while the reader is able to see all the main characters, including the narrator or autobiographical hero, both from within and without. The writer of fiction is free to invent significant dialogue to express the clash of characters and ideas. He is free to invent a plot out of real life events. The autobiographer, on the other hand, is more limited. As the Scots poet Edwin Muir complains in his *Autobiography* (1954), he has 'to stick to facts and try to fit them in where they fit in', a phrase which curiously suggests not only factual restraint but also the author's possession or creation of a superior structure of truth ('where they fit in'), which somehow transcends mere adherence to facts. He has, as Hal Porter insists, to be especially truthful about the world of childhood, knowing that he alone can say what it was like. 'No one but I will know if a lie be told, therefore I must try for the truth which is the blood and breath and nerves of the elaborate and important facts.' Autobiographers cannot see themselves from the outside with complete objectivity, although they may invent various techniques for establishing themselves as objects for detached contemplation, an 'other' in relation to the writing 'I'. To achieve such detachment Donald Horne mockingly calls himself 'young Donald' and sometimes 'D. R. Horne'; similarly, Bernard Smith adopts a variety of names to identify his earlier selves, thus making his autobiography a parable about naming and the sense of identity, while Hal Porter skilfully switches from the pronoun 'I' to the impersonal 'he' when he wishes to create a more objective and dispassionate view of his past self.

In an autobiography the other characters exist mainly in relation to the autobiographer, even when they are as memorable as Hal Porter's mother, who continues to sing the songs of the music hall on her death bed, or Robin Eakin's eccentric father, a Kings Cross doctor who lived for years in the same house as his mother-in-law and her sisters but never spoke to them. Compared with English autobiography however, Australian is less rich in a supporting cast of colourful eccentrics.

What, then, are some of the distinguishing marks of Australian autobiography? A facetious answer might be that the dunny or outside lavatory occupies a place quite unknown in European autobiography. It is the sacred site of sexual initiation, the throne of solitary contemplation and the lurking place of the deadly red-back spider. For Barbara Hanrahan, as for many male writers, 'at night the lavatory became a confessional booth, an altar to the past.' A more serious answer is that Australian autobiography is primarily secular. The struggle for self-identity rarely involves revolt against an oppressive religious creed, as it does for example in Edmund Gosse's *Father and Son* and other classics of European autobiography. This is not to say that religion plays no part. It does. Bernard Smith describes the conflicting claims of his mother's Roman Catholicism, Old Dad's Bible readings, the Salvation Army Sunday School and his foster-mother's Congregationalism; Paul Hasluck records his upbringing in a Salvation Army household; Vincent Buckley gives a vivid picture of his Catholic education in Melbourne. But for none of these writers does the climax of self-discovery coincide with a dramatic moment of religious acceptance or rejection. Perhaps only in Australian autobiography could a moment of potential religious conversion be fixed by such a sentence as Bernard Smith's: 'It was the first week of November; the year Wotan won the Melbourne Cup'; only in Australian autobiography could British-born Graham McInnes discover his Australian identity in angry reaction to English bodyline bowling.

It is not patriarchal religious authority that the growing Australian child has to escape but an authoritarian educational system and the demand for social conformity. The picture that emerges from Australian autobiography is of a strongly authoritarian society, intolerant of human differences, timidly conventional, highly class-conscious, thoroughly materialistic and utilitarian in its values, and either distrustful or positively hostile towards the arts. It is a very different picture from the one described by Russel Ward in *The Australian Legend*, which celebrates myths about the noble bushman, the free democratic spirit and an egalitarian society. It was an egalitarianism that did not extend to 'protected' Aboriginals who had their own mythology and scale of values, as is evident in Dick Roughsey's *Moon and Rainbow*.

One scholar, Richard Coe, detects a common dialectical pattern in most Australian autobiographies.[3] It consists first of a glimpse of an innocent rural paradise, second of a plunge into a suburban or urban world of cultural materialism and mediocrity, which must be rejected to discover the true self, and third the discovery that 'Australia is to be found neither wholly in its magic, nor yet wholly in its ugliness, but in the two elements taken together, their force of opposition still intact.' Over-schematic as this may appear when we remember how Donald Horne found primitive nature in Sydney and sophisticated society in Muswellbrook, it does draw attention to the fact that the quest for personal identity involves asking fundamental questions about national culture and identity.

In recreating the worlds that formed them and from which they felt obliged to escape, many of the writers give memorable accounts of childhood houses and gardens, family rituals, popular songs, and the impact of the early cinema and radio on the pattern of family life. These first-hand accounts of a rapidly changing world are especially valuable to the social historian. But to the writers some details acquire a symbolic significance and serve to define the whole pattern and meaning of their lives. They become, in James Olney's phrase 'metaphors of the self'.[4] For Hal Porter, the cast-iron balcony in his childhood house comes to symbolise the solitude, detachment and objectivity required by the artist. For David Malouf, a brass jardiniere containing ill-assorted oddments symbolises the endless quest of the Self for a lost Other. When Patrick White says 'Till well into my life, houses, places, landscape meant more to me than people', he probably speaks for the majority of Australian autobiographers.

Yet landscape plays a smaller part than one might expect from the evidence of Australian poetry and painting. Donald Horne provides a possible reason when he confesses that he was totally incapable of recording his youthful impressions of the Blue Mountains because of his ignorance of nature and the lack of a literary tradition. 'Since the grapes also reminded me of John Keats, when I looked at the valley I

3 Richard N. Coe, 'Portrait of the Artist as a Young Australian: Childhood, Literature and Myth', *Southerly*, XLI (1981), 126–62.
4 James Olney, *Metaphors of the Self: The Meaning of Autobiography*, Princeton University Press, N.J., 1972.

wondered how John Keats would have described it. I had no way of describing it. I did not know the names of anything I saw. Australia was an inadequate country, not written about in good literature.' The naturalist A. H. Chisholm confirms one of Horne's points when he writes in his significantly titled autobiography *The Joy of the Earth* that there 'was no place in the curriculum for natural history, and thus we were not taught even the simplest facts in the story of the world about us, as contained in the rocks and plants and birds.'

As if to compensate for their ignorance of the natural world, Australian autobiographers describe their urban landscapes in great detail. 'I am a city child', one of Barbara Hanrahan's fugue sequences begins, and her world is 'a concrete one', 'hammered by a ceaseless rain of cigarette packets, sweet papers, chewing-gum, dog shit, and gobs of yellow phlegm'. For both Barbara Hanrahan and Bernard Smith it is the suburban garden rather than the untouched Australian bush that becomes the image of an Eden once enjoyed but now 'a garden that was not a garden', but where 'death was all about'.

Self-doubt, disenchantment and gratitude for small mercies play an important part in Australian autobiography. The sense of 'the Uncertain Self', which Professor Heseltine sees as a recurrent element in Australian literature, is more obvious in autobiography than in any other form.[5] It is as apparent in Donald Horne's anxious truculence at Sydney University as in Hal Porter's desire to 'escape oneself, the versions of the self compelled into existence by others'. The conflicting loyalties towards European and Australian cultural models is only one source of self-doubt for the embryonic artist, but it is an important one. There is also the struggle between the developing self and the pressures of a highly conformist society. Contempt for the intellect, worship of sport and a deep suspicion towards the arts have made it difficult in Australia for the artist as a young man to pursue his calling with any confidence.

The position has been even more difficult for women, as many of the writers included in this anthology testify, from Miles Franklin to Joyce Nicholson. It was not until the age of forty-nine that Joyce Nicholson

5 Harry Heseltine, 'The Uncertain Self: Notes on the Development of Australian Literary Form', *Review of National Literatures*, special issue on Australia, ed. L. A. C. Dobrez, vol. 11, 1982.

overcame those self-doubts enforced upon her by a male-dominated society and discovered that she had the necessary talents to take over her father's run-down publishing firm and make it a great success. In her case, as in so many others in life, she had accepted her subordinate and ill-paid position because of her deep love for a man, her father. Even the life of a great battler like Kylie Tennant was dominated by the expectations of her tyrannical father and her demanding husband. The new wave of feminist autobiography should prove a great liberating force in Australian society.

The voices of new migrants and Aborigines are beginning to be heard through autobiography. These too should help to change national consciousness. In such first-hand accounts as Mary Rose Liverani's of arrival in Australia as a child and Kevin Gilbert's of his early life, the reader comes to see the misleading nature of such stereotyping labels as 'migrant' and 'Aboriginal'. We see the experience of individuals from the inside with a consequent increase in our sympathetic understanding and humanity.

Perspective is all-important in autobiography. Alan Marshall learned that to return to a time when the grass always seemed taller, he needed to go out walking with his three-year-old granddaughter, keeping his head always level with hers. Clem Christesen, in his reminiscences of his Townsville boyhood, recalls Walter de la Mare's question to Russell Brain 'Can you go back in memory to your childhood and if so, how big are you then? Can you remember putting your fingers on the edge of the table when your eyes were first level with it?' Hal Porter registers the significance of the first time he looked into the eyes of a boy his own height and saw in the face an image of human mortality. Contrasting perspectives are often the means of differentiating and linking past and present.

Pattern is even more crucial. A book of extracts can give some sense of the rich diversity of Australian autobiography, but it can do little to suggest the process by which individual writers discover the truth about themselves by uncovering a pattern in their lives and creating a literary structure to embody that pattern. With some writers, however, it has been possible to illustrate something of this process. The extracts from Bernard Smith's *The Boy Adeodatus* form a clear pattern, while those from *The Watcher on the Cast-Iron Balcony* show how Porter sees his life as a series of initiations and how the discovery of the self is made

made through writing about the other – mainly his mother. The whole book is structured around his love of her, in life and in death. This is only an extreme form of a process common to many autobiographies: the achievement of self-definition through exploring relationships with others. Porter's meeting with Victor first establishes the pattern and the sustaining theatrical metaphor: 'Victor is my first playmate and, though scarcely a friend and scarcely loved, is a first reading for the rehearsal for the first scene of the first act in the long comedy of friends I am stumbling through.' Family and friends serve this important but subordinate role in defining the self. But fathers are less important than brothers (who perhaps are more manageable as father-substitutes), other siblings go unnamed, close male friendships are unexpectedly rare for a country that still cherishes the myth of mateship. Love too plays a minor role. Patrick White's moving tribute to a love that has survived the strains and stresses of over forty years stands out like a beacon of light in a dark loveless world.

The greatest single landmark in the history of Australian autobiography was the publication of Hal Porter's *The Watcher on the Cast-Iron Balcony* in 1963. This proved beyond question that sophisticated fictional techniques could be applied to personal reminiscences in order to transform them into a fine art. Among many others, George Johnston was profoundly influenced by Porter's example. Nevertheless, the outstanding success of A. B. Facey's *A Fortunate Life* suggests that there is still a place for a vividly told tale by a largely uneducated man, always provided that the teller has lived an interesting life, has a good memory, is observant, sensitive, and does not put on literary airs and graces. Such a tale of youthful hardship as Facey tells is a testament to the strength and fortitude of ordinary folk in the face of adversity. And the same is true of Alan Marshall's popular trilogy, which begins with his boyhood triumph over the effects of polio in *I Can Jump Puddles* and ends with his success as a writer in *In Mine Own Heart*.

The fact that biography and autobiography are two of the most popular forms of reading today suggests that the often proclaimed 'death of the author' is something of a myth. Both forms satisfy a basic curiosity in the mysteries of the human personality and the processes of growth and fulfilment. They also illuminate the extent to which human beings are moulded by domestic and social pressures. In the case of famous writers, their autobiographies provide us with fascinating insights into patterns of early reading, literary influences and much else besides. Only the famous become the subject of biographies and truth is subordinated to public praise. Autobiography, on the other hand, presents us with fallible creatures more like ourselves and, because the writers place themselves in the centre of the world they recreate, we live in and through their experience with peculiar immediacy.

At the time when oral history and the 'slice' method of reconstructing the past are being canonised in official bi-centenary histories, it is important that the unique value of literary autobiography should be recognised. The truth it presents is the product of the writer's unique handling of language. On the other hand, the onlooker's account of 'how it was' is as likely to be a muddled memory of newspaper reports or a borrowing of journalistic cliché as a vivid record of personal experience. Of this there is a memorable example in Stephen Spender's autobiography *World Within World* (1951). When interviewed, his fellow firemen in the London Blitz described what they had seen not in their own words, which they distrusted, but in the tired clichés of the daily press. In reading autobiography we as readers actively participate in the long and often painful process of searching for the truth about the self and its relation to the ever changing social world. Apart from the unique insights that autobiography may give into personal psychology and social process, it should create an ineradicable scepticism towards the official myths offered us by our literary critics and social historians.

PROLOGUE

♦ ♦ ♦ ♦

MILES FRANKLIN

♦ *My Brilliant Career?*

Possum Gully, near Goulburn,
N.S. Wales, Australia, 1st March, 1899

MY DEAR FELLOW AUSTRALIANS,
Just a few lines to tell you that this story is all about myself – for no
other purpose do I write it.

I make no apologies for being egotistical. In this particular I
attempt an improvement on other autobiographies. Other autobiographies weary one with excuses for their egotism. What matters
it to you if I am egotistical? What matters it to you though it should
matter that I am egotistical?

This is not a romance – I have too often faced the music of life to
the tune of hardship to waste time in snivelling and gushing over
fancies and dreams; neither is it a novel, but simply a yarn – a *real*
yarn. Oh! as real, as really real – provided life itself is anything
beyond a heartless little chimera – it is as real in its weariness and
bitter heartache as the tall gum-trees, among which I first saw the
light, are real in their stateliness and substantiality.

ALAN MARSHALL

♦ *I Can Jump Puddles*

This book is the story of my childhood. In these pages I have described those influences and those incidents that helped to make me what I am.

But I wanted to do much more than record the experiences of a little boy faced with the problem of his crutches; I wanted to give a picture of a period that has passed. The men and women here described are a product of that period and they too are passing. The influences that made them self-reliant, forthright and compassionate, have given way to influences that can develop characters just as fine, but the mould has changed and the product is different.

To give a picture of life at that time, I have gone beyond the facts to get at the truth. I have sometimes altered scenes, made composite characters when this was necessary, changed time sequences to help the continuity and introduced dialogue that those who shared my experiences of the horse-days may find confusing.

I ask their pardon. A book of this nature demands a treatment that facts do not always supply; the truth it seeks to establish can only be revealed with the help of imagination.

HAL PORTER

♦ *The Paper Chase*

An autobiographical writer, one who rides a horse to catch a horse, rounds up in half a century of jog-trotting, cantering, and outright galloping a limitless host of characters. He is compelled, therefore, severely to limit the number of them he lets out at one time from the overcrowded concentration camp crowning the ridge of his mind, from that Ark straining at the seams like a lunatic asylum or bargain-sale department store on the Ararat of memory. Were he to attempt to let all free, the avalanche would dance and roar over him, mouthing the unmouthable, scorching him to flinders, mashing him to silence and nothing beneath a torrent of flaming soles. Out of control, the cascade of square-open mouths and hyper-eager eyes, of hair streaming like a storm of oriflammes, of billows of ardent flesh and hot hearts, would hurtle operatically into the quick-sands below, carrying optimism and cowardice, modesty and flattery, honour and menace, guilt and grace, forever out of hearing, forever out of sight.

The outlet must be kept narrow; a few figures beckoned into the flood-lit outer world; the gate slammed – oh, quickly. Even so he finds himself reeling back a little from the power of life left in these long-time internees, finds himself drawn into a frieze of posturing profiles, hemmed in by the inhabitants of that Wagnerianly bloated cliché, a Cavalcade of Humanity. Hemmed in, nose to nose, it is difficult to see beyond the warts.

DONALD HORNE

♦ *The Education of Young Donald*

Technically this is an autobiography, but 'autobiography' seems to suggest a sense of self-importance that is so far from what I had in mind that when people first used the word I had the feeling of someone who looks over his shoulder to see what is being talked about.

It is true that I have used facts, not fiction, to tell how a happy boy turned into something else as a youth and then as a young man, and that the happy boy and the young man were my 'self', but since the central character is presented as a social animal, his adolescent revolt shaped and coloured by social circumstance, I would use the word 'sociography' rather than 'autobiography'. Although parts of it are concerned with the kinds of accident that affect character and affront human dignity with the importance of their triviality, other parts attempt to show what social history can look like when told through *people*, and in some of the ideas that beset the central character – reform, revolution, experimentalism, freedom, nihilism, fraudulence, 'reality', alienation – is to be found some of the intellectual history of our times, in a particular context.

GEORGE JOHNSTON

◆ *Clean Straw for Nothing*

It will all come together, I am sure, like the pieces of a mosaic or the scattered chips in a kaleidoscope. At the moment it's a mess. Ruptured syntax. This wild leaping around through time and space. First person one minute, third person the next. It doesn't matter. I am not trying to write, just setting things down to get them straight. After all, none of us is first person all the time; we can be third person, too, and sometimes no person at all, only a space filled around by other people: we can no more claim a consistency of εγώ in the Greek sense than we can really believe we are a part of a sustained and forward-flowing chronology. I think I prefer the kaleidoscope image. The shaking of the fragmented chips, the patterns forming at random. This is easier than believing in a planned design.

CLIVE JAMES

◆ *Unreliable Memoirs*

Most first novels are disguised autobiographies. This autobiography is a disguised novel. On the periphery, names and attributes of real people have been changed and shuffled so as to render identification impossible. Nearer the centre, important characters have been run through the scrambler or else left out completely. So really the whole affair is a figment got up to sound like truth. All you can be sure of is one thing: careful as I have been to spare other people's feelings, I have been even more careful not to spare my own. Up, that is, of course, to a point.

Sick of being a prisoner of my childhood, I want to put it behind me. To do that, I have to remember what it was like. I hope I can dredge it all up again without sounding too pompous. Solemnity, I am well aware, is not my best vein. Yet it can't be denied that books like this are written to satisfy a confessional urge; that the main-spring of a confessional urge is guilt; and that somewhere under-neath the guilt there must be a crime. In my case I suspect there are a thousand crimes, which until now I have mainly been successful in not recollecting. Rilke used to say that no poet would mind going to gaol, since he would at least have time to explore the treasure house of his memory. In many respects Rilke was a prick.

Premature memoirs can only be conceited. I have no excuses against this charge, except to say that self-regard is itself a subject, and that to wait until reminiscence is justified by achievement might mean to wait for ever. I am also well aware that all attempts to put oneself in a bad light are doomed to be frustrated. The ego arranges the bad light to its own satisfaction. But on that point it is only necessary to remember Santayana's devastating comment on Rousseau's *Confessions*, which he said demonstrated, in equal meas-ure, candour and ignorance of self. However adroitly I have calcu-lated my intentional revelations, I can be sure that there are enough unintentional ones to give the reader an accurate impression. I had an absurdly carefree upbringing. If my account of it inspires disap-proval, that can only serve to help redress the balance. One doesn't expect to get away with it for ever.

DOROTHY HEWETT

♦ *Autobiographically Speaking*

In the process of observing, let alone recreating, I'm even changing myself, even as I write I am changing. When I sit down to write the last word of my autobiography, I'll be a very different person from the writer who struggled with the first paragraph. The actual pro-cess of writing, let alone living, has changed me. Remembering, plus all the external events that have occurred as I wrote, these have all changed me as a human being. The process of recording the past has probably changed my writing self even as I write the words, everything is fluid and everything is flux. And the writer addressing the reader, can no longer be the writer she was at twenty-five or forty or even last year.

So it seems to me that in order to write autobiography, the writer invents a pseudonym, a character, and follows that character through a series of events that appear to make up a life. The character speaks in the name of 'I' and this is very suborning. The reader thinks I'm getting it straight at last now, this is the real thing, the truth, what actually happened, smoking hot off the page. This is all an illusion. The act of creation has altered what really happened. From the inception of the autobiography, that self-conscious dramatic pseudonym has become this character called 'I', and yet there's this terrible compulsion on the writer to try and tell the truth, to get it right. But one can no longer, if one ever did, possibly, know what the truth was and at the back of one's mind there's always the libel laws. Who will be infuriated by this? Hurt, horrified, vindictive? What husband, wife, lover, ex-husband, ex-lover, friend, child, parent, relative, passer-by, will rise up in outrage, pain and even revenge at their depiction in this essentially fictionalized past?

JAMES HARDY VAUX

James Hardy Vaux (1782–?) was born in England and
transported three times: for theft in 1801 and 1810, and
for forgery in 1830. A compulsive liar and thief, three
times married, he used his undoubted talents to impress
his employers. *The Memoirs of James Hardy Vaux*
(1819) was the first full length autobiography to be
written in Australia.

♦ ♦ ♦ ♦

I continued to labour in double-irons, (locked up every night in the
jail,) for about a month, when a draught of men being ordered to the
public agricultural settlement of Castle-hill, twenty-four miles from
Sydney, I was included in the number, and about twenty of us were
immediately sent up, escorted by constables. Notwithstanding my
condition in the jail-gang was deplorable enough, I felt a greater
depression at the thoughts of going to this settlement, a place of
which from every account, I had conceived the most unfavourable
idea. Though I suffered much in Sydney, by being obliged to work
till three o'clock in so disgraceful a situation, yet when that hour

released me from the restraint of the overseer, I was enabled to visit my friends and acquaintances, with whom I enjoyed myself till sunset, when I was obliged to return to the jail, and was locked up for the night. On the contrary, Castle-hill being considered a place of punishment, the prisoners there, who were sent up under circumstances like mine, were not allowed to quit the settlement at all.

On arriving at Castle-hill, I was first employed at the hoe, which severe labour was so fatiguing to me, that it had nearly the effect of breaking my heart. However, I contrived at times to obtain a lighter employment: and during the term of my remaining at this settlement, I had a spell at almost every kind of work peculiar to the place.

After a few weeks had elapsed, I prevailed on the superintendent (Mr. Knight,) who had conceived a partiality for me, to grant me a pass to Parramatta, eight miles distant, and sixteen from Sydney. I had an anxious wish to visit the latter place, but Mr. Knight had no power to extend his permission so far, and I knew that application to the magistrates at Parramatta would be fruitless. I, therefore, determined to hazard a flogging, which would be the consequence of my detection, and to take the wished-for trip without leave or license. This being Friday, and my week's work done, I accordingly set off, accompanied by two or three others, similarly circumstanced, and after six hours' walking arrived at Sydney. Here I lay concealed in the house of a friend till Sunday noon, when I again set out proceeding with the utmost caution, and arrived at Castle-hill the same night, conformable to the tenor of my pass.

As I experienced nothing but misery and privation during five days in each week, and found such enjoyments in Sydney, I repeated my excursion almost every succeeding Friday, but was not always equally fortunate in my proceedings. The police in Sydney having some information of my visits, were constantly on the lookout for me, and I was at last apprehended, punished with fifty lashes, and sent back in custody of a constable. This did not deter me, however, from running the same risk at several subsequent periods, only redoubling my precautions, and travelling in the night.

MARTIN CASH

Martin Cash (1808–77) was born in Ireland and
transported in 1827. After serving a seven-year term his
later adventures included cattle-duffing, imprisonment
for larceny, several escapes, bush-ranging, a death
sentence commuted to transportation for life, Norfolk
Island and, eventually, a conditional pardon. His autobiography *The Adventures of Martin Cash* (1870) was
edited and possibly written by James Lester Burke. This
extract deals with life on Norfolk Island.

♦ ♦ ♦ ♦

I could see at a glance that the convict regulations were not strictly
carried out, and also that a free-and-easy style pervaded the whole
establishment. At meals the prisoners formed themselves into
messes, having six men in each mess, but who the six were that con-
stituted a company was purely a matter of chance, the men pairing
off as fancy or inclination prompted. At the time of my arrival there
were about two thousand prisoners on the island, who were all in
possession of gardens which they were permitted to cultivate, having all the Saturdays throughout the year for the purpose. At six
o'clock in the evening we were marched in single file from the

lumber yard, each man being searched on passing through a gate leading from the latter to the barracks, which was a large stone building three stories high, with a wooden frame running down the sides, to which the hammocks were suspended. The lights in the dormitories were extinguished every night at eight o'clock, but I was much surprised to see that a number of the prisoners lit their candles, and after rigging up stalls with their blankets they commenced to work, some at shoemaking, others tailoring; in fact, each at his own particular trade or calling, which enabled them to procure a supply of tea and sugar, a prisoner's chief comfort.

The following morning, when the gangs were formed, I was told off to an old man named Dalton, who was employed in the engineer department, and on taking me to the Military Barracks he told me to sit down and make myself comfortable. I did not well know what to make of this, and seeing him engaged in laying down some tiles I offered to assist him in the work, but he said my help was quite unnecessary, as he did not intend to do much himself. He worked for about an hour and then knocked off. I found him to be a most ingenious character, having been at one time employed in cleaning and repairing watches, and at another in mending umbrellas. He could also build ovens, set grates, etc. and, in fact, could do almost anything. On seeing that this state of things was likely to continue, I procured some straw, which I split when in the prison at night and carried with me in the morning when going to my work. I was therefore employed the best part of each day in making hats and bonnets, for which I found a ready sale in all quarters, and was soon enabled to contribute largely to the mess I was attached to.

J. F. MORTLOCK

John Frederick Mortlock (1809–82) was born in
England. *Experiences of a Convict* (1864–5) is the autobiography of a proud, well-educated man transported in
1843 for the attempted murder of his uncle who, he
believed, had defrauded him of his inheritance. The
extract illustrates the extreme social mobility of the
penal colony.

◆ ◆ ◆ ◆

Having thrown up the police, I tried a lawyer's office, which, owing
to his habits, in a short time proved very distasteful. Necessity,
therefore, obliged me to become once more a denizen of the 'Barracks,' where the officers having become acquainted with me, a
little favour was shown; and being employed as a writer without
pay, I now and then contrived to have a stroll. I made several ascents
up Mount Wellington, commanding from its summit a superb and
extensive prospect, and once when in company with a party, including a (transported) French lady, Madame La Marquise de la Grange,
nearly perished in a snow-storm. Enveloped in icicles and snow, we

passed a miserable, doleful night, the frost of which was only prevented by a huge fire that I made, from becoming fatal – in the winter time a Greenland temperature prevailing on the tops of the mountains. In the early part of 1848, the kind interference of the Ns placed under my charge a school of six-and-thirty boys, the master having been taken suddenly ill from the breaking of a blood-vessel. He, Mr. Mummery, was a queer little man, about five feet high – in holy orders – formerly of St. John's College, Cambridge; what transported for I never knew – it could not have been for breach of trust, no penalty being then attached to that delinquency.

A former rather celebrated governor, Sir George Arthur, employed him to instruct his children. Afterwards, when his sentence had elapsed, he married an emigrant governess, of no great beauty, and, for several years, kept a school with much success. Here was another metamorphosis, – one day, helping a gang to unlade a ship, I laboured on the wharf (having lost my unpaid writership); on the next, behold me cane in hand, installed in the head master's awful arm-chair, on a salary of £14 per annum. To impress myself with a sense of my dignity, and to lighten my spirits, I immediately, on the slightest occasion, belaboured several of the boys, particularly those whose parents had never been transported; this refreshed and consoled me.

JOSEPH JENKINS

Joseph Jenkins (1818–98) was a wealthy scientific farmer
in Wales until he emigrated at the age of fifty-one,
leaving wife and family behind. He became just a
swagman but his shrewd criticism of Australian farming
methods reveals his expert knowledge. Of the diary
that he kept continuously for 58 years, 25 years cover
the period in Australia. *Diary of a Welsh Swagman,
1869–1894* was first published in 1975.

January   *The wrong and the right of it*
1873
If this fine land were to be properly cultivated, I do not see that she
could find a market for the sale and consumption of her products
anywhere nearer than Europe. During this present harvest, farm
labourers are far too numerous. Nearly one half of them are out of
work and the other half is obliged to work hard for a wage of 4d an
hour, and are harassed by their employers into the bargain. Moreover, young Colonials are employed to the exclusion of the labourers, so that some two per cent of the fine crops is wasted through

the employment of unskilled hands instead of paying proper labourers to perform the work in a husband-like manner:

> The staff of life deserves to be
> In more efficient hands;
> Let ev'ry one, in his degree,
> Perform what it demands.
> The land is rich from North to South.
> From West and East the same;
> We would not meet a hungry mouth
> Should all add to its fame.

The state of Victoria may take many, yes scores of years, before it is converted to its proper use. A general craving for gold completely checks any advancement in this direction. Only the squatters have the urge to plan for posterity. As long as mutton and wool are harbingers of the general welfare, it is short-sighted to rear one sheep to the acre when twelve could be husbanded with little additional care and labour, while we read that a million people have lately died from hunger in Arabia, and the hard-working man pays so dearly for his loaf of bread.

Our present and former legislators are to be blamed for handing over so much good land to the same people. When land is taken from one tenant and given to another, it is expected that the latter improves it, but the lands of Victoria have diminished in value from the time they were so barbarously taken from the natives, and when the golden rules of humanity were so deliberately flouted.

◆

January   Man's inhumanity to man
1878
At the commencement of this my thirty-ninth diary it occurs to me that should all my manuscripts be kept and examined, it will be found that no days or even hours have gone unrecorded in those

thirty-eight years. This has given me more pleasure than labour, and I am in sympathy with the phrase, 'Habit is second nature'.

> *See yonder poor, o'er-laboured weight,*
> *So abject mean and vile,*
> *Who begs a brother of the earth*
> *To give him leave to toil.*
>
> (From Robert Burns' poem, 'Man was made to Mourn'.)

Should that witty poet be obliged to swag this country at the present time, he would find that these four lines of his would be most appropriate. The working men in this Colony are suffering from want of the necessities of life, both in regard to aliment and shelter, where millions of acres of the richest land in existence, remain in their natural state, and which have been claimed by a few 'dogs in the manger', who do not keep a single sheep on each two acres of such productive, but neglected land.

These deny a fellow-creature even water from their creeks and reservoirs to quench their thirst. It is plain that the world is steeped deeper and deeper in tyranny. How different from the days of Abram and Lot, for Abram said unto Lot, 'Let there be no strife, I pray thee, between me and thee, and between my herdmen and thy herdmen, for we be brethren. Is not the whole land before thee? Separate thyself, I pray thee, from me. If thou wilt take the left hand, then I will go to the right, or if thou depart to the right hand, then I will go to the left'.

Shortly past midnight, I was awakened by a loud report from guns nearby. This hailing of the New Year was new to me, and it seems a foolish idea. The Scotch and the Irish regard it as a sporting day. They assemble at the Sal-Sal falls where over 3,000 attend horse-racing. There is too much gambling in the country, but the people will have it. Most of the race-goers were farmers, and half of them had neither water nor grass at their farms for the cattle, all through lack of preparation against drought conditions.

Bush fires are likely to be numerous before the end of the month because of the dry grass. To drop a lighted match, carelessly or deliberately in revenge, can burn fifty square miles of grass and

corn, as well as homesteads and animals. The guilty person is not
always the one punished. When a rogue is well dressed he is very
often mistaken for a gentleman.

A load of timber boards arrived from Melbourne for the making
of jam-boxes. Many thousands have already been made. They measure 2 x 1½ x 1 feet. The man that makes them gets 5s per 100 and he
makes 130 a day. At home I doubt whether carpenters would manage sixty in a day. Labour on this farm is got on the cheap.

I have finished singling a three-acre paddock of mangolds. A ser-
mon at the house as usual this Sunday evening. I cannot understand
why people in the face of common sense, believe in the teaching of
John Calvin.

It was a miserable journey by waggon to Ballarat. At times visi-
bility was down to two yards from dust rising from the rough road.
Dust lies six feet deep in parts; it drifts like snow in the hollows.
Since the 1st of January the toll gates no longer function.

I opened roads in the cornfield with a scythe in preparation for
the reaper. It was so hot that I could not handle with my bare hands
the stone to sharpen the scythe.

Bush fires rage and the air is foul with smoke. Some think it is
caused by heat from the sun on broken glass-bottles, others consider it is caused through negligence, but most happen when
hungry swagmen call at farms in search of work, and are sent away
by ferocious dogs and foul words. A lighted match in the dry grass is
their way of retaliating.

Harvest men are numerous and are obliged to sleep and starve on
the dusty roads. They will not be employed before Monday in order
to save their Sunday meals. The drought continues. No water for
man or beast. Prospect of a scorching summer, and a dry Fall to
follow. It is time for Joe to leave the husks and return to Wales!

I managed to mow 2¾ acres of barley in 11 hours and 5 minutes,
and that by one in his sixtieth year. I must never repeat this
frolic.

Ten days ago I could not hold the stone to hone the scythe
because it was so hot; today I could not hold the rake and fork
because of the cold, so changeable is the weather. The mangold
crop is a complete loss, the vegetable is devoured to ground-level by
the locusts, and they have now started on the potato haulms.

Took the waggon to Ballarat for a load of sugar for jam-making. I arrived there at 11 o'clock and found that my watch which had not been cleaned for twenty months coincided with the time by the town clock.

The temperature is 103°F. The Master drove back in his heavily loaded carriage from a journey of twenty-six miles. The horse was covered in white foam from sweating. There is no sense in it.

♦

[In hospital] When we were allowed out in the grounds during the day and resting on seats conveniently arranged in the shade or facing a northern aspect, we chatted on various topics. One time, the Australian natives (the Aborigines) were discussed. The majority of the patients held it was a right and even a Christian obligation to be rid of them all. In the name of everything, whence came such authority?!!!

♦

I met an Aborigine. He seemed half-starved. I took him into my cottage, and invited him to share a meal with me, and I shared my blankets with him during the night. He could speak fair English. The railway commissioners from Melbourne were to visit Maldon, and I advised my new friend to meet them at the railway station and to hand them the undermentioned note:

To the railway commissioners.   Maldon
                                                           28 July 1887.

Gentlemen and Brothers too.
I am the last of the Aborigines tribe in these parts. I do humbly wish
you to compare two lots of Title Deeds.

> *I received mine from the Author of Nature, while the land*
> *occupied by all the railways is titled by the white man's lawyers.*
> *Always humble. Praying for your charitable consideration.*

> 'Equinhup', but nicknamed by whites – 'Tom Clark'.

The response to the short petition brought him 20s in silver, with a promise of more.

ROLF BOLDREWOOD

Rolf Boldrewood (1826–1915), pseudonym of Thomas
Alexander Browne, arrived in Australia from London in
1831. In 1844 he took up land in Western Victoria,
calling it Squattlesea Mere, a name taken from Walter
Scott. After various changes of fortune as landowner
and police magistrate he established his name as a
novelist, best known for *Robbery Under Arms* (1882–3).
The extracts are taken from his autobiographical essays
Old Melbourne Memories (1884).

♦ ♦ ♦ ♦

Standing in the gathering winterly twilight, at the intersection of
Elizabeth and Flinders Streets, one instinctively remarks the long
crowded suburban trains, laden with homeward-bound passengers,
quitting the city and care for the night's charmed interval. All the
streets of busy Melbourne are yet thronged, in spite of the apparently rapid diminution which is proceeding. The indefineable hum,
noticeable in large urban populations at the close of the day, as the
lamps are lit, which mark for most men the boundary between
work and recreation, is increasingly audible. The grand outlines of
the larger public buildings become suggestively indistinct. If your

ear be good, you may hear the steam-whistle and the roar of the country trains at Spencer Street Station. The senses of the musing spectator are filled to saturation with the sights and sounds proper to the largest, the most highly civilized, the most prosperous city in the world, for the years of its existence. Stranger than fiction does it not seem, that in the month of April, in the year of grace 1840, we should have migrated *en famille* from Sydney to assist in the colonization of Port Phillip, in the founding of this city of Melbourne? The moderate-sized schooner which carried us safely hither in a few hours under a week, had been chartered by Paterfamilias, so that we were unrestricted as to many matters not usually left to the discretion of passengers. It was a floating home. Colonists of ten years' standing, we had many things to bear with us, which under other circumstances of transit must have been left behind. There were carriage horses and cows, the boys' ponies, the children's canaries, poultry, and pigeons, dogs and cats, babies and nurses, furniture, flower-pots, workmen, house servants – all the component portions of a large household shifted bodily from a suburban home, and ready to be transferred to the first suitable dwelling in the new settlement. One can easily imagine to what a state of misery and confusion such a freight would have been reduced had bad weather come on. But the winds and the waves were kind, and on Saturday afternoon the harbour-master of Williamstown partook of some slight alcoholic refreshment on board, and welcomed us to Port Phillip. Well is remembered even now the richly-green appearance of the under-stocked grassy flat upon which the particularly small village of Williamstown stood. A few cottages, more huts – with certain public-houses, of course – made up the township. More distinctly marked even was the succulence and juiciness of the first Port Phillip mutton-chops upon which was regaled our keenly hungry party. We had just quitted the enfeebled meat markets of Sydney, scarce recovered from that terrible drought which wasted the years of 1837, 1838 and 1839. We had reached a land of Goshen evidently – a land of milk and butter, if not of honey – a land of chops and steaks, of sirloins and 'under-cuts' – of all youthful luxuries well nigh forgotten – of late unattainable in New South Wales as strawberry ice in a canebrake.

Among other trifles which our very complete outfit had com-
prehended was a small steamboat adapted for the tortuous but
necessary navigation of the Yarra Yarra, of which noble stream,
moving calmly through walls of ti-tree, we commenced to make the
acquaintance. This steamerlet – she was a *very* tiny automaton, puffing out of all proportion to her speed – but the *only* funnel-bearer –
think of that, Victorians of this high-pressure era! – had been sent
down by the head of the family the voyage before, safely bestowed
upon the deck of a larger vessel. The *Movastar* was a better boat, I
daresay, but the tiny *Firefly* bore us and the Lares and Penates of
many other 'first families' – in the sense of priority – safely to *terra
firma* on the north side of what was then called the 'Yarra Basin'.
This was an oval-shaped natural enlargement of the average width
of the river, much as a waterhole in a creek exceeds the ordinary
channel. The energetic Batman and the sturdy Cobbett of the
south, Pascoe Fawkner, had thought it good to set about making a
town, and here we found the bustling Britisher of the period
engaged in building up Melbourne with might and main. Our
leader laid it down at that time, as the result of his experience of
many lands, that the new colony, being outside of 36 degrees south
latitude, would not be scourged with droughts as had been New
South Wales from her commencement. In great measure, and absolutely as regarding the western portions of Victoria, this prophecy
has been borne out.

Sufficient time had elapsed for the army of mechanics, then established in Port Phillip, to erect many weatherboard, and a few
brick houses. Into a cottage of the latter construction we were has-
tily inducted, pending the finishing of a two-storeyed mansion in
Flinders Street, not very far from Prince's Bridge. Bridge was there
none in those days, it is hardly necessary to say; not even the
humble one with wooden piers that spanned the stream later, and
connected Melbourne people with the sandy forest of South Yarra,
then much despised for its alleged agricultural inferiority: still there
was a punt. You could get across, but not always when you wanted.
And I recall the incident of Captain Brunswick Smyth, late of the
50th Regiment, and the first commandant of mounted police, riding down to the ferry, from which the guardian was absent –

'sick, or drunk, or suthin' – and, with military impatience, dashing on board with a brace of troopers, who pulled the lumbering barge across, and fastened her to the further shore.

◆

Pride and successful ambition swelled my breast on that first morning as I looked round on my run. My run! My own station! How fine a sound it had, and how fine a thing it was that I should have the sole occupancy – almost ownership – of about 50,000 acres of 'wood and wold', mere and marshland, hill and dale. It was all my own – after a fashion – that is, I had but to receive my squatting licence, under the hand of the Governor of the Australias, for which I paid ten pounds, and no white man could in any way disturb, harass, or dispossess me. I have that first licence yet, signed by Sir Charles Fitzroy, the Governor-General. It was a valuable document in good earnest, and many latter-day pastoralists with a 'Thursday to Thursday' tenure would be truly glad to have such another. There were no free-selectors in these days. No one could buy land except at auction when once the special surveys had been abrogated. There were no travelling reserves, or water reserves, or gold-fields, or mineral licences, or miner's rights, or any of the new-fangled contrivances for letting the same land to half-a-dozen people at one and the same time.

There was nothing which some people would consider to be romantic or picturesque in the scenery on which I gazed. But the 'light which never was on sea or shore' *was there*, to shed a celestial glory over the untilled, unfenced, half-unknown waste. Westward stretched the great marshes, through which the Eumeralla flowed, if, indeed, that partially subterranean stream could be said to run or flow anywhere. Northward lay the lava-bestrewn country known as the Mount Eeles rocks, a mass of cooled and cracked lava now matted with a high, thick sward of kangaroo grass, but so rough and sharp were the piles and plateaux of scoria that it was dangerous to ride a horse over it. For years after we preferred to work it on foot with the aid of dogs.

MARY GILMORE

Dame Mary Gilmore (1864–1962) was brought up in
the bush in New South Wales, became a schoolteacher
and was active in the labour movement in the 1890s.
She joined Lane's New Australia experiment in
Paraguay in 1897. On her return, she established
herself as a leading Australian poet. In *Old Days: Old
Ways, a Book of Recollections* (1934) she records a
vanishing way of life.

◆ ◆ ◆ ◆

When I was older whatever I read I was; whatever I thought, I felt;
and thought began very early with me. When I was about seven or
eight I used to think with bleak terror, '*What if nothing ever moved
again!*' And I used to try to make the other children feel as I
did.

'Eternities and eternities and no movement; and after that eternities and eternities and eternities, *and still no movement!*' I punc-
tuatingly would say. But the others went on catching grasshoppers
or hunting birds. A bird in the hand was to them what such a
problem was to me.

Youth troubles over eternity; age grasps at a day and is satisfied to have even the day. So another of my childhood's troubles was eternity itself. So also was space. And yet another was the terror of when there would be nothing. The doctrine of the indestructibility of matter, the creativeness of change, had not then reached Australia – at least not as far as children were concerned. So I used to stand with shut eyes, and with my fingers in my ears, trying to compass the silence of creation, when all would be consumed, and the heavens rolled up as a scroll, and there was nothing – nothing – nothing –

When that came to pass there would be no moon, no sun, and no stars; no wind on the face, no rain on the head. And how I loved the wind on my face and the rain on my head! I was like a bird in these things; I lived among them like a bird. But, though I could imagine the sun and the moon and the stars and the round world of geography all gone, I still never thought of a time when there would not be a solid earth, and two feet, mine of course, standing on it. As to space! Think of beyond the moon, space; and beyond the stars, space; and after that still space; with no end and no horizon, no matter how far you went! In spite of that the horizon was to me a concrete line round the earth; sometimes I used to see myself cutting holes in it and peering through into the nothing – into space – into eternity – perhaps even seeing heaven, and God on the great white Throne.

I was fourteen years old before the horizon became an imaginary line, the groans of hell ceased, and the implacability of God went like a mist.

HENRY LAWSON

Henry Lawson (1867–1922) was born on the goldfields at Grenfell, New South Wales. After a bush education he worked on building contracts and as a coach-painter. Later he became a regular writer for the *Bulletin*. Many of the short stories on which his fame rests are partly autobiographical. Deafness from an early age contributed to his tragic view of life. He began *A Fragment of Autobiography* in 1903, taking his life up to 1888, but it was not published in his lifetime. The extract throws light on the sources of some of his stories and the pattern of his early reading.

◆ ◆ ◆ ◆

I was eleven or twelve when I first began to talk about being a writer some day; but I may have cherished the idea earlier. It exasperated Father, but Mother encouraged. Mother had a copy of Edgar Allan Poe's poetical works. I often heard her read 'The Raven' aloud and the other short poems and I read them myself later on, over and over again. Not very healthy reading for a child, was it?

Home life, I might as well say here, was miserably unhappy, but it was fate – there was no one to blame. It was the result of one of those utterly impossible matches so common in Australia. I remember a child who, after a violent and painful scene, used to slip out in the dark and crouch down behind the pig-stye and sob as if his heart would break. And a big black mongrel dog who'd come round with slobbery sympathy. And the child would put his arms round the dog's neck and bury his wet white face in the shaggy hair. But that child had a stubborn spirit and would not kiss the rod.

Spencer had given up his selection to a man who was mining mad, and taken in exchange a little two acre freehold, up near the Old Bark School, at the foot of Sapling Gully – a piece of land which the man had prospected exhaustively and had sunk a good deal of money in. The tenant on Spencer's old selection was an Irishman named Page, and there was a feud between him and our family until we left. It was about a boundary fence, of course, with a stray bull thrown in. Page 'didn't want to be onneighbourly', but 'he'd be aven wud 'em some day'. We bought a small secondhand harmonium, and Page got a barrel-organ next week. Both houses were close to the fence, and so sure as we started the organ of an evening Page would grind his hurdy-gurdy, and a digger across the road a concertina, and Fred Spencer would thump a kerosene tin in the still moonlight, and there would be music on Pipeclay. Page said that the hurdy-gurdy would go 'rippin' wid him if he only had the noats'.

One day, after our rooster and Page's rooster had crowed defiance at each other – each on the top of his own haystack – for several days, our bird went down, and got on Page's haystack and tackled the other fowl. We watched the fight until both birds fell down on the other side of the stack. We dared not go through the fence, but, some half-hour later, we heard Page's familiar 'Insoide there – come out!' He had our rooster and [was] handling him gently. 'Yere cock beat my cock!' he said, 'but I bear no malice – 'twas a grand fight. There he is.' And he set him down carefully.

We boys – the Spencers and we – used to annoy Page a good deal. 'I'll tell the masther on ye!' he'd say. We used to like to run barefoot along the moonlit road and plough up the thick white dust with boughs until we were enveloped in a dense cloud. Page had a score or so of turkeys and they roosted along the top rail of the fence in front of his place; and sometimes, as late as possible, we'd slip down and brush those turkeys from end to end with a bough, and they'd gobble, gobble, gobble, all down the line like a new musical instrument. And Page would come out, sometimes in his shirt, and then we'd vanish. In my memory my childhood, or boyhood, if I had any, went out with the gobble of those turkeys. There was a flicker when I got a horse of my own, and again when I got a gun, but it went dead out.

♦

I went for a few months to a Catholic school in Mudgee. I don't know why I was sent there; but probably because my mater had become disgusted with our own churchmen as they were then. I remember one day, Pat Tovey, the coach driver, who was taking the mails out on a pack-horse because of the bad weather and flooded creeks, gave me a lift home on the pack-horse. He stayed to deliver a bag at a post office near our place kept by a bigoted Protestant family with whom our family were at feud.

'What are they sending that boy to a Catholic school for?' asked the post-mistress.

'Sure he's bein' educated for a priesht,' said Pat: and a little further on he said, half to himself and half to me: 'Let her put that in her pipe and shmoke it.' Then he added with a chuckle, 'It'll be all round the dishtrick be tomorrer mornin'.'

I was given a weedy riding hack and used to ride to school. I usually milked six or seven cows and had to catch the horse before riding to school, and was never late that I remember. Some children had to rise before daylight and milk ten or fifteen cows in [the] bitter cold frosty morning before starting for school. I don't suppose there was ever such a collection of young fiends as were in the Catholic school in Mudgee when I went there. One had thrown a slate at the last master, who broke a blood vessel and died. Several masters had resigned, but the present one, Mr. Kevan, was a strong man and kept the young devils well in hand without the assistance of Father O'Donovan. His successor, a better scholar, a younger and cleverer man (who nevertheless said things like 'Don't do that no more') had a tough fight but got the school under after using up two or three canes a day for a week or so. I got a sharp cut once by mistake, but, somehow, I didn't seem to mind. Of course, there were no girls in this school.

◆

The few Protestant pupils were sent out during prayers in the morning, but woe betide the Catholic boy who threw the Protestant boys' religion in [their faces], whether he fell into the hands of the schoolmaster afterwards or Father O'Donovan. 'I'll have none of that sort of thing,' said Father O'Donovan, with no softness in his voice. 'I want that understood once for all.'

Once or twice Mr. Kevan came and sat beside me, as I sat lonely and unhappy, by myself on a stool in the corner of the yard, and drew me out of myself and talked to me about poetry and Edgar Allan Poe. He'd heard something of Mother, I suppose.

I was tormented a good deal by the town boys, after school hours, and used to get to the paddock where I'd left my horse, and get off home as quickly as possible. I was called 'Chummy' by some, and by others 'Barmy Harry'. Years before there had been another Barmy Henry in Sydney, a pale delicate shy and sensitive boy, carrying a tray of pastry on his head, to customers, for his master, a fancy baker, and mumbling verses to himself. It was the habit of 'talkin' to hisself', as his companions thought he did, that won him the nickname and the reputation of being mad. Henry Kendall.

I read Dickens. Got him at the School of Arts in Mudgee and read *The Old Curiosity Shop* first I think. I have read Dickens over and over again and can read him now at any time. Next I read Marryat – *Jacob Faithful* and *Peter Simple*. I paid a visit to my mother's people at Wallerawang, and, on leaving, one of my aunts presented me with a volume of Bret Harte's, entitled *Some Folks*, and containing 'Tennessee's Partner', 'Mliss', etc. I read that book on the journey home and it fascinated me; it seemed to bring a new light, a new world into my life, and this with Dickens still fresh. But Dickens stayed by me and Bret Harte did not. I read *Don Quixote* before I was fourteen, but that was an accident – somebody had left the book at our place. I remember being greatly puzzled and worried about the loss and recovery of Sancho's ass. It was only the other day I read somewhere that Cervantes did not read his proofs and that it was doubtful if he had even read his copy. And oh! of course we read *Robbery Under Arms* when it first appeared in the *Sydney Mail* – Browne, by the way, touched an Australian sore when he described the Marsden family as being, the girls Catholics and the boys Protestants. We read *For the Term of His Natural Life* (as Marcus Clarke wrote it) in the *Australian Journal*. The introduction was, I think, equal to Dickens's style. The sight of the book with its mutilated chapters and melodramatic 'prologue' exasperates me even now. And we read *Jack Harkaway* – I was going on for thirty before I read *Dead-wood Dick*, and then I used to read him to put me to sleep. And Mother used to recite Gordon from the *Australian Journal*. I liked tailing the cows amongst the gullies, for it gave me opportunities for reading – though I was supposed to do some ring-barking. But when I was about thirteen I went to work with Father.

HENRY HANDEL RICHARDSON

Ethel Florence Lindesay Robertson (1870–1946) was
born and educated in Melbourne. In the autobiographical novel *The Getting of Wisdom* (1910) she
presents with ironic detachment the growth in
self-knowledge of her alter ego, Laura Rambotham.
Myself When Young (1948) is an unfinished autobiography and there are strong autobiographical
elements in her novels, *Maurice Guest* (1908), based on
her music studies in Leipzig and *The Fortunes of
Richard Mahony* (1917–1929), based on her father's life.

♦ ♦ ♦ ♦

♦ *The Getting of Wisdom*

And Laura? . . . In Laura's case, no kindly Atropos snipped the
thread of her aspirations: these, large, vague, extemporary, one and
all achieved fulfilment; then withered off to make room for more.

But this, the future still securely hid from her. She went out from school with the uncomfortable sense of being a square peg, which fitted into none of the round holes of her world; the wisdom she had got, the experience she was richer by, had, in the process of equipping her for life, merely seemed to disclose her unfitness. She could not then know that, even for the squarest peg, the right hole may ultimately be found; seeming unfitness prove to be only another aspect of a peculiar and special fitness. But, of the after years, and what they brought her, it is not the purport of this little book to tell. It is enough to say: many a day came and went before she grasped that oftentimes, just those mortals who feel cramped and unsure in the conduct of everyday life, will find themselves to rights, with astounding ease, in that freer, more spacious world where no practical considerations hamper, and where the creatures that inhabit dance to their tune: the world where are stored up men's best thoughts, the hopes, and fancies; where the shadow is the substance, and the multitude of business pales before the dream.

In the meantime, however, the exodus of the fifty-five turned the College upside-down.

Early the following morning Laura made her final preparations for departure. This, alas! was not to be on so imposing a scale as the departures of her schoolfellows. They, under special escort, would have a cab apiece, and would drive off with flying handkerchiefs and all their luggage piled high in front. Whereas Laura's box had gone by van: for she and Pin, who was in Melbourne on a visit, were to spend a couple of days at Godmother's before starting up-country. Even her farewells, which she had often rehearsed to herself with dramatic emphasis, went off without éclat. Except for Miss Chapman, the governesses were absent when the moment came, and Miss Chapman's mind was so full of other things that she went on giving orders while she was shaking hands.

But Laura was not destined to leave the walls, within the shadow of which she had learned so much, as tamely as all this. There was still a surprise in waiting for her. As she whisked about the corridors in search of Mrs Gurley, she met two girls, one of whom said: 'I say, Laura Rambotham, you're fetched. Your pretty sister's come for you.'

'My . . . who?' gaped Laura.

'Your sister. By gum, there's a nose for you – and those whopping eyes! You'll have to play second fiddle to *that*, all your days, my dear.'

On entering the reception-room Laura tried hard to see Pin with the eyes of a stranger. Pin rose from her chair – awkwardly, of course, for there were other people present, and Laura's violent stare was disconcerting in the extreme: it made Pin believe her hat was crooked, or that she had a black speck on her nose. As for Laura, she could see no great change in her sister; the freckles were certainly paler, and the features were perhaps beginning to emerge a little, from the cushiony fat in which they were bedded; but that was all. Still, if outsiders, girls in particular, were struck by it . . .

A keener stab than this – really, she did not grudge Pin being pretty: it was only the newness of the thing that hurt – a keener stab was it that, though she had ordered Pin repeatedly, and with all the stress she was master of, to come in a wagonette to fetch her, so that she might at least drive away like the other girls; in spite of this, the little nincompoop had after all arrived on foot. Godmother had said the idea of driving was stuff and nonsense – a quite unnecessary expense. Pin, of course, had meekly given in; and thus Laura's last brave attempt to be comfortably like her companions came to naught. She went out of the school in the same odd and undignified fashion in which she had lived there.

The wrangle caused by Pin's chicken-heartedness lasted the sisters down the garden-path, across the road, and over into the precincts of a large, public park. Only when they were some distance through this, did Laura wake to what was happening to her. Then, it came over her with a rush: she was free, absolutely free; she might do any mortal thing she chose.

As a beginning she stopped short.

'Hold on, Pin . . . take this,' she said, giving her sister the heavy leather bag they were carrying in turns to the tramway.

Pin obediently held out her hand, in its little white cotton glove.

'And my hat.'

'What are you going to do, Laura?'

'You'll see.'

'You'll get sunstroke!'

'Fiddles! – it's quite shady. Here're my gloves. – Now, Pin, you follow your nose and you'll find me – *where* you find me!'

'Oh, what *are* you going to do, Laura?' cried Pin, in anxiety.

'I'm going to have a good run,' said Laura; and tightened her hair-ribbon.

'Oh, but you can't run in the street! You're too big. People'll see you.'

'Think I care? – If you'd been years only doing what you were allowed to, I guess you'd want to do something you weren't allowed to, too. – Good-bye!'

She was off, had darted away into the leaden heat of the December morning, like an arrow from its bow, her head bent, her arms close to her sides, fleet-footed as a spaniel: Pin was faced by the swift and rhythmic upturning of her heels. There were not many people abroad at this early hour, but the few there were, stood still and looked in amazement after the half-grown girl in white, whose thick black plait of hair sawed up and down as she ran; and a man with mop and bucket, who was washing statues, stopped his work and whistled, and winked at Pin as she passed.

Cross and confused Pin trudged after her sister, Laura's hat and gloves in one hand, the leather bag in the other.

Right down the central avenue ran Laura, growing smaller and smaller in the distance, the area of her movements decreasing as she ran, till she appeared to be almost motionless, and not much larger than a figure in the background of a picture. Then came a sudden bend in the long, straight path. She shot round it, and was lost to sight.

◆ *Myself When Young*

And one day I vented my irritation by flinging out: 'I don't know I'm sure how I ever came to write *Maurice Guest* – a poor ignorant little colonial like me!'

My husband glanced up from his writing-table, and said in his wise, quiet way: 'But emotionally very experienced.'

At the moment I rather blinked the idea, being unprepared for it, then went away to my own room to think it over. And the more I thought the more I saw how true it was – though, till now, the connexion had never occurred to me. That is to say, I had written *Maurice* quite unaware of what I was drawing on. Later events had naturally had a certain share in his story. But his most flagrant emotions – his dreams, hopes and fears, his jealousy and despair, his sufferings under rejection and desertion – could all be traced back to my own unhappy experience. No wonder the book had come easy to write. I had just to magnify and re-dress the old pangs. – But the light thrown by my husband's words did not stop there. It cleared up other knots and tangles in my life, which at the time of their happening had seemed stupidly purposeless. Now I began to sense a meaning in these too, to see them as threads in a general pattern. And gradually the conviction deepened that, to a writer, experience was the only thing that really mattered. Hard and bitter as it might seem, it was to be welcomed rather than shrunk from, reckoned as a gain not a loss. – Since then, I think I may say that the natural rebel in me has been considerably less to the fore.

JOHN SHAW NEILSON

John Shaw Neilson (1872–1942) was born in South
Australia. His father was a bush poet, entirely
self-educated. The son became an itinerant worker
alongside his father and began to contribute poetry to
the *Bulletin* and the *Bookseller* in the 1890s. The style
and spelling of *The Autobiography of John Shaw Neilson*
(first published in 1978) reveal his limited formal
education and his diffidence in the company of editors
such as A. G. Stephens of the *Bulletin*, and other poets,
but in fact he was intelligent and widely read.

◆ ◆ ◆ ◆

About the middle of Oct Dad & I went away to the SE of S Australia shearing. We returned a few weeks before Xmas. We got
work wheat clearing. After that was over, we followed a trashing
[threshing] machine, (a steam one) this time. We were out till March
& made about thirty shillings a week each. The red rust was very
bad that year and I got sore eyes, which stopped me from doing any
reading or writing till the middle of Winter. All that Autumn &
Winter we were working contract fencing.

I think the sore eyes was about the beginning of my very discontented period which lasted for several years. I was very like Mother, there was a good deal of the pessimist in me. I remembered while we worked at that contract fencing, Dad was a good deal of his time writing a Ballad. I thought it was a very good ballad, but he never got it printed. I believe Ward & Lock would have printed it, but they did not want to pay for it, and they only wanted to give him a book, in which it was going to appear.

When my eyes got better, I tried to write verse and Stories. I got eight lines of rhymne into the *Leader*. My first appearance in Print was under some pen name.

They were very raw lines, but Dad praised them, and said, they were very much better than what he did at the same age. He also thought that one of my stories was fairly good.

♦

I packed up about the middle of December. I arrived in the harvest city one evening & got lodgings somewhere out near Paddington. It was a very noisy place on the tram-track. I did not know that the trams ran all night in Sydney. They cease at midnight in Melbourne. A couple of days after I met A.G. by appointment at the Post Office.

He was still a very fine looking man. He must have been very handsome when younger. One of the first things he told me was that his ancestors were flemish pirates who settled in Wales three hundred years previously.

Most of the Stephens he said had been editors. They were good at looking over other people's work, but did not have much creative power themselves.

I forget what day of the week it was. I remember we went for a ferry-ride & afterwards he came back & showed me his den & we had a long talk there. He had a wonderful collection of all sorts of scraps written & printed. We talked little about my verse but much more about other peoples.

He really had a fervant love for Australian verse & prose. He had known so many writers and helped so many. He had a marvellous memory. He spoke with genuine feeling of many who had passed out.

There was a touch of something like genius about the man. His mind seemed to remind me of lightning. He was a difficult man to understand. One person who knew him well said that he was several men in one. He was extremely emotional & yet a stranger would not think it of him.

I think it was that day we went to see Mrs Gilmore. This warm-hearted lady was very anxious that I should meet Prof. Brereton & Christopher Brennan.

She managed both these things. I believe she had great difficulty in finding Brennan because he was at some remote address. It was on the following evening that I met the charming John le Gay Brereton. We spoke [for] several hours & he saw me home about midnight. He spoke very feelingly of Henry Lawson whom he had known so well.

I think it was the following day, a Saturday, that I met Brennan. A very kind soul named John Quinn invited A.G. and myself to dine with him at a cafe. The proprietor was French. French was spoken & I believe I was the only person there who did not understand the language. I was at once struck by the resemblance of Chris Brennan's head to that of the great Dr Johnson. One man said of Brennan that he had the greatest mind in the Commonwealth.

MILES FRANKLIN

Stella Maria Miles Franklin (1879–1954) was born to a
New South Wales squatter family and spent her early
years with her wealthy grandmother before moving to
her family's much poorer property. Much of her
writing is direct or fictionalised autobiography. The
extracts are taken from *My Brilliant Career?* (1901)
written when she was only sixteen, *My Career Goes
Bung* (1946) which was rejected by publishers in 1910
for its audacity, and *Childhood at Brindabella*, published
posthumously in 1963.

♦ ♦ ♦ ♦

♦ *Childhood at Brindabella*

The rhythm of horses came to me earlier than walking. In those
moments – rare with me – when the sense of actuality has been
slightly loosened by over-fatigue or a high temperature, there recurs

for ever like the movement of a stream or the pattern of leaves flickering in a zephyr, the sensation of a well-bred horse being released, or about to be released, into action. Unforgettable are the pleasant odour of the warm satiny skin and the noble animal's every sensitive gesture as he waited a-tingle. He might rub his head on his fore-leg or stamp against a fly, test or mouth the bit, his alertness firmly reined to endure the finishing touches of departure. Then off, the instant the weight was on him, settling to the required gait as he cleared his breathing with a ruffle of good-will and good-going in his skilled responsibilities.

Deeply etched are the proportions of a tall easy horse controlled by a slim tall man with a natural beard and a very small child bundled on a pillow in front of him. The man was my father, one of my maternal uncles or one of Mother's cousins. The pillow, made by Mother, was stuffed with feathers in an outer case of purple sateen of the kind used for dress-linings.

Except on the rarest occasions we went about on horses – horses that *were* horses, with a dash of blood – the whalers so much sought for the Indian Army. My father and his brothers bred horses of full stature. The eldest brother had scorn for what he dismissed as 'dunkies'. A pony was a rarity among us. We liked to be up out of the water or bogs of the string-heads and streams of our domain. The men rode far and fast: the children could not have kept with them on mere ponies.

My confidence and pleasure in horses was inborn. Mother rode seventy miles or more two months before I was born, from Bobilla to Ajinby the long way round. She went by impossible tracks negotiable only by a mountain-bred horse, at such angles that those unaccustomed could not retain a seat. For miles the horse plunged to the girths in snow. She rode her own blood horse, Lord Byron, who had borne her to her new home as a bride. His shoes had not been removed and snow collected in hard balls in the arches of his hoofs. Mother never forgot that punishing journey. There would have been fewer jolts had Lord Byron shed all his stilts at once, but he went off one at a time, and no surety from which point the next jerk would come, which increased the strain. She rode too on a hard new side-saddle in an elegant habit, tight-fitting and boned.

She was so exhausted at the end of the first gruelling day of over

thirty miles that she had to rest for three days at the home of a
selector. The motherly wife won Mother's unfading love, though I
do not know that they ever met again. Mrs H. had the usual pioneer
brood herself. She put Mother in her own bed as the warmest place
for her bruised body, and placed her youngest, a child in arms, at
Mother's feet to keep them warm.

When I was three months old Mother rode home by a different
route over the daisied plains by the sparkling rivulets where some of
our longest creek-rivers began. My second uncle, a capable and
humorous young man, carried me before him on the purple pillow.
He says that I yowled when I grew hungry and the dairy, as he
expressed it, had ridden too far ahead. Thus – straight from the bed
in which I was born to the back of a horse with no perambulator
intervening.

There was no gangway for prams in our bailiwick. My parents'
home was a mile or more from the main homestead of my father's
second brother, and his more advanced family. Between was little
level track that took no heed of a creek or a fence or a swamp where
the wild ducks used to 'sing their long-drawn note of revelry rejoic-
ing at the spring.' And why would people of any age be pottering
along on foot when there were horses of varied accomplishments
for all?

But sometimes on Sunday afternoons the two families met half
way on foot as a little company for the two young mothers and a
change for the men from constantly catching and saddling horses.
On such occasions I rode on my father's shoulder. No head so
much as poked out of doors unhatted. Sunstroke was considered
more likely than snakebite and when my father took off his hat to
get it out of my way I desperately spread my fat paws on his crown to
save him from death.

♦ *My Brilliant Career?*

'Sybylla, what are you doing? Where is your mother?'
'I'm ironing. Mother's down at the fowl-house seeing after some
chickens. What do you want?'

It was my father who addressed me. Time, 2 o'clock p.m. Thermometer hung in the shade of the veranda registering 105½ degrees.

'I see Blackshaw coming across the flat. Call your mother. You bring the leg-ropes – I've got the dog-leg. Come at once; we'll give the cows another lift. Poor devils – might as well knock 'em on the head at once, but there might be rain next moon. This drought can't last for ever.'

I called mother, got the leg-ropes, and set off, pulling my sunbonnet closely over my face to protect my eyes from the dust which was driving from the west in blinding clouds. The dog-leg to which father had referred was three poles about eight or ten feet long, strapped together so they could be stood up. It was an arrangement father had devised to facilitate our labour in lifting the cows. A fourth and longer pole was placed across the fork formed by the three, and to one end of this were tied a couple of leg-ropes, after being placed round the beast, one beneath the flank and one around the girth. On the other end of this pole we would put our weight while one man would lift with the tail and another with the horns. New-chum cows would sulk, and we would have great work with them; but those used to the performance would help themselves, and up they'd go as nice as a daisy. The only art needed was to draw the pole back quickly before the cows could move, or the leg-ropes would pull them over again.

On this afternoon we had six cows to lift. We struggled manfully, and got five on their feet, and then proceeded to where the last one was lying, back downwards, on a shadeless stony spot on the side of a hill. The men slewed her round by the tail, while mother and I fixed the dog-leg and adjusted the ropes. We got the cow up, but the poor beast was so weak and knocked about that she immediately fell down again. We resolved to let her have a few minutes' spell before making another attempt at lifting. There was not a blade of grass to be seen, and the ground was too dusty to sit on. We were too overdone to make more than one-worded utterances, so waited silently in the blazing sun, closing our eyes against the dust.

Weariness! Weariness!

A few light wind-smitten clouds made wan streaks across the white sky, haggard with the fierce relentless glare of the afternoon sun. Weariness was written across my mother's delicate careworn features, and found expression in my father's knitted brows and dusty face. Blackshaw was weary, and said so, as he wiped the dust, made mud with perspiration, off his cheeks. I was weary – my limbs ached with the heat and work. The poor beast stretched at our feet was weary. All nature was weary, and seemed to sing a dirge to that effect in the furnace-breath wind which roared among the trees on the low ranges at our back and smote the parched and thirsty ground. All were weary, all but the sun. He seemed to glory in his power, relentless and untiring, as he swung boldly in the sky, triumphantly leering down upon his helpless victims.

Weariness! Weariness!

This was life – my life – my career, my brilliant career! I was fifteen – fifteen! A few fleeting hours and I would be old as those around me. I looked at them as they stood there, weary, and turning down the other side of the hill of life. When young, no doubt they had hoped for, and dreamed of, better things – had even known them. But here they were. This had been their life; this was their career. It was, and in all probability would be, mine too. My life – my career – my brilliant career!

Weariness! Weariness!

◆ My Career Goes Bung

Life among boys and girls at an institution such as the Stringybark Hill Public School, ere adolescence has arrived to mess things up, is a good example of democracy. There were no wealthy within competitive reach, money did not count to any extent, and beauty and birth did not count at all. We never heard of such things. Only the merit of brains and honesty weighed in the school room, and athletic prowess coupled with fair play on the playground.

Any sort of lessons except long addition sums were a joy and sinecure to me. On the playground, though small, I was fleet of foot and exceptionally agile, could vault as high as any boy of my own age till I was twelve, and was always chosen as captain whether the game happened to be cricket, rounders or prisoners' bar. A balance was preserved in my status by the fact that the dunces at lessons were always the best bats or runners outside, and that athletes when grown up had so much more glory than mere scholars.

I was impatient to be done with school so that I could take hold of life in the big world. I could not understand why people stayed in some lone hole with no more spunk in them than a milch cow, while the universe elsewhere teemed with adventure.

I expected to continue in enjoyment of the friendship and affection of my fellows, working for and winning a high place in all the activities that I essayed. I thought that there would be any number of activities to choose from. I was sure of winning love and acclamation because I never cheated in a game or put on airs over my ascendency in them, and eagerly shared anything and everything within my power.

Thus came the last day under the rule of the gentle old teacher in the little slab school house among the tall trees on the stringy bark range. Old Harris, as we called him behind his back, got drunk on occasion but was condoned by the kindly settlers because he knew and loved each child individually. He could bring what there was out of the thickest skulls and I rioted unrebuked and highly encouraged within his jurisdiction. He had been educated at one of the great colleges in England. I don't know which as he never mentioned it to the simple circle of Stringybark Hill. He was supposed to be related to big swells but that likewise he never mentioned unless he was a bit tipply and some flash intruder was putting on airs. He had the manners of an angel, a dear kind face, and wouldn't have harmed a grasshopper. These qualifications earned him the protection of the rudest and crudest. He taught a mere handful of children the rudiments of education for less than £3 a week and boarded with a family who were industrious, honest and kind, but could offer him no congeniality of mind or companionship of knowledge.

Ma condemned his fecklessness to be stuck there, but Pa would rub the top of his head – his own head – and remark, 'At Old Harris's age life boils down to a decent bed and a good feed, and those things are his.'

At the end of my last day with him he patted me on the shoulder

- an unusual liberty for this diffident soul. He never seemed to have any egotism except when he was drunk. It must have been ingrowing like squeezed toenails. He made a little speech over me, the kind which youth accepts as drivel at the time, but which comes back vividly when youth has grown towards this drivelling knowledge itself. It returns to me now in the drivellage of my twentieth year, and here it is.

'Sybylla, you are a good girl – clean and true – and a gifted one to boot. You are as game as a young lion but I fear that the opposing forces will break your heart. You are a glad young thing now, but with your ability and temperament, alas, it will take more than ordinary conditions to keep you happy. You have a quicker brain than any scholar I ever had, but that will not help you unless you use it to hide the fact of its existence and to enhance your beauty; and of beauty you have ample to secure what would satisfy most of your sex, but which will never content you, so I might as well hold my tongue. At any rate, good fortune attend you. The old school house will be dull and lonely without you.'

I thought that he must have had a drop, but now when he is dead and six years have passed, I simply know that his experience of life was more than mine.

I was let out in advance and he stood looking after me as I swung down the path between the young trees which I had helped to plant on by-gone Arbor Days. Affection is a terribly binding thing. It always keeps me from breaking bonds, so I turned back every few steps to wave to the old man with a wistful regret that he was a finished chapter and that I could not take him with me into the glamorous young world towards which I was headed.

I had two miles to go by a short cut, which I followed for the joy of fallen logs to vault, and I sprang high every yard or two for the gum leaves that splashed their outline on the ground. The sky was a washing-bag blue with mountainous white clouds of thunderous splendour piled in the west. What a sunset it would be! I revelled in every scrap of beauty that came my way, and was excited to picture the beauty and adventure that I was going to broach beyond the ragged horizon to be seen from the tall fence post. The loveliest most thrilling thing in sight was the road that led from the front paddock to Goulburn, then on and on to Sydney – first port of call in my voyage of conquest. I climbed on to the garden post for a view before entering the house, my school days past.

'What are you doing there like a tom-boy?' inquired Ma. 'You must change your ways now. The happiest days you'll ever know are over – all play and no work and worry. You'll find life a different matter.'

LIFE a different matter – I should hope so! – like a blue ocean of adventure calling with a deafening invitation to embark.

A. H. CHISHOLM

Alexander Hugh Chisholm (1890–1977) was born in
Victoria. He became a journalist, literary editor, and
distinguished naturalist. In *The Joy of the Earth* (1969)
he criticises the neglect of nature study in schools. This
throws light on Donald Horne's sudden realisation as
an adolescent in the Blue Mountains that he could not
name any tree or flower.

♦ ♦ ♦ ♦

When, at the age of four and a half years, a quaking boy began
attending a public school in the town of his birth, the first sight of a
brisk feminine teacher, equipped with a cane, caused him to break
into a startled wail; and when, at the more or less mature age of
twelve and a half years, he left that school to take to 'the bush', it
was the farewelling teacher, this time a man, who shed tears.

A fair balance!

Those episodes remain clearly in mind. I remember how my sister Margaret, leading me by a clammy hand, knocked at the door of
the infants' class-room (then known as the A.B.C.) and how a

teacher who opened the door casually swished a cane against her long skirt, upon sight of which I, bursting into anticipatory tears, tried to run away. It is curious that isolated incidents of childhood having no special significance should cling to one's memory, but I recall without effort the sequel of eight years later, when the headmaster stood near the school gate nodding goodbye to the children as they 'broke-up' for the Christmas holidays.

'My boy', he said to me, 'I heah you are leaving school?'

'Yes, sir', I replied.

'What are you going to do, my lad?'

'I'm going out in the bush, sir'.

'What are you going to do there?'

Here was a tricky question. I had given no thought to what I was going to do in the bush other than look at trees and flowers and birds, varied perhaps by a trifle of fossicking for gold, and it seemed quite unlikely that 'Dad', the headmaster, would be impressed by that vague venture, self-imposed, in what is now termed vocational guidance.

So, then, when he asked again, 'What are you going to do there?' I said, 'Please, sir, I-I don't know'.

Without further ado, 'Dad' produced a handkerchief, blew his nose, and wiped his eyes. He had lost again. The bush had robbed him of another scanty-educated scholar, just as the district mines had done many times – those deep gold-mines where a sturdy lad could earn 'four bob a day' at 'truckin'', from which job he would in time 'go below' at a higher wage, and, as like as not, die at an early age of 'miners' complaint', a form of lung trouble.

'Dad' knew all this. He knew what 'the mines' implied and he knew that virtually the sole occupation offering in the bush near the town was wood-cutting, and so, when he lost a boy of any brightness to the mines or the bush, 'Dad' became upset.

A highly emotional man. In a considerable experience of school-teachers, subsequently, I have never known one whose temperament was anywhere near as mercurial as that of my first (and only) headmaster. Stirred to sudden rage by a slip or a misdemeanour on the part of a boy, he would shout 'Come out he-ah!' thrust a pencil between his teeth and bite furiously upon it (more than once he bit it into pieces), and reach for a cane. He struck us upon hands rendered stiff by the frost of winter mornings. If hands were pulled back involuntarily he struck on legs or arms. Sometimes, though rarely, a reckless boy attempted reprisals, and then the whole school seethed with excitement while awaiting the outcome.

In brief, our head was a kin-spirit of the young Sam Johnson's bogeyman, Hunter – 'very severe, and wrong headedly severe', in that 'he beat us unmercifully and did not distinguish between ignorance and negligence . . .'

Once, in an attempt to ease the effects of one of the master's excesses, I paused in our public gardens on the way home and treated myself to something in the nature of a psychiatric exercise. 'Try to forget it', I advised myself. 'Your name is only a name, anyway, and it might easily have been given to someone else. Tell yourself that your body might also belong to someone else. Forget that it belongs to you'.

I must have impressed myself with that quaint little mind-over-matter adventure on the part of a boy of about ten years – even now I can recall the precise spot where it occurred – for a little later I began to wonder at the nature of the thoughts, and then I laughed and felt rather better: after which I pushed on home and, without bothering Mother with my troubles, gained practical solace through that staple medium, a slice of bread and dripping.

Perhaps, by the way, Mother was to some extent the cause of my attempt to forsake bodily awareness. For, quite often, she chanted the verses about the old woman who when staggering home from market in darkness – and being dazed concerning her own identity – was growled at by her own dog, upon which she cried, 'Lawks a' mercy on me – this is none of I!'

Another curiosity in kind that has chanced to persist in memory has for basis the fact that Mother's morning formula when sending me off to school was always, 'Goodbye; be a good boy'. But, on a particular occasion, probably through being busy, she limited herself to a simple 'Bye-bye'. And I, having got me into the street, suddenly felt only partly equipped, or, maybe, mentally half-dressed: wherefore I returned to the house and stood in the kitchen doorway. 'Gracious!' Mother exclaimed, 'what is wrong?' And, quite solemnly, I told her the trouble: 'You didn't say "Be a good boy" "! Mother smiled broadly. 'Oh', she said, 'I'm so sorry. Now, run along – *and be sure to be a good boy!*'

That action on my part, I suspect, was not prompted by a desire for moral stimulus so much as attachment to a familiar phrase – as with the sense of loss we feel whenever a familiar line of verse is dropped. At any rate, the admonition was somewhat superfluous, for, certainly, I had no inclination to be other than 'good' when the headmaster was on view.

◆

Returning to the class-room: it seems desirable to record that, as with Australian history, there was no place in the curriculum for natural history, and thus we were not taught even the simplest facts in the story of the world about us, as contained in its rocks and plants and birds.

Furthermore, no teacher ever found any cause for complaint at our attending school with the scalps of unfortunate honey-parrots in our caps; nor did any one raise an objection when, on the odd occasions of our being taken on aimless bush rambles, every vandal amongst us devoted most of the time to robbing as many birds' nests as could be found.

It follows, then, that my desire to leave school in favour of the bush, however firmly based on an interest in birds and other wild-life, was not prompted by the guidance of any teacher. A more potent factor, indeed, was the simple play of life, season by season, in my own household yard and garden.

Nor was either of my parents directly responsible for the school-deserting enterprise. Mother, on her part, had serious qualms about it. But, being aware that I had scored the flimsy distinction known to youth as 'the certif' (sometimes gained at the age of twelve), and as she, like most other local parents, was quite unable to pay the fees required by each of the town's two private schools, she probably reasoned that her restless son might as well be working. And my father, having already often pressed me into service in his fruit-growing and fruit-selling activities, probably figured that he could turn me to further use on his orchard. Thus, the shackles of formal education were discarded.

But there was, at least, one episode arising from school attendance that exercised influence concerning natural history. This came to pass when a boy of my age, then about eight, whispered to me in class that he had made a notable discovery in the way of birds' nests – he had found a colony of 'bottle swadgies' in a cave on his side of the town. He was, he said, quite willing to reveal the find; but, being moved by thoughts of profit rather than the spreading of knowledge, he indicated that an escort fee would be required.

'Wattle-y'-gimme?' he asked. Negotiation followed. Cash payment being out of the question among penniless boys, we closed the deal with the next best thing – something to eat – and so, next day, I bestowed upon that rising businessman a large quince plucked from one of our household trees.

We went then to a ragged hillside and clambered down and through the tunnels of a long-abandoned mine; and there, with the aid of a lighted scrap of candle, I saw for the first time a group of the remarkable bottle-shaped nests of the small birds which I later came to know, quite well, as fairy martins. Doubtless my companion of that expedition, if he be still living, has long since forgotten our adventure, but the sight of those mud-pelleted nests, so neatly attached to the roof of the cave, and with the elfin swallows darting in and out, has remained with me.

◆

Perhaps it should be said that my first clear recollection of contact with the world of Nature, the play of non-human activities, dates from about the age of three. In brief, the memory relates to my action – very smart action – in diving beneath a sofa each time thunder broke loose. It needed many smiling reassurances from Mother, together with an elder brother's pronouncement that the noises were merely 'beer barrels rolling in the sky', to convince me that the end of the world was not at hand.

That triviality aside, I advance a little in time and reflect upon the glory of a flowering peach-tree that grew at one side of the old home. The pink chasteness of those blossoms rivalled in appeal a mass of white blooms on an almond-tree growing nearby; and together they seemed to me, from the age of perhaps five years onward, to be very gracious sights – beautiful in their own right and additionally welcome as harbingers of Spring.

The almond-tree, moreover, was a banquet-hall for birds. Silver-eyes frequently flitted among the blossoms. So did other small honeyeaters. But, most of all, the guests were lorikeets, gay little nectar-loving parrots, the one kind green-bodied and purple-crowned and the other green-bodied with a red face.

I gazed at those blossoms and birds often and earnestly in the days of late winter. And, from time to time, Mother rested from her domestic labours and gazed at both her son and the tree-pageant, meanwhile murmuring verses or melodies acquired as a girl in the peace of rural Perthshire.

So, then, when the question is asked, 'How did you begin to study birds?' the best reply would appear to be:

'Appreciation took rise, at a very early age, under the combined influence of the birds themselves and a spiritual heritage from the Scottish highlands. Especially was the influence exercised by birds of many colours that visited a blossoming almond-tree in our household yard in early spring, by the sight of numerous remarkable nests of small swallows seen in the half-light of an old mining cave, and by the colours of both the forms and voices of various birds seen or heard, either by day or night, in or near a sequestered bush orchard'.

MARTIN BOYD

Martin Boyd (1893–1972). One of a large artistic and
cosmopolitan family, Boyd, born in Switzerland, grew
up in Victoria but spent much of his adult life in
England and Europe. In World War I he served in the
English forces. His autobiographies are *A Single Flame*
(1939) and *Day of My Delight* (1965). The extracts come
from the second.

◆ ◆ ◆ ◆

There was more point in 1938 than there is now in writing of my
war experience. Since then horrors beyond imagining and outside
the range of any crimes of history have been inflicted on humanity
by its rulers, and what I say would be negligible in comparison. Also
I have put most of it into *When Blackbirds Sing*, though the hero of
that book has no resemblance to myself. But as one of the excuses
for this autobiography is to make a contribution, however slight, to
'human evidence' and to give the effect of experience on character,
and as the war must undoubtedly have had a considerable effect on
me, I shall put down some of my more vivid memories, even
though, as in life, a proportion of them may be trivial.

On the night before I left England I was driving through the darkened streets to the Grosvenor Hotel, where I slept to be in time for the morning train, when a horse lorry came out of a side street and the shaft went clean through the door of the taxi, missing me by inches. I took this as a good omen.

With two or three other subalterns from my depot, I was dumped at about three in the afternoon at a railway siding near Calais. It was cold and wet. The name Calais had always suggested to me the English queen and the six burghers, and Bloody Mary's broken heart, and Wordsworth's sonnet, but here there was nothing to see beyond sheds and cinders and a lot of railway line, gleaming under the grey sky. At last we entrained for Étaples. The local Nord trains were never very luxurious. During the war, with their broken glass and bedraggled seats, they were like trains in hell. It took us several hours to make the short journey to Étaples. Someone found a candle-end and stuck it in its own grease on the window ledge. It flickered dismally in the draught, and went out when at rare intervals the train jolted forward. I was excited at being in France and peered greedily out at the dark flat countryside. I had always looked forward to going to France as to a supreme experience. As I strained my eyes at the broken windows it was as if some youth who had dreamed of, but never met a woman, had at last been confronted with a bald and toothless hag.

We arrived at Étaples at midnight, and the next day we had to march out with our draft of men to the Bull-ring, a place with quite as unpleasant memories as the front line. The Bull-ring was a part of the huge sand dunes across the river from Le Touquet. We marched out there against a biting wind, on ground that had been frozen for weeks. We were handed out gas-masks while a flustered captain shouted, unheard against the wind, how they were to be tested and worn. The bewildered men were then herded into a pitch-dark tunnel dug in the sand, where the gas was two or three hundred times as strong as it would ever be in the open. It penetrated our masks as we stumbled choking through the dark. A man fell over and was trodden on by those pushing behind him. It was rumoured that a man a day was killed through carelessness at the Bull-ring. This must be an exaggeration, but the worst aspect of a war is not the danger of wounds and death from the enemy, but the submission of one's body and soul to brutes and fools in authority.

♦

By 1917 no private soldier had the faintest idea what he was fighting for, so that the generals ordered more and more raids to keep the blood-lust simmering, and to try to key up the necessary hatred of the enemy, to whom the Tommies referred without rancour as 'old Jerry'. We were ordered to lecture our platoons on bayonet fighting and the spirit of offensive, to try and stir them to a vicious hatred of the Germans. I thought: 'There is no escape from doing this filthy thing, so I will go the whole hog.' In an old barn, built of thatch and clay and smelling of cows, I gave them a lurid and savage harangue on the delights of murder, on kicked genitals, and jabbed guts. Unless they cultivated these pleasures, the war for civilisation could not be brought to a successful conclusion.

When I had finished and they were dismissed, the men walked away in embarrassed silence, feeling that an attempt had been made to corrupt their core of human virtue.

Once when I was orderly officer, there was a man undergoing field punishment No. 1, which entailed being tied to a cart. I was expected to see him on my rounds, but the N.C.O. edged me away from the barn where he was supposed to be tied. At first I insisted, thinking that the man might be suffering, but then I realised that he was not tied up at all, and that there were certain human indignities demanded by the war machine, which the men would always resist when possible.

♦

There are two attitudes of mind that lead to a contented old age. One depends on ourselves, the other on the condition of our times. The first is to look back on the good things we have known, the delight of youth, and the capacities of manhood, not with regret, but with satisfaction, regarding them as an asset of memory.

The second is to realise that those assets are not lost forever, but will be enjoyed by others through centuries to come. When a young man of a thousand years ahead feels delight, the delight we felt is immortal. When he feels the same response to a girl's face, or to an orchard in bloom, or to an aspect of truth, to that extent, apart from all theological speculation, we continue to live. Therefore our personal happiness in our later years depends partly on how far we think present conditions are conducive to the perpetuation of our own experience. I do not mean that art forms or social habits or games must be the same, but that man's essential self must cherish the values which the good men of every known civilisation have held to be eternal.

However it is useless to speculate on millenniums ahead. What we may be concerned with is how the young people we know, and possibly their children, are to achieve the conditions for a good life. Old men are proverbially inclined to view the world as going to the dogs, so I shall try to regard present tendencies objectively, and see truthfully how they help to give me the second attitude of mind.

There are two things which seem to threaten the immortality we have in the survival of our values. They are the myths of the 'atomic age' and 'modern man'. I have seen a review which condemned a book for affirming traditional standards in 'this atomic age'.

About a dozen men have gone into space in a Sputnik. The remaining hundreds of millions of humanity either go to work by bus or train, or plod across the fields, and the groceries are still delivered by a boy on a bicycle. They do not come whizzing into the store cupboard by atomic energy. None of these millions are affected in any detail of their lives by the 'atomic age' and their interest in the man in the Sputnik is rather less than that in the divorce of a filmstar or the price of vegetables. As Archbishop Fisher said, these flights 'have not solved one human problem'. No discovery of science, no rocket into outer space, can alter in any way the laws of our essential being, or of our obedience to the forces of good. The only effect the atomic age has had on man has been to give him an underlying sense of nervous apprehension, which also must have been felt during the Black Death, and by the Christians under Diocletian.

'Modern man' is another myth without meaning. There is no such thing. The young Italians playing football on a vacant piece of ground near my room are identical in every emotion and shout and gesture with the boys who sixty years ago used to play impromptu football at Kew, while waiting to go into school.

The man who goes up in a Sputnik is identical with the one who fifty years earlier hacked his way through ice to the North or South Pole; and he is identical with the Elizabethan who went in search of the North-West Passage; and he is identical with Odysseus; while the unhappy refugees from modern tyrannies are identical with the Holy Family fleeing into Egypt; and when we relate them to the true Myth, they are not merely political victims, but our brothers and the eternal children of God.

A. B. FACEY

Albert Barnett Facey (1894–1982) was abandoned by his
mother and lived with his grandmother in the
Coolgardie goldfields. From the age of eight he earned
his own living on the land in Western Australia,
brutally exploited by harsh employers. After being
wounded at Gallipoli he taught himself to read, tried
farming, and became an active trade unionist while
working in Perth tramways. *A Fortunate Life* (1981) has
been made into a television 'mini-series'.

♦ ♦ ♦ ♦

When there was a crowd stopping the night I had to sleep in the
back of the stables on bags of chaff and corn, or a pile of empty bags.
This time Bill came and slept there with me. On Christmas Eve we
talked for a long time after we had made our beds. Bill suggested
that we hide some of the grog. He pointed out that by doing this
there would be less to drink and it would help to stop any brawling.
He said, 'It is only when they get very drunk that they brawl.'

After we had talked about this we decided that we would hide
some of the grog. Bill said he knew where it was because he had seen

Alec and Bob putting it in the large hessian cooler used for the milk.

The cooler stood out on the back verandah. It was very large and had a container on top that would hold about eight gallons of water. There were strips of bag running from the water down the hessian sides and the water soaked up into these, then onto the sides of the cooler making the inside very cold. Being outside on the verandah in the fresh air made it cooler still. The bottom shelf was packed with the drinks for Christmas Day.

Bill and I agreed that when the lights up at the house went out, and we were sure that everyone was asleep, we would carry out our plan. Bill said, 'If they find out some is missing they will never expect us to be the ones who took it.' I asked, 'Where do you think we should hide it?' Bill suggested that the top of the stable roof would be the ideal place because it was covered with about twelve inches of straw.

It was a very dark night and we carried out our plan in the early hours of the morning. We took three bottles of whisky, three bottles of rum and four bottles of wine. They were all quart bottles. We weren't seen by anyone. Bill climbed up onto the roof of the stable and I handed the bottles up to him. Bill put them in holes that he made in the straw, then covered them over.

Next morning, Christmas Day, everyone was asleep when I went up to light the fire. Bill went with me to get the cows, then we filled up the water-troughs at the soak. That took nearly an hour, but there was still no movement over at the house. They were still asleep. We fed and watered the pigs and Bill milked the two cows that had to be milked. We took the milk up to the cooler and then the old lady came out and told us to get our own breakfast. After we had our breakfast we took the sheep out to graze and arrived back near midday. The women were busy preparing Christmas dinner. The men were all under the weather, some couldn't walk.

When Bill and I went in to dinner everyone was drinking. Some were so drunk they couldn't sit in their chairs properly. We had our dinner and then went and refilled the water-trough. After that we had a sleep in the stable until it was time to bring the cows in. I went for the cows and Bill filled the water-trough again. Besides the cattle and horses, the sheep had to have extra water in the summertime.

This Christmas Day it was really hot – a hundred and one degrees fahrenheit in the shade.

When I got back with the cows it was nearly sundown. Bill came to meet me and said that there was a big row on at the house. The grog had run out and Bob was blaming everyone for getting away with it, or stealing it, even the old lady. This made Bill and me very scared. Bill had heard Bob say that last Christmas he had found some bottles planted in the stable and he would search it this time from end to end. Bill suggested that we take the grog that we had planted and put it somewhere else.

We got the bottles off the stable roof (it was getting dark), and put them into two bags. We put these on top of the pig shed roof. A little while later Bob and three others commenced looking for the missing bottles. They were still pretty drunk, so we felt sure they wouldn't find them.

About half an hour later Bill's brother George came and told us that Bob wanted Bill up at the house. Bill went up to Bob and I stayed in the stable. Later I heard Bill yelling and I knew then that he was copping a belting. They were trying to make him tell them where the grog was. This made me frightened so I thought I would shift the bottles from the roof of the pig house in case Bill gave in and told.

It was very dark by then so I went to the pig house and brought the bottles down to the ground. I intended to put them in a bag and hide them. The pigs were all asleep, so I knocked the heads off the bottles and emptied them into the trough with the pig feed. This would save me two trips to get rid of the grog, as I couldn't have carried all the full bottles but the empties were easy to manage in a bag. I put the bag, full of broken bottles, over the fence and took it down into the gully close to the soak.

When I was clear I heard loud voices going towards the pig house. I couldn't see who it was, but one of the voices was Bob's and I could also hear Alec. I was safe as it was very dark, and as long as I didn't make a noise I would be all right. All at once it came to me to let the bag and broken bottles down into the water. There was always about eight feet of water in the soak and the weight of the bottles would hold the bag down, and no one would be able to find it. Having done this I sneaked back to the pig house and could hear

that Bill was copping it again. They were belting him and calling him
a liar, then Bob's voice came above the others and said, 'Find Berty.
Then we will get to the bottom of this.'

They all started looking for me. I had no boots on so I quietly got
away into the bush and stayed hidden. They never came near where
I was. Then a terrible din came from the pig shed. Two or three pigs
started to squeal, then a few more, then finally all the pigs were
squealing. Oh, what a noise. This brought all the half-drunk men
and the women to the pig house. I sneaked up as close as I dared,
wondering what was wrong. Then I heard. Bob yelled out, 'The
young sod has poured the grog into the pig trough and they're all
drunk. Wait until I get hold of him, he'll be sorry for this. I'll skin
him alive.'

This made me go back into hiding in the bush. About two hours
later things became quieter. The pigs were not so noisy and everyone seemed to be settled down for the night.

It was in the early hours of the morning when I ventured into the
stables to get my blanket. Bill was not there. Everything was quiet.
My idea was to wait until daylight came, then clear out and try to get
to Uncle's place. I was very tired and fell asleep and when I woke it
wasn't only daylight but the sun was well up, and standing over me
was Bob with a stock-whip in his hand. I had not undressed for bed.
I still had on my pants and a shirt, and an old rag hat. These, along
with my red blanket, were all my belongings.

Bob said, 'Well, how much grog did you and Bill put into the pig
trough last night? Now there's no use denying it, we thrashed it out
of Bill last night and you've still got yours coming. Come on get up,
where's the rest of the grog?' I didn't speak, just stood looking up at
him. He gave me a cut around the legs, then he lashed me three or
four times around the shoulders and body. I jumped up and tried to
run out of the stable. As I got out of the doors he caught me around
the legs again and I fell to the ground. He continued to whip me.
The whip was one he used to tame the horses with and he was an
expert. He knew how to use that whip. I don't know how many
times he cut me because I must have fainted.

◆

When we were called to our sections our officer gave us a briefing on the proper instructions for landing. We were told that our ship would move as close as possible into shore but would keep out of range of the enemy's shelling. He said, 'They will throw everything they've got at us as soon as they wake up to what we're doing. Now, when the ship stops you will be called to the side and lined up. On the side of the ship is a rope net already in place. A destroyer will come alongside and you will climb over the side and down the rope onto the deck of the destroyer when ordered. When the destroyer has enough men it will pull away and go towards where you are to land. Close to shore you will be met by a small motor boat towing rowing-boats. You will climb into the rowing-boats and the motor boats will take you as close to shore as possible. There will be sailors in the rowing-boats and they will take you into the beach. Now you are to get ashore as best you can and then line up on the beach and await further instructions.'

This was it. We were scared stiff – I know I was – but keyed up and eager to be on our way. We thought we would tear right through the Turks and keep going to Constantinople.

Troops were taken off both sides of the ship onto destroyers. My platoon and other 'D' Company men were on the same destroyer. All went well until we were making the change into rowing-boats.

Suddenly all hell broke loose; heavy shelling and shrapnel fire commenced. The ships that were protecting our troops returned fire. Bullets were thumping into us in the rowing-boat. Men were being hit and killed all around me.

When we were cut loose to make our way to the shore was the worst period. I was terribly frightened. The boat touched bottom some thirty yards from shore so we had to jump out and wade into the beach. The water in some places was up to my shoulders. The Turks had machine-guns sweeping the strip of beach where we landed – there were many dead already when we got there. Bodies of men who had reached the beach ahead of us were lying all along the beach and wounded men were screaming for help. We couldn't stop for them – the Turkish fire was terrible and mowing into us. The order to line up on the beach was forgotten. We all ran for our lives over the strip of beach and got into the scrub and bush. Men were falling all around me. We were stumbling over bodies – running blind.

The sight of the bodies on the beach was shocking. It worried me for days that I couldn't stop to help the men calling out. (This was one of the hardest things of the war for me and I'm sure for many of the others. There were to be other times under fire when we couldn't help those that were hit. I would think for days, 'I should have helped that poor beggar.')

We used our trenching tools to dig mounds of earth and sheltered from the firing until daylight – the Turks never let up. Their machine-guns were sweeping the scrub. The slaughter was terrible.

I am sure that there wouldn't have been one of us left if we had obeyed that damn fool order to line up on the beach.

♦

After the first lot of interviews, the two returned soldiers and I were left. Then my name was called again. This time it looked like I had been chosen for the job. The man doing the interviewing was the owner and manager. He asked me a lot of questions about myself and what I knew about ironmongery, and I explained that my step-father had an ironmongery shop in Hay Street, West Perth and that I had had quite a bit of experience with all plumbing requisites before I enlisted in the A.I.F. He looked up and said, 'You're our man. Now I want to ask you a few personal questions. Do you get a war pension?' I said, 'I do.' He asked me how much. I replied that I hadn't been notified yet and asked him why he wanted to know. He said that they would have to know to be able to fix my wages. I asked, 'What has the war pension got to do with my pay?' He replied, 'Well, you don't expect to receive a war pension plus full wages do you?' This made me see red. I said, 'What in the hell are you coming at? Are you trying to get cheap labour? If you are, try it on some other mug. What did you do about enlisting and doing your bit or are you one of those cold-footed bastards that stayed home to take advantage of the enlisted man's wife or girlfriend for your own filthy lust!' With that he called an assistant and told him to call the police.

I walked out and slammed the door and told the other returned men not to go in there, that he was only looking for cheap labour. That was my first experience of finding a light job. Some thanks after all the promises given to us, and this firm had a large placard displayed outside saying: *Your Country is in danger. Enlist now.* After this episode I was expecting to be confronted by a policeman at any time to answer for what I had said to the firm's owner, but nothing happened.

It upset me to find people who were just out to take advantage of you, especially when it was something like this. After I came back from the war that was the only time that I came across that sort of exploitation, but apparently it went on quite a bit.

There were also a few times when I ran into larrikins who would jeer and sling off at me for going to the war, but I soon sorted them out. I would clout them quick and lively – they would all show a fight until then, but a good straight left would fix them.

Generally though, people were marvellous – trying to get down the street sometimes was impossible. People would stop me to talk, to find out what had happened and what it was really like. They probably had someone who was away in it, or who had been killed, and wanted to know. I was worried sometimes that the police would be after me for blocking the footpath.

People at home were all a hundred percent behind the war. They were all sad about what was going on at Gallipoli, but the feeling was to send more troops to help. They'd have sent everyone they could get hold of to help. Some men who didn't go got a rough time, but we never said anything to them because we thought that they had some brains. I would have stayed behind if I had known.

STELLA BOWEN

Stella Bowen (1895–1947) was born in Adelaide, studied
art in England, met the novelist and literary
entrepreneur Ford Madox Ford and with him mixed in
artistic circles in England, France and Italy. Her
autobiography *Drawn From Life* (1941, reprinted 1984)
presents a vivid picture of North Adelaide society
before World War I and gives a compassionate account
of her life with Ford. During World War II she was an
Official Artist of the Australian War Memorial Board.

◆ ◆ ◆ ◆

The land where I was born is a blue and yellow country, although
when the sun pours out of a cloudless sky, there is very little colour
to be seen. The blazing sky itself is almost empty of blue, and the
yellow ochre of the dried grass is silvered by the glare. Even the
shadows are less blue than painters like to pretend, and the air is so
dry that the distance has the same quality as the foreground, and
you can judge of space and perspective only by the diminishing scale
in size. Local colour – flowers in the garden, or a little girl's dress – is
sucked out and bleached by the sun, and the extreme visibility is
tempered only by a shimmering heat-haze rising in the middle dis-

tance from the baked earth. The world is seen as a pattern of light and shade.

If you want to see a pattern of colour, to see the flower-beds as a rich mosaic and the child's frock a miracle of pink, you must come north where the sun is veiled in mist, and to your undazzled eyes, colour comes into its own. I never knew verdure until I came to England, and I have never forgotten my first surprised delight in the separate veils of blue which define each stage of the English distance.

On the first day of an Australian heat wave, you shut and darken all the doors and windows of your home. Underneath the corrugated iron roof lies a layer of insulating seaweed. The hours pass in a dim and listless obscurity, until eight o'clock – or perhaps nine – when it has become cool enough outside to open up the windows. After dark, all the houses are empty, and from every garden comes the sound of quiet voices, relaxing into sociability.

Perhaps at midnight you carry your mattress on to the lawn, where a mass of pinky-white oleander flowers, sweeping to the ground beside you, reflect such brilliance from the moon that you must needs turn the other way. You wonder whether what your nurse said is true, and that the moon can change you into an idiot with a crooked face; but you are too tired to care much.

When the early dawn arrives, to chase you indoors with its dog-barkings and its cock-crowings and its glare, you are still unrefreshed and quite unready for to-morrow. The house is closed again before the sun gets up, and you go back to bed to sleep again till breakfast-time.

Your English cousin, seeing trees bending in the wind, says: 'Doesn't it look fresher? Couldn't we go out?' But if she ventures her nose into that scorching oven-blast, straight from the desert – 'I don't think it would be safe,' she'll say.

Sand and grit are everywhere, and flies of course, and no water for the garden. And all the talk is of the bushfires to the north.

But the business of the town goes on as usual, the men don't even wear white suits, and the hours of work are the same as on the days when it is cool. When the change comes, which may be in five days, or in fifteen, the wind swings round quite suddenly, and a great freshness blows up from the sea. Doors bang and the trees bend the other way and the temperature may drop 20° in half an hour. Everyone collapses.

After that, comes a period of the kind of weather that good Australians refer to when they talk about their wonderful climate. The kind of weather in which you remember bathing all day long in the bluest sea in the world, and eating all the fruit you could stomach – figs warm from the trees, grapes (we were very fussy about the kinds we thought worth eating), oranges, of course – and once you really start eating oranges there is no reason why you should ever stop – passion-fruit, apricots, peaches and nectarines, all the fruits of the earth and no stint. It was considered inevitable, but unimportant, that we children should make ourselves a little ill sometimes in the fruit season.

And you remember the grey-green gum trees which give no shade, and the pine trees and the pepper trees which are not much better in this respect, and the great light spaces of the open landscape, in contrast with the luxuriant gardens, painfully maintained in times of drought, with their green lawns and deep shade, verandas screened by trellised vines and flowering creepers, plumbago, bougainvillea, hibiscus, mimosa (but we call it wattle) and dozens of flowers whose names I have forgotten.

And of course there were hammocks under the vines.

I wish I knew the truth about that strangely dim and distant life in Adelaide before the war. I have reconstructed it in my memory as a queer little backwater of intellectual timidity – a kind of hangover of Victorian provincialism, isolated by three immense oceans and a great desert, and stricken by recurrent waves of paralysing heat. It lies shimmering on a plain encircled by soft blue hills, prettyish, banal, and filled to the brim with an anguish of boredom.

I must be wrong. There must have been more in it than ever met my eye. My poor small eye was placed very close to the ground, and my view was doubtless a worm's-eye view. But it was the only view I had . . .

I was born in the sort of house that must inevitably end its days as a boarding house. It was sizable, rather gloomy, at a sufficiently good but not fashionable address, detached, with two little lawns and a summer-house in front and a back yard behind containing clothes

lines, a stable and a coach house, a see-saw and a swing. Being in
Australia, it had a front veranda with balcony above, and its roof was
largely smothered in Banksia roses, bougainvillaea and other greenery. There was a trellis of vines covering the path from the front to
the back and figs, apricots, lemons and oranges grew around the
back yard.

There was a pampas-grass in the garden, and an aspidistra in the
drawing-room.

There were no modern conveniences. The nicest thing about it
was the view. Being placed high on the edge of the town's oldest
suburb, it looked down over low-lying park lands where cattle
grazed, over the distant slums surrounding Port Adelaide, where
factory chimneys trailed smoke wreaths, and delicately drawn ship-
masts reared themselves against the most spectacular sunsets I have
ever seen.

Trains going north ran across the middle of this view. They ran
for three days as far as the desert, and then came back again. I hated
the thought of that dead-end!

I never went more than a few hours north on that line myself,
when visiting those of my girl friends whose parents had sheep
stations in the fertile belt near the coast. The life on those stations
was the most characteristically Australian life I ever saw. It had its
own style and its own flavour and it could never have been the same
anywhere else. In the towns, except for the modifications imposed
by the climate, we were just pale imitations of something which was
already moribund in England . . .

Going to England was called 'going home,' even by people who
had never been there and whose fathers had never been. We all
talked with varying degrees of Australian accent, of which we were
ashamed when we became aware of it. We regarded a real English
accent with positive reverence.

At Christmas, which came at midsummer with the temperature
at – perhaps – 100° in the shade, we sat down at midday to turkey
and flaming plum pudding, having sent each other cards depicting
robins in the snow.

We were, in fact, a suburb of England. But it was different in the
country. If you were a hearty sort of person who liked riding, and
the great open spaces (and they certainly were very great and very

open), and if you did not mind living in an ugly bungalow with a corrugated iron roof, and liked rough-and-ready polo, and racing, and driving big distances in derelict cars to visit your nearest neighbours; if you liked jogging on horseback through the dusty sunlight behind a herd of sheep and had no hankering after the Arts or other sophistications, then you might well hold the view that life on a station was the only life worth living.

But I was a town girl.

JOAN LINDSAY

Lady (Joan) Lindsay (1896–1984), author of *Picnic at Hanging Rock*, was born and educated in Melbourne. She married the artist Daryl Lindsay in 1922. The extracts from *Time Without Clocks* (1962) describe the impact of the Lindsay clan on the young bride.

♦ ♦ ♦ ♦

Time – whether you are burning it up by falling in love or spreading it out thin in a dentist's waiting room – is a commodity that cannot be weighed out and measured by clocks. The genius who first thought up a concoction of little cogwheels and pulleys and striking bells for the slicing of our days into twenty-four hours has considerably increased the muddle and confusion of the civilised world.

For most of the years of this book Daryl and I managed very happily without man-made time. Although on New Year's Eve we would hang up in the studio the gift calendar from the local store – a blonde with a sheaf of wattle blossom, a misty eyed spaniel with a hangover – neither the kitchen clock nor the figured squares of the calendar could measure our first golden summers at Mulberry Hill. They were the timeless clockless summers of a dream.

♦

We were to lunch with Daryl's three artist brothers: Norman, Percy and Lionel at their favourite Greek restaurant long since changed hands or disappeared. Like most painters the Lindsays all had a nose for the best places to eat and drink. Where was this one? I only remember my footsteps suddenly dragging as we walked up a sunny hill towards Macquarie Street. It was my first meeting with my three new brothers-in-law.

They were all there waiting for us over a glass of sherry, all talking at once and all addressing each other by the family name of 'Joe'. I remember Lionel embracing me warmly in his own delightful manner – a cool hand pressed on either cheek: I could feel my head being tilted backwards my hat sliping sideways. Then smack! the brisk downswooping Lindsay kiss! 'Delighted to meet you, old girl!'

'A dozen oysters to start off with Joe?'

'You know Joe you must admit old Joe here can *paint*. That was a damned good study, old man.'

'I say! Joe was telling me there's a cracking portrait by Tom Roberts kicking about at Gills in Melbourne . . .'

'A stumer!' puts in Lionel Joe, using a favourite word of his own coining.

'Joe you old bastard! give your poor wife some hock!' Daryl asked: 'Has anyone seen old Henry about lately? We heard in London he was pretty sick.' (A few days later, in Macquarie Street, we *did* see the poet Henry Lawson shuffling along with fever bright eyes in a shabby brown suit. Lionel slipped a coin into the half-opened hand as we passed but no word was spoken.)

The Joes were gregarious to a man and the meal was punctuated by a hundred alarums and excursions as one or other of the Lindsays sprang from the table to greet a friend, lift a glass to someone on the other side of the room or examine a drawing pinned to the wall. I remember Lionel leaving his seat to throw both arms round the shoulders of a dignified individual in a tarboosh who willy-willy remained locked in a python embrace for several minutes while Lionel chatted of this and that. Finally he released the embarrassed manager with a hearty slap on the back and resumed his seat. 'That fellow makes the best Turkish coffee in Sydney. Superb!' The talk ranged over a vast international terrain that took in Proust and privvies and always, as a recurring theme song, painting. The brothers drew on a rich and inexhaustible store of shared experience family jokes wisdom and wit. There was much hilarious venom-spitting – the exclusive Lindsay brand of venom which I later came to recognise – laced with the milk of human kindness even as they tore their victims limb from limb. (Bores, public and private, any kind of pomposity in a top hat, the contemporary 'Wowser' in various guises.) Of an unpopular relative Daryl said: 'I've got nothing against the poor bastard but by God I could slit his throat!' Actually not one of the Joes would have willingly hurt a fly. During the oysters I had seen a strong family resemblance. By the time the lobster arrived – an item personally supervised by Percy as the expert – they had become four clear cut individuals alike only in the exuberant vitality that made everyone else in the room look like waxwork dummies. Percy the eldest could be tough when occasion demanded as when he quelled a quarrelsome drunk outside a Melbourne fish shop with a length of barracouta – an excellent substitute for a rubber truncheon. Today however he was gentle fresh-faced and shining as an elderly cherub, attired in spotless white and panama hat and carrying as he often did a string shopping bag. Dear happy-go-lucky Percy for all his casual ways was a very domesticated man and a good cook. Lionel in spite of the warm day was wearing his customary scarf about his neck, tossing it lightly over a shoulder as he talked with the graceful gesture of a matador with a cape. A passionate lover of Spain he might with his expressive eyes gracious manners and beautiful speaking voice easily have passed as a light complexioned Spaniard. Although our table was a focus of attention I noticed that most of the patrons were unashamedly staring at Norman, already acclaimed a genius by the

Australian public on account of his powerful cartoons in the Sydney *Bulletin*. While the man in the street gloated on the horned demons mealy-mouthed parsons and misunderstood prostitutes the more aesthetically minded admired the astounding mastery of technique. Norman Lindsay was a distinguished local celebrity – somebody to be pointed out strolling down George Street or lunching at the Hotel Australia with his strikingly handsome wife. I had expected him to be 'tall dark and handsome' something like the figure of Don Juan swaggering through hell in his own etching. One should never build up a mental image beforehand of a celebrity one is just about to meet. Mine of Norman was so wrong that it took several minutes to adjust myself to the reality of the frail-looking man across the table engaged on an impassioned analysis of Nietzsche's philosophy. As he talked a heavy lock of dark brown hair continually fell unnoticed across his forehead. The glass of wine at his elbow stood forgotten. The climate in which the dismal German thrived was far far away from Cytherea. As soon as he stopped talking it struck me as a sad over-sensitive face dominated by the too large nose and extraordinarily luminous eyes. With Nietzsche finally beaten and left for dead and the advent of the gorgonzola, the genius of *The Magic Pudding* and *Saturdee* took over and a wild internal gaiety shot up like a flame. Here was the great comic artist who like Phil May saw the cosmic humour of ordinary things that most people pass by . . . an amorous rooster in a back-yard . . . an old sleepy dog woken by its own fleas . . . small-town little boys sniggering behind a fence . . . Prime Ministers, Prima Donnas, cockatoos . . .

The restaurant was beginning to empty, the waiters clearing away the glasses and shaking out the tablecloths. The four Lindsays were still talking. More wine was called for, more coffee. 'A brandy Joe! . . . Waiter! A black coffee for the lady!' far into the sultry afternoon. All the Joes as they talked used their hands with the expressive gestures of painters who make more than ordinary play with the thumb. The air above our table seemed aflutter with hands as the air above a dovecote is aflutter with wings.

Now in the warm shuttered room the slats of sunlight are creeping across the litter of coffee cups and wine glasses. The tablecloths the menu a handkerchief and every other available surface is scribbled over with pencil notes and sketches. 'Wait a minute Joe . . . it was like this . . . and this.' A stub of pencil, a burnt match, a fountain pen, anything will do. The tired waiter who knows these customers of old folds his napkin over his arm opens a newspaper and sits down in a corner. At least they will tip him well when they remember to get up and go home. The wine the laughter most of all the talk – the sense of having suddenly landed on a new planet – has gone to my head. I long to tell these entrancing creatures that I love them all. Words fail me and I can only sit agape in admiring silence. Now and forever I know without any doubt (I was never quite certain at home) that the pen and brush are indeed mightier and ever so much more fun than the sword or even the cricket bat. In this illumined moment a web of tangled schoolgirl values is swept away and I begin to live in the free Lindsay world of ideas and imagination.

SIR KEITH HANCOCK

Sir Keith Hancock (1898–), born in Melbourne and
educated at Melbourne and Oxford, became Professor
of History at Adelaide, Birmingham and Oxford
Universities and Director of the Institute of
Commonwealth Studies in London 1949–57. He
describes his autobiography *Country and Calling* (1954)
as the record of 'a man's endeavour to discover himself
in relation to his native land and his work and his idea
of history'.

♦ ♦ ♦ ♦

About this time I found myself in a gang of Protestant heroes who
used to exchange taunts and threats with a Roman Catholic gang.
We would chant:

> *Cathlick Dogs*
> *Jump like Frogs*
> *Eat no meat on Fri-ee-days.*

And they would sing:

Proddy Dog, Proddy Dog,
Sitting on a well,
Up comes the Devil
And pulls him down to hell.

Then we and the Catholic boys would pelt each other with cow-
dung. There was plenty of it lying about on the river bank, some of
it too new and wet to pick up, some of it too dry and light to hurt;
what every boy looked for was a piece that was dry and hard outside
but with a centre of green sticky muck. But even when we scored or
suffered a hit or two with these stinking bombs we never threw
stones, nor, so far as I can remember, fought with our fists. When
we had flung enough cow-dung we chanted our doggerel again and
went our separate ways jeering.

Thus I managed to show a brave face to the world despite my
pugilistic débâcle. If I doubted my courage, nobody else did. Indeed,
I soon had the good luck to get myself acclaimed as a young hero not
only in Bairnsdale but throughout Victoria. Some of us were playing hide-and-seek one evening on the river bank and I sped away
with a boy called Ronnie at my heels. He was a year or two younger
than I and had not yet learnt to swim and as he followed me along a
slippery track under a little bluff he fell into the water. I promptly
jumped in after him and pulled him out; then, with a proper sense
of dramatic effect, I allowed myself to be scolded by Mother for
coming home dripping wet – for I knew that I would appear doubly
heroic if I let others bring the news of my exploit. Before long a
message came from Ronnie that he would give me all the money in
his money box (drat him, he never did!) as a reward for saving his
life. Next morning a policeman took me down to the river to show
him where the event had happened and tell him the details. The
water was running fast and the policeman's measurements showed
that it was deep; yet I seem to remember that I had one foot on the
bottom while I was getting hold of Ronnie and bringing him in. Can
it be that the place I showed the policeman was not precisely the
place where Ronnie fell in? The published account of my exploit
says that Ronnie flung his arms around me and nearly choked me –
'Hancock freed himself, turned onto his back, put the boy on his
shoulder . . .' – but how in the world could the policeman get to

know all this except by my telling him? Did I tell him the truth? I was taken down to Melbourne to be presented with the bronze medal of the Royal Humane Society; but to this day I simply do not know whether I was a little hero or a little liar.

◆

One afternoon in the early nineteen-twenties, when six or seven Rhodes Scholars were gossiping with me in Balliol, I said something prim and another Australian jeered – 'Listen to the parson's son!' He was a parson's son himself, as I quickly pointed out. And when a Canadian chipped in I said at a venture, 'You're one too.' He was. Then the three of us turned inquisitor against all the others. Everybody in that room, so it turned out – Australian, New Zealander, Newfoundlander, Canadian, Rhodesian, South African – was a parson's son. The coincidence was not quite so unusual as might be thought, for the Rhodes Scholars of those days, despite their wide diversity of geographical background, had for the most part a closely similar background of family upbringing. And from their similar families they went to schools of pretty much the same stamp. Although I did not know it, the path that I was following between the ages of nine and nineteen was little different from the paths that my contemporaries were following in the widely different landscapes of Natal, Taranaki or British Columbia.

For ten years or more I was being shaped for Oxford without ever imagining that this was my destiny. Rhodes Scholars I understood, when I first began vaguely to hear about them, were confident young men of immense athletic prowess, initiative, brilliance and popularity; whereas I was good at jumping examiners' hurdles but shy of most others. A most unexpected and unwelcome change had befallen me after I left Gippsland. The boisterous young tough whom I portrayed in my last chapter became the shy bookworm who belongs to the present one. I did not want to be a bookworm, I wanted to be an athlete. Jim could knock up fifty runs in fifty minutes, Justin could race and dodge the whole length of the football field; but I became so clumsy with my hands and so slow on my feet that I lost the confidence necessary for success in games. Perhaps our migration from country to city was the cause of this? But, at the time, it seemed to make little difference. Our suburb, I must confess, was a drab place unglamorously named Moonee Ponds; but it had glamour for me and my schoolmates – ragged allotments where we could play cricket on a dirt pitch with a kerosene tin for a wicket, plenty of dried cow dung to pelt each other with, a mysterious drain down which we could track each other in our gang games to its outflow in the Moonee Ponds Creek – this creek was, indeed, a pitiable contrast to my gleaming river, but I romped along its banks as if they had been Gippsland and even broke my leg in climbing its miserable muddy cliffs. No, the dreary suburb may have stunted my delight in beauty, but I cannot blame it for my athletic incompetence or the shyness which crept gradually upon me.

XAVIER HERBERT

Xavier Herbert (1901–84) was born at Port Hedland, Western Australia, worked as a hospital dispenser in Melbourne and later moved to the Northern Territory, where he gathered experience for his two famous novels *Capricornia* (1938) and *Poor Fellow My Country* (1975). This extract from his autobiography *Disturbing Element* (1963) throws considerable light on the themes and dominant imagery in *Capricornia*.

♦ ♦ ♦ ♦

My very first memory is of being on a beach, watching my father and my half-brother and half-sister sporting in the sea. That's all there is to it, except a feeling of detachment. But I believe it to be one of the most significant of my memories, its import the fact that I was standing apart from those nearest and dearest to me, which I take to mean that I was experiencing the revelation that I did not truly belong to them.

Such perception in a tiny child (I could have been no more than three) might be thought incredible. But without allowing for it in any child, how account for lifelong memory of seemingly trivial things? My theory is that preoccupation with the puzzle of all puzzles, the riddle of the reality of one's own existence, begins with the very dawning of awareness, and that lasting memory is always concerned with it. Certainly it turned out that I didn't belong to my family as closely as most people do to theirs, as closely as I would have liked for the comfort of my soul. Whose fault it was is beside the point. What seems remarkable to me about the revelation I claim is not that it came to me so young but that I was so old before I would accept it.

I believe that what caused me to be standing apart from the group to make the observation was mistrust of them in what I considered a dangerous situation. I assume that I had been frightened, most likely on a previous occasion, by my father's rough handling of me in the sea, and knew I could expect no help from the others. There is ground enough for the assumption. I was always afraid of Dad near water, until first I could outrun him and then outswim him.

Dad was rough like that in all other play he had with me. I say 'he had with me', because I would never be in it unless forced. My memory of our play is a hotch-potch of being held under water, bubbling green sea water or the murky weedy waters of rivers and creeks, by those great vices of hands; of having my head knocked off by those hands in slaps delivered in boxing contests I was compelled to stand up to through having one small foot clamped to the ground by one of his huge feet; of being flung up by those hands on to tall horses that immediately bolted with me in response to a slap on the rump.

Many a scarey kid has had to go through that sort of thing at the hands of a father whose only intention was 'to make a man of him'. But few kids have been driven to the lengths I was by failure of the intention. Apart from convincing myself that my father was my enemy, I have been preoccupied for most of my life with trying to overcome the cowardice I believed due to his malicious mishandling of me.

Surely Dad could not be blamed for clumsiness in handling me when he made a man of my half-brother? Phillip, only three when Dad took to fathering him, had known no other father. It wasn't that he was superior to me in physique. On the contrary, I am of rugged type, while he was spindly. As Mother used to say in comparing us: 'Phillip's the lean, well-bred aristocrat, like his grandfather. You're the peasant type, like your father.'

I never saw Phil do anything particularly courageous, except on horseback, and his sister was just as daring a rider. Nevertheless, he didn't appear to have the slightest difficulty in adjustment to the rough and tumble of masculine life whereas I went into it a complete mess.

As for that malice I believed Dad bore me as a child, if it had been real it must have expressed itself in much more violence than I suffered at his hands. Such were the cuffings I had from him in anger that I scarcely remember them, and it is pretty evident that the one and only thrashing he gave me was due more to conflict over me within himself than to rage against me. Several times I flew at him in defence of Mother, when I thought he was going to do violence on her in quarrelling, and he did nothing to me. He did get in blind rages at times, but he always took them out on a horse or a goat.

Yes, he was really a mild man. Yet I literally made a monster out of him. I mean I made him one in my imagination. Even long after I'd come so far from fearing him as to pity him, the monstrous symbol that stood for him in my subconscious being still lurked there, watching, menacing, a great bull-thing.

I think I can recall the occasion of his establishment as a monster in my imagination. I was very young, too young, presumably, to be left to sleep alone, which was why I was put to bed with him. Maybe Mother was having a baby and the other children had been sent away. I have no recollection of anyone else in the house, indeed of any human presence at all during the critical period. There was only that grunting, roaring, bellowing beast, which pursued me in dreams and was there in the dark room when I woke, so that I braved the unknown terrors beyond in flight from it. Dad was always a prodigious snorer.

I have an idea that my earliest animalizing conception of him was as a great kangaroo. That was natural enough, seeing that a big buck kangaroo, significantly called an Old Man, would be the first large and dangerous animal I would know of. We used to see kangaroos from trains, giants eight feet high, grey or red, according to terrain, all the more menacing-seeming because they were suddenly there, staring at you, before you were properly aware of them. Also, the favorite sport of Dad and his horsy mates was hunting kangaroos, and I grew up on tales of what a fearsome thing a bailed-up old man 'roo could be, how with a slash of a great horned hind toe he could bring a horse down tangled in its own guts, or pick up a dog and crush him, or take a man and drown him in a water hole. What could not such a beast do to a little boy?

Another of my earliest recollections is of telling the family a story of the running down of a kangaroo by a train we were travelling in. It is the first story I remember telling. Description of the event will also serve to show what my relations with the family were like in the matter of my story telling. The highlights of the scene are vivid in my mind, and even some of the words remain with me. I take the liberty of giving the conversation fulsomely on the ground that I remember only too well from subsequent experience how it used to go when the family were in a mood to lead me on to indulge myself as the Romantic Liar they declared I was.

I was kneeling on a seat and looking out of the window at the inland scene, seeing the stunted trees, the mulga and the wilga and the gimlet gum, doing a kind of dance, spinning past, seeming to swing away from the train to the horizon and race ahead, to come back to meet us and go waltzing past and round again, the same set of trees in endless gyration.

I turned to the family to report the fascinating phenomenon: 'I seen trees dancin'.'

A general chuckle as Mother said: ''Ere 'e goes!'

'Trees goin' roun' an' roun'.'

Mother would use my story-telling as an exercise for her sardonic wit, if in the mood: 'Pulling up their roots and doing the polka, eh?'

'Yes.'

Smirks and giggles.

'What else'd you see?'

'Big kangaroo.'

'What's it doing – picking its teeth with a telegraph pole?'

Much mirth.

'No – kangaroo got runned over.'

Kangaroos were often run down by trains, as I, son of an engine driver, knew well. Men got run down, too, so that death to me at that stage would be something first concerned with the railway. Here was material for out-letting my preoccupation with the terrible father-beast, an opportunity for slaying him in fantasy.

'Engine runned over old man kangaroo – bunka-lunka! All bleed come out . . . oh!'

Squeals and howls of mirth. I can't say how I felt about the reception of my story then. However, I know that later on I used to feel a sense of loss over their treating what I told them as merely funny. Still later I deliberately made the stories droll. Finally I stopped telling them.

JACK LINDSAY

Jack Lindsay (1900–) was born in Melbourne but
brought up by his mother in Queensland. He came
under the influence of his father, the artist and writer
Norman Lindsay, from 1919 to 1926 and moved in
colourful Sydney Bohemian circles. In 1926 he moved
to London and has lived in England ever since. His
autobiographical trilogy, *Life Rarely Tells* (1958), *The
Roaring Twenties* (1960) and *Fanfrolico and After* (1962)
is a great contribution to cultural history.

♦ ♦ ♦ ♦

When I first felt myself the member of a group, detached from the
broad lap of the family, we were living in a house built over the spot
where the train from Milson's Point plunged into a tunnel on its
way to North Sydney suburbs. Between our house and the landing
stage of the ferry at Lavender Bay was a stretch of beach with some
weatherboard shacks of fishermen (soon to be pulled down). There,
playing under the afternoon-eyes of my mother, I had come to
know half a dozen lads, fishermen's sons, who knocked down my
sandcastles and kicked my cap seawards, charged on broomhandle-
horses, jumped over me like the wind, disappeared into damp cran-

nies under their derelict homes. Barefooted lads, about my own age or a little older, with stubborn untidy hair and torn breeches, scrambling with scarred toes among the driftwood and smelling of tar, putty, and crushed ants. My mother, when not taken up with watching that Ray didn't swallow too much sand, made friends with the whooping pack and reconciled them to me. She asked them up to our house for tea, and they ate loudly and hungrily, leaving sand and seaweed on the floor. After tumbling me about and falling on me, they communicated something of their own seashore smell to my hair and clothes, and took me in as one of themselves.

We played on the beach, skimming stones across the waves and racing the mongrel-dogs. We put jellyfish down one another's backs. We stood between the rails at the tunnel entrance as the trains came roaring up, stood there defiantly, shouting, as long as we dared. We went on rambling walks, planned with piratic strategies, over the hills of sparse grass and lantana bushes that lay inland.

We sang as we went, because we had a common purpose which could be uttered only in song. We were together and defiant. We chafed all the while against one another, taking a dare or giving it, wrestling, tossing a penny, running, climbing trees. 'I saw it first. I got higher than you did. I touched it first.' I felt myself distinct because I was part of them; I was part of them because I detached myself in the ceaseless dares and claims.

We sang in a tramping yell, about moonlight and somebody's daughter washing her feet in soda water, and Hell O Hell O Helen most divine. Also, without any intention of championing the policy of White Australia:

> Rule Britannia, Britannia rule the waves,
> No more Chinamen in New South Wales –

though we liked Chinamen and merely felt that the words were somehow a defiance of authority. Also:

> Forward Christian Soldiers
> to the Battle of Waterloo.
> The wind blew off my trow-ow-sers
> and I didn't know what to do.

For the moment it seems that I too could sing. Indeed the echoes from the dry gritty hills must have somehow drifted under the arch of our front gate. For my mother taught me the words of *We Sailed by the Lowlands Low*, and once I was cajoled into singing the ballad in the drawing-room, to ladies in a rustling circle, all dressed in lilies and lavender, white kid gloves and clouds of lace. Ladies who exclaimed at the clever and well-behaved little boy, and whose voices had the tinkle of frail silver teaspoons on bone china, in a light of milk. But my mother was far too absorbed in her children to entertain much, and the ladies soon receded into the bright domes of their fringed parasols, patting a dear little boy on the cheek and climbing into carriages curved like the sepals of their own flowering selves. There remained only the clash of my mother's many thin silver bracelets, the froufrou of her petticoats with their eyelets of broderie anglaise into which I wanted to thread pieces of string.

And the voices on the hills. The singing was indistinguishable from the movement of arms and legs, and loudest when all sound was torn from the mouth by the wind of our speed as we ran down the stony slopes. Grey grass and lantana bushes with hard green unripe berries in clusters; stones and grey grass and a tin-shack mouldering red and old barbed wire with a few dirty tufts of wool. Endlessly shelving sunlight, a silent explosion of light, and birds squawking on the telegraph poles. Nothing but hills of harsh gold, spiky with grey grass.

Afterwards, the crunch of stolen apples in a hollow of snug heat, among the tumbling sandboys who laughed and used lots of words that I hadn't heard before – words which I knew by some masonic understanding must not be repeated in adult company. The body as a secret source of delight, one's own inestimable possession, and an awareness of the forbidden.

My fifth birthday was nearing. We discussed it in a big back room of the house where we played with various objects found in its lumber, a genuine blunted cutlass and a phonograph with cylinder records that emitted Negro songs across the hiccups of cracks. Perhaps because the whole gang had gathered in a room that was mine, I saw them all together, saw them as *my friends, myself, us*. We drank water out of discarded beer bottles. 'I've drunk beer,' said the eldest boy, Harry, wrinkling his snubnose and reeling about. 'I drank a whole bottle.'

That evening my mother, coaxing me to bed, remarked, 'You can do whatever you like on your birthday.'

And I replied, feeling very sly and somewhat frightened, doubling up in the armchair, 'Oh no, I can't.'

♦

I went camping also with boys from the school and often tramped with them from One Tree Hill among the ridges and gullies around. I learned how easy it was to get lost in the criss-crossing gullies where one vista seemed much like another. From a bush-wise friend of these wanderings I acquired various maxims. If you haven't got a compass (and I never had), keep your eye on the sun and watch your relation to its movement. Work towards a watershed. Better still, go down a creek: you'll come sooner or later to a larger creek and some sort of house – in the wilds, a shepherd's hut or a small farm or at least a paddock fence. At first glance it may well seem hard to tell whether you're going up or down a gully; but if you look at the way the bushes grow along it, you could make out the flow of the stream in torrent-time.

Climbing along the scattered bones of a dry course, we found a pool left in some deep bowl of rock and had a dip, then lay about trying to smoke dry pieces of lawyer-vine in which the small perforations allowed at least something of a free passage for the smoke. Or we slid down a slope, catching at the roots or the saplings when the pace threatened to get out of control, and ending in a green nook from which we watched a brown-green water snake slide in a sinuous zigzag across the stream. Or listened to a flight of chattering lories among the tree tops.

Alone and naked on a flat stone like the opened palm of the sun lifting me out of time and space, I still felt a compelling union with the earth. As though moving through successive rings of tightening light, and yet at the same time flowing outwards to clash against the

horizon. Aware with crystalline intensity of a leaf shape, the shadow
of an ant, the pleats of a water plant, and yet lost in the undulating
fields of gold, the earth spinning below like a small shadowy globe.
The universe broke into countless pieces of bright glass and I rose
steadily from the dark centre, a frail eternal fountain, going up
against the ghostly debris, falling. And at last, coming back from the
four corners of the rounded distance, I heard my heart beating deep
in the earth and waited with a patience beyond all thought till it had
crept back into my breast.

♦

Alone, with water, fire and air, I was happy. The prinking flow of
the water was not distinct from the rhythmical structure of the
song; the leap of the wind and all the moods of the sky. The beautiful drowned woman smiled up at me from the river depths and
became the sly nymph; every flowering shadow was a tryst with
Keats and with Amaryllis.

My solitude was a marriage with the earth. One night, formally
so. Mary had had a couple of trees cut down and the fall of a tree was
always a belly blow, a pang of humiliation, a crash of loss. A great
heap of boughs and leaves was piled at one end of the garden. The
moon came up at midnight and made me restless with a flickering
breeze. Mice of shadowy light stole under the door. A leaf-finger
tapped. I went on to the moonpyre of greenery and lay there naked.
Dozing a moment, I woke on a fear, clinging to the boughs. The raft
of the earth shook on the dark waters, the moon was veiled, something fluttered across the sky, and the cradle of greenery rocked me,
comforted me. My sister the tree had also been severed from the
earth and we were one in the buoyant bed of darkness. Far away,
inside my head, a bird wailed. And then, as the wind slid the cloud
away, the fountain of light burst up out of the earth, out of a hole in
my side.

Mostly the spell held. But there were moments when it slipped
and I was lost in the mockery of chaos. Sometimes I couldn't stop

saying the same word over and over till it ceased to have meaning and became a strange clot of alien life, a cut-off thing, lodged hostilely in my head and refusing to go. The word of magical meaning became the clot of madness, the blind ticking death of meaning. Words were then locusts in the crops, stripping the earth of green and familiar life. And this treachery of the word was the very loss of self. The alien and hostile world swelled up inside and burst like an abscess and left a raw void; and an obliquity of angles entangled the world. Reach out and the object moved aside, ever so little, but enough to make you miss it. The gap between your straddling feet grew wider. You felt the turn of the mad earth in every pause. Whatever you did was broken apart, a separate mechanism in which you were inexplicably and agonizedly caught. Time, the mad clot beating; death, a dusty spiral in the dank repellent smell; sleep, the pit of the body in which lurked terrible snakes. Fear of involuntary emission, of V.D. (obscurely learnt about from warnings in public lavatories and the tantalizing pedantries of encyclopaedias), of blindness and strange privies, of people talking and talking on the other side of the wall, beyond the window pane, of absolute cruelties seen in the street, a kicked dog or a fallen horse between two trams, a man glimpsed through a window savagely beating a small girl with a belt. Lying in bed, you felt on the edge of sleep your body puffing up, grown huge and doughy, floating away out of control; nothing of you left but a peculiar hot taste in the mouth or your heart rattling and swinging at the end of a piece of string tied to the iron bar of the bed.

Mary however knew that I wrote verse and wanted me to do something about it: have it read, published, utilized. I resisted her with a stubborn silence, but she had helped to break the spell, the single-minded independence of my movement. I couldn't help thinking for the first time how my verses would seem to someone else; and once I thought like that, I couldn't rest calmly on my delight in the sun-game, the prismatic modulations among the cubes and arcs of nature.

I needed Plato for my defence and I found him through Shelley, in the Everyman translations, and then (as I learned more Greek) in the original.

Till now the separation of poetry and world, of sensuous essence (or spirit) and everyday experience, had been a matter of simple and direct oppositions – even if it had its moments of anger and despair. The world was interested in things that seemed to me futile: money-making and sausage machines and fashions and shop windows. The world was concerned with penning large numbers of people in unclean prison systems called towns. And I was absorbed in what I thought the real things, colour harmonies and symmetries of rhyme, the relation of a Shakespearean sonnet to the balances of a bough in the wind. The only person who could enter into my sphere was another preoccupied with the same problems – and though the advent of such another was theoretically possible, it seemed so remote a chance that I never thought about it. My mind to me a kingdom is; in a cell I still own the universe of my body.

But now an argument had begun in the cell, in the universe; and I couldn't halt it. For, unforeseeably, I was arguing with myself. My aunt's frowned-off intrusion had merely opened the door to the stranger, myself. Experience had to find an intellectual idiom.

The exultations had previously faded out in a sick dizziness, a bacchic wrenching at the roots of my hair, a sense of milky light-nings in the blood, a straining of the entire body upwards as if by becoming cruelly aware of the limiting structure of bone I could achieve a liberating discipline of wings. But now my thoughts had to pass beyond this annihilating moment, into some schoolroom of Apollo, where they would be required to explain and justify them-selves. They could no longer rely on the blank and blind opposition of the world; they had to find ways of speaking which would at a pinch enable them to smile with a safe guile.

Now it was not a matter of my spirit-self against the lumpish world, with a neutral mask between. The mask was also myself, also the world. I was myself double, inside and outside, and two voices claimed the mouth of the mask. Mask and face could change places and roles with indefinite address and prolixity. The flame spiral of song, consuming the world and escaping into ethereal acrobatics, was no longer the only possible graph of the free spirit. The social extension of the inturned and organic experience was discovered to be possible, necessary – an unexplored aspect of the single reality. Yet my total rejection of the world's values made that extension conceivable only as an imaginative act peopling solitude.

♦

A harsh land, but I loved it in its own right, in its particular existence, not simply as the given example of water, air, fire, earth, from which I might draw the poetic essences. Witherby pointed to the lack of variety as compared with an English landscape. Every tree trunk straight as the next, every ridge as stony and meagrely grassed as the next. Tall scraggy trees soaring into nothing in particular, into an indefinite entanglement of thin leaves; ragged broken rocks. Miles and miles of ring-barked trees, killed off to make the grass grow thicker, without any concern for the ultimate effect on the soil, on the climate. Box-flats with the leaves gone scantily into the sky, the bark hanging scabbily in festoons, the scrabbly undergrowth. Thick scrubland, with odd bunya-pines and criss-crossing creepers. And then a broad vista, where the delicate distance of hazy blue and purple was born from the endless dull green tree tops; and a strange mirage of luxurious beauty shimmers out of the dry gritty earth.

'I like it because man has yet done so little to it,' Witherby said.

I could not appreciate that remark until I had seen England; but I felt the untamed grandeur, the infuriatingly labyrinthine mess, as part of myself. Now I no longer experienced the ecstatic communion of my early adolescence, no longer could slide from the human world by leaving the houses behind me and listening to the tongues of water. Yet I at moments felt myself rooted in a new way, a mere visitor to the seething life of nature but happy in its sufficiency and coming back into it by devious roads, overcoming my exclusion. For the elemental union I substituted a meditative calm, in which the blue distance, the waterfall-plume, the pillared strength of a silver gum, became images so deeply brooded on as to express the whole of reality.

I read Henry Lawson and found many elements of this new self in his work; but still could not see where I next went as poet.

I watched the carpet snake, about a dozen feet long, marked on the back and sides with a pattern of rich brown and yellow. It lay gorged on something that showed as a lump in the middle of its body – maybe a bandicoot or even a whole wallaby. There was nothing to fear in it any more than in the frilled iguanas that looked like baby dragons as they scampered over rocks or ran up a tree. But it made me think of the adders and the brown snake with its iridescent drabness and the snake with the neat white rings and the black snake with red stripes on his sides and a salmon belly. An earth crawling with many horrors. Any stick you leaned carelessly to take up might leap and lash and sting you to a blackening death.

'Death adders, nothing to scare a bloke in those cross-eyed buggers,' said the hairy chap in the pub down on the flats, scratching himself and spitting at a spider on the wall. 'You can catch 'em on the hop any day in a pear clump. When they strike, they hoop 'emselves up and whack their head and tail together, real comics they are. Some bloody fools say they stick you with the horny end of their bloody tails, but they bloody well don't. Many a one I've held by the blasted tail. They can't do a thing in hell then. But when they've got their goddam danders up, they'll come hell-for-leather at you, rearing up like a mad Irishman. But you can knock the buggers silly with a stick and pick 'em up by the bloody tail. I wish I had one here. I'd soon make all you bastards run.'

He spun a coin. 'My shout.'

A hard earth. I began to fear it, but I fought my fear down.

ALAN MARSHALL

Alan Marshall (1902–84) was born in Western
Australia. His long writing career covers the period of
the Great Depression and celebrates his triumph over
physical infirmity, especially in the
semi-autobiographical trilogy: *I Can Jump Puddles*
(1955), *This is the Grass* (1962), and *In Mine Own Heart*
(1963).

◆ ◆ ◆ ◆

◆ *I Can Jump Puddles*

Next day I rode Starlight home during lunch hour. I did not hurry. I
wanted to enjoy my picture of father seeing me ride. I thought it
might worry mother but father would place his hand on my

shoulder and look at me and say, 'I knew you could do it,' or something like that.

He was bending over a saddle lying on the ground near the chaff house door when I rode up to the gate. He did not see me. I stopped at the gate and watched him for a moment then called out, 'Hi!'

He did not straighten himself but turned his head and looked back towards the gate behind him. For a moment he held this position while I looked, smiling, at him, then he quietly stood erect and gazed at me for a moment.

'You, Alan!' he said, his tone restrained as if I were riding a horse a voice could frighten into bolting.

'Yes,' I called. 'Come and see me. You watch. Remember when you said I'd never ride? Now, you watch. Yahoo!' I gave the yell I sometimes gave when on a spirited horse and leant forward in the saddle with a quick lift and a sharp clap of my good heel on Starlight's side.

The white pony sprang forward with short, eager bounds, gathering himself until, balanced, he flattened into a run. I could see his knee below his shoulder flash out and back like a piston, feel the drive of him and the reach of his shoulders to every stride.

I followed our fence to the wattle clump then reefed him back and round, leaning with him as he propped and turned in a panel's length. Stones scattered as he finished the turn; his head rose and fell as he doubled himself to regain speed: then I was racing back again while father ran desperately towards the gate.

I passed him, my hand on the reins moving forward and back to the pull of Starlight's extended head. Round again and back to a skidding halt with Starlight's chest against the gate. He drew back dancing, tossing his head, his ribs pumping. The sound of his breath through his distended nostrils, the creak of the saddle, the jingle of the bit were the sounds I had longed to hear while sitting on the back of a prancing horse and now I was hearing them and smelling the sweat from a completed gallop.

I looked down at father, noticing with sudden concern that he was pale. Mother had come out of the house and was hurrying towards us.

'What's wrong, dad?' I asked, quickly.

'Nothing,' he said. He kept looking at the ground and I could hear him breathing.

'You shouldn't have run like that to the gate,' I said. 'You winded yourself.'

He looked at me and smiled, then turned to mother who reached out her hand to him as she came up to the gate.

'I saw it,' she said.

They looked into each other's eyes a moment.

'He's you all over again,' mother said, then turning to me, 'You learned to ride yourself, Alan, did you?'

'Yes,' I said, leaning on Starlight's neck so that my head was closer to theirs. 'For years I've been learning. I've only had one buster; that was yesterday. Did you see me turn, dad?' I turned to father. 'Did you see me bring him round like a stockhorse? What do you think? Do you reckon I can ride?'

'Yes,' he said. 'You're good; you've got good hands and you sit him well. How do you hold on? Show me.'

I explained my grip on the surcingle, told him how I used to take Starlight to drink and how I could mount or dismount with the aid of my crutches.

'I've left my crutches at school or I'd show you,' I said.

'It's all right . . . Another day . . . You feel safe on his back?'

'Safe as a bank.'

'Your back doesn't hurt you, does it, Alan?' mother asked.

'No, not a bit,' I said.

'You'll always be very careful, won't you, Alan? I like seeing you riding but I wouldn't like to see you fall.'

'I'll be very careful,' I promised, then added, 'I must go back to school; I'll be late.'

'Listen, son,' father said, looking up at me with a serious face. 'We know you can ride now. You went past that gate like a bat out of hell. But you don't want to ride like that. If you do people will think you're a mug rider. They'll think you don't understand a horse. A good rider hasn't got to be rip-snorting about like a pup off the chain just to show he can ride. A good rider don't have to prove nothing. He studies his mount. You do that. Take it quietly. You can ride – all right, but don't be a show-off with it. A gallop's all right on a straight track but the way you're riding, you'll tear the guts out of a horse in no time. A horse is like a man; he's at his best when he gets a fair deal. Now, walk Starlight back to school and give him a rub down before you let him go.'

He paused, thinking for a moment, then added, 'You're a good bloke, Alan. I like you and I reckon you're a good rider.'

♦   This is the Grass

There was a time when I had imagined that even hunger could not drive a man to eat that which naturally revolted him. I learnt that he reached that state in stages, down, down to the level of animals.

In Fitzroy there were a number of cafés that supplied a three-course meal for sevenpence. In the early morning a spring cart drawn by a bony horse pulled up in front of these cafés. It was laden with hessian bags stuffed with vegetables and fruit swept from the stalls of the Victoria Market or gathered from the gutters where it had been tossed for disposal by the council cleaners and their brooms.

I had spoken to the old man who owned the spring cart and horse, had watched him at the work he did before he reached the cafés.

He walked stiffly and slowly. ('Bloody arthritis, I've got. There's no cure for it, they tell me. Bugger them anyway.')

On the nights when the market was open and the greengrocers of the city and suburbs had collected to buy from the growers, he hung around with his broom and bags collecting the outer leaves of cabbages torn from these vegetables as useless and flung in the gutters.

Lying on the ground around the stalls were carrots and parsnips crushed by the hooves of horses that brought the market carts in from the country farms round Melbourne.

Apples bearing brown patches of decay, sprouting onions, shrunken potatoes sat amid the sodden horse dung that had spread along the gutters.

He swept them all into his bags, sometimes removing with a wipe of his hand the filth that clung to them. These bags of vegetable refuse were bought by the cheap cafés and tossed into stock-pots for soup or use with servings of meat in place of the unpolluted and fresh vegetables sold on the stalls of the market from where this refuse had been discarded.

Cabbage was one of the vegetables that helped to fill the plates of every meat course supplied in these cafés. Coarse and unpalatable, it nevertheless was a serving of vegetables and justified the café's claim that it supplied three-course meals.

These cafés were patronised by people whose wealth consisted of the few coins in their pockets.

I ate regularly at one of them. It had marble-top tables, cold and uninviting, and a linoleum-covered floor foot-printed with the dirt of the streets. But the meals were a little better than those of its rivals and there was no obligation to leave after your meal was finished. You could sit and talk to those who like yourself were loth to return to the isolation of the streets.

One evening I ordered steak and fried onions. The proprietor brought the laden plate to me, sliding it across the marble table top, then holding out his hand for the money.

One always paid before eating. So many men had robbed him by eating first then showing their empty pockets that he refused to supply a meal unless it was paid for in advance. I paid him then began eating.

The knife was sharp. The proprietor believed that customers who found their steaks easy to cut would never regard them as tough. He kept his knives extremely sharp. Even so the steak seemed to resist with more than average obstinacy the sawing of my knife.

I sat chewing the first mouthful while gazing straight ahead of me, my thoughts centring on the movements of my jaws which after a few minutes began to tire.

I took the piece of steak from my mouth with my fingers and looked at it. It was a fibrous, grey ball of juiceless matter that my fingers found difficulty in breaking. I returned the shredded remains to my mouth and resumed chewing, but after a while I took it from my mouth again and placed it on the edge of my plate, unable to reduce it to a size and consistency I could swallow.

I told myself that I had received nourishment from its juices and that the fibre could not add more to this contribution, but after half an hour when with aching jaws I gazed at a dozen pallid lumps of chewed meat encircling the onions and selvage on my plate I felt cheated. Where was the energy I needed? I sat drooping in my chair.

The onions had grown cold and a layer of congealed fat like thin, grey ice covered them. Through this shield there projected strands of flaccid onion that curved over and lay inert upon it.

I pushed the plate away in distaste and sat looking at it with features twisted into an expression of revulsion.

A man who had been sitting alone at a table against the wall came over and touched my shoulder. He was not a young man nor was he old. He had sunken cheeks and tired eyes and his eyes looked into mine slowly and deeply, offering for my inspection in this space of complete honesty the suffering of all men who had experienced poverty and hunger.

'Do you want that, mate?' he asked, pointing at the plate.

'No,' I said. 'I've finished.'

'Can I have it?'

'Yes.'

He took the food away to his table and began eating it. He ate all the chewed lumps of meat I had taken from my mouth, all the stiffened onion, the fat . . .

When he had finished he lifted the plate to his face and licked it.

♦   *In Mine Own Heart*

The boarders began to tell me their troubles, feeling I was not part of their world. I could not compete with them. Revelations of little weaknesses to one with many obvious weaknesses would not discredit them.

'I'm getting a stye on the eye. Do you think a wedding-ring

rubbed on the eye stops it? I want it to clear up by Saturday as I'm visiting friends,' said Mr Gulliver.

'When they engage you to sing at a party, they should introduce you to the guests and treat you as one. It's only right; I'm going to demand it,' said Stewart Mollison.

'There is little real appreciation of talent in Australia. There are times when I feel like giving up study and finding an easier way to make money. I should have been a hairdresser,' said Mamie Fulton.

They were kind, considerate people who always saw I had a chair to sit on, a free passage to walk through the lounge. They would hurry to get me things to save me having to rise, to walk – a glass of water, maybe, a book . . .

They thought crutches were 'terrible' and told me so with comforting voices. They wished 'something could be done about it', and professed themselves willing to get me the addresses of masseurs who, you never know, might do me a lot of good. Mr Burmeister recollected a pulled muscle he had suffered in his youth. A masseur had cured him and the cost was negligible, all things considered.

'Things should be made easier for you,' they claimed, and they all agreed that no one could imagine how great was the handicap from which I suffered unless they had walked on crutches. Not one of them had walked on crutches, but they all knew people who had and these people were quite definite that it imposed a great strain upon the heart.

There were staircases and the difficulty of getting on trams and the dangers of slipping on the roadway when it was wet. So many things.

And, of course, people . . . They were so inconsiderate. Mr Gulliver had, himself, witnessed old people standing in trams while young healthy men retained their seats and Mamie had seen blind men pleading to be helped across the road and 'no one stopped'.

Of course, blindness was the worst thing that could happen to anyone, though Mr Gulliver wasn't so sure about this. Deafness, he thought, would be a far greater handicap. Never to hear music was too terrible to contemplate.

Mrs Birdsworth felt that, after all, I had much to be thankful for: 'You have such a happy disposition no one would realise you were crippled,' she told me.

They all agreed that this was just what they felt themselves.

'When you are sitting at a table talking and laughing no one would know,' was Mamie's way of putting it.

Stewart Mollison concluded the discussion with a final compliment.

'Well, Alan, we all like you and you will always have our sympathy.'

A murmur of agreement greeted this declaration that called for a humble thanks to them all.

The feeling the boarders regarded as compassion was a sentimental pity that served to strengthen them against suffering in others. It destroyed what it was intended to strengthen – resolution in the afflicted. It sapped the will to fight, killed ambition, weakened hope.

The emotions they experienced when looking at a cripple hurt them, roused a primitive fear of a suspected deterioration in their own bodies and they rid themselves of it by the release of a spoken compassion.

They sympathised from a position of strength, increasing their respect for themselves by declarations of understanding and concern, believing these emotions sprang from their unselfishness and kindness, not from self-protection.

They were never inspired to action by their conclusions, only to retreat. They moved back from the obligations placed upon man by man through individual misfortune, shrinking from action that would have disturbed their complacency and brought them to a realisation of their own ephemerality.

None of them was aware of handicaps in themselves, handicaps that made them restless, frustrated, swallowers of aspirin and frequent visitors to doctors. The lines of tension engraved upon their faces, the sleepless nights of which they sometimes complained, the restless walking from room to room on spring nights, sudden bursts of irritation – these said as much about them as my crutches said about me.

We were all suffering from handicaps. My handicap lay in the minds of people I met, in their attitude towards me, not in my crutches.

♦

'Never leave anyone any the worse for knowing you,' Arthur had once said. That was my creed.

I wanted to write books that meant something. I could never do that while burdened by lack of confidence, a sense of inferiority, a sense of being different from other men. Anonymity amongst the people was what I had to achieve, a merging with them.

And I had to experience love as they did. I was sure that behind a man's achievement was the love of a woman. Before I could establish myself as a writer I must first of all establish myself as a man. The knowledge that a woman could love me would release me from the bonds that bound the cripple of the bookshop and that even now were tightening around me.

From now on I would no longer be an observer of life; I would be a participant. I would fling myself into the torrent in which all men struggled.

I left happy, uplifted, inspired. I rose from my seat on the bed and stepped out of the door of my bungalow to breathe the night.

I looked up at the full moon. I was hemmed in by fences, by the peaked roofs of houses, by thrusting chimneys, but away above them where the moonlight was untouched was the place for my soaring spirit. In a lovely dream I sped upwards on wings. I rolled and dived and met the flood of light as from a welcoming sea.

And, beside me, her hand in mine, drenched by the same beauty, inspired by the same love, was a girl I had not met and did not know. Together we looked upon the cities and the people and the bush to which we belonged.

How bright was this night!

KATHLEEN FITZPATRICK

Kathleen Fitzpatrick (1905–) was born at Omeo,
Victoria. She became an associate Professor of History
at Melbourne University where she taught for
thirty-two years. Her autobiography *Solid Bluestone
Foundation* (1983) covers her childhood in Melbourne
and student days in Oxford.

◆ ◆ ◆ ◆

After private study came indoor recreation, which was rather pleasant, because we could talk (a rare treat in convent life) or even read,
and at Portland Convent I made my first acquaintance with Dickens
by reading *Oliver Twist*. It strikes me now as rather an advanced
work for nuns to let little girls read in the full, unexpurgated edition. After indoor recreation we had supper, which was like morning refection, except that there was hot cocoa instead of cold
jam-water. Then evening prayers and ablutions, carefully supervised, and the evening ended with a strenuous bout of hair-
brushing, one hundred strokes of the brush and not one less being

the required number. I felt it hardly fair of the nuns, who had solved the hair problem once and for all by shaving it off, to insist on meticulous hair-culture for us and, indeed, a dangerous thought weakly fluttered across my awakening mind, a question as to whether there might not be some inconsistency between shining hair and the renunciation of worldliness so constantly urged on us as an ideal.

In all seasons we washed in cold water but once a week we had a hot bath on whatever night we were rostered for. I imagine that the convent had no hot water system and that the water for the hot baths was heated nightly in coppers. 'Utterly ridiculous' Mother had said, on finding on the list of items Lorna and I must bring to the convent, the words 'bath robes'. From the specifications it was clear that these were not what we called dressing-gowns, for putting on before and after the bath, but just what the words said, bath robes, long-sleeved ample dresses right down to the ground, for wearing in the bath. At home we had long bathed ourselves, Mother attending only briefly to make sure we had not skipped the harder bits, but at Portland even the oldest girls, like Lorna, were bathed by one of the lay sisters. Each bath took a long time, because not only did the lay sister do a perfect, AMDG job, but in order not to offend against modesty, she folded back only a few inches of the bath robe at a time, washed and re-clothed the bare bit and began on another area. The same regard for modesty was shown in the dormitory where, although we had curtained cubicles, we were taught how to undress and dress without seeing any of our own flesh by making a kind of tent of night-dress or dress.

Protestant friends, when regaled with these details of convent life, have asked whether such attitudes towards our bodies did not make us prurient little beasts. No, I do not think so. Our view of the matter was that all adults were mad and nuns the maddest. We did not ask the nuns their reasons for giving us a bath in so laborious and inefficient a manner because, being children and therefore not mad ourselves, we knew that it was a waste of time to ask mad people reasonable questions. The same principle held good for the ban on what were called 'particular friendships', a curious term since friendship is, *per se*, particular: what was meant was making a favourite playmate or companion of any particular girl. No doubt it is necessary for nuns, in their sexually segregated communities, to guard against lesbianism. We, of course, had not the faintest idea of what they were guarding us from, nor did we have any curiosity about it: the rule against particular friendships was, in our opinion, only another instance of the madness of nuns.

What I remember as chiefly being stressed in our Portland curriculum was the correct way of doing things. Training was all, education (in the literal sense of bringing to light and developing individual character or talent) was nothing. What was in us, the nuns believed, was original sin and their duty was to drill it out of us by insisting that there was one and only one right way of doing everything and tolerating only that way. Sitting, for example, required the head to be up, shoulders back and down, feet side by side, heels and knees together, hands (unless usefully occupied) perfectly still and never engaged in hair-smoothing, ear-exploring or any other activity pertaining to the person. I can recognise a convent girl of my generation still by her posture and deportment. Slumping and sprawling were unladylike and anyway, impossible, because the only arm-chairs and sofas in the convent were in the parlour for visitors; for us there were only backless benches and stiff wooden chairs. An upright posture was further encouraged by a daily exercise of walking briskly round a room with blocks of wood balanced on our heads. Our speech had to be clear and our vowels correctly pronounced, and in the course of a year (for we did not return to Melbourne for the holidays) this became habitual, so that when Lorna and I at last re-appeared at 'Hughenden' our young uncles, Ack and Len, pretended to be unable to understand a word we said because, they averred, our lingo was so lah-di-dah.

C. B. CHRISTESEN

Clement Byrne Christesen (1911–) was born in
Townsville and educated at Queensland University.
He is a poet, short story writer and founder of the
magazine *Meanjin*. The extracts come from an
autobiography in progress, *The Generous Sun*, part of
which has been published under the title *The Island*.

◆ ◆ ◆ ◆

Memories are like dreams which vividly illuminate a moment in
time, perhaps experienced very many years ago, so that what is
remembered has far greater clarity than events of yesterday. The cry
of a plover, the subtle fragrance of frangipani, the feel of assam silk,
the taste of guava – these and other sensations quicken imagination,
help us recall in a flash a whole world of fragmented sensibilities
which had long since faded from conscious memory.

'Obsessions grow from uncertainties'. And yet my earliest childhood 'obsessions' were rather the product of absolute certainties of
place and time, of seemingly immutable factors governing a well-

ordered, secure, and loving world. People around me did not change, the environment of ocean beach and tropical garden did not change. Tides moved, the seasons moved, but they did not really change. The sea remained, waves breaking against beach in regular rhythm. The trees did not shed their leaves in what passed for winter; birds flew away but always returned, as did the sun and stars; flowers withered but bloomed again. There were no uncertainties, no doubts, no anxieties. And the island, and the great rock behind the town, could never move away.

These 'obsessions' were very real to me during the first six years of childhood – so real that even today I can recall them with varying degrees of precision. Many of the physical features of Townsville have altered drastically: the wide beach spreading back to the Strand has mainly been filled in, and between retaining wall and sea is now a mere strip of sand. Much of the beauty, the magic of the place as I knew it as a child, has gone. All the coconut palms and most of the Moreton Bay fig-trees bordering the Strand have been cut down. Houses now creep up the slopes of Castle Hill, and on the westward side suburbs and industries sprawl toward Mount Stuart and the Flinders Range. On Magnetic Island the riotous tropical vegetation which once bordered the little coves and bays now exists only in a few isolated pockets. The destroyers have been at work. The far North Queensland outpost has now become the State's second largest city.

But in imagination I can still inhabit a realm which has long disappeared. Time present, time past . . . memory can partly bridge the gap, help recapture reality. 'Can you go back in memory to your childhood and if so, how big are you then?' Walter de la Mare asked Russell Brain in one of their conversations. 'Can you remember putting your fingers on the edge of the table when your eyes were first level with it?' Yes – oh yes, and the very objects on the table: the pack of 'Post-toasties' at breakfast, a china egg-cup, the heavy silver cruet and soup tureen at night, and the high green-shaded kerosene lamp – these and other objects trigger a stream of elusive recollections. But not of faces. Figures, yes, even the texture of clothes, and the colour of clothes, but faces remain indistinct. I can 'see' my mother's blue-black hair which she wore piled high on her head but not her lovely young face. She sits in a cane chair in the garden beneath a wide-spreading banyan, reading a leather-bound book with pages of thin paper: the leather is green and has the touch of velvet. I walk with my father in the noon-day sun. He is wearing a white drill suit buttoned to the neck, and carries a huge black umbrella to protect him from the heat; but his face is indistinct. At night we walk 'around the block', the three of us, past the army barracks, past the convent, hearing the harsh rustle of palms and the distant sound of waves, past houses and glimpse lamplight filtering through lattice-enclosed verandas.

And yet there is one face which is almost clear – that of a little Aboriginal girl, Dolly, a year or two older than I, and my first playmate: a round dark face which is always smiling. She was my devoted friend and followed wherever I went. It was she who taught me to taste the fruit of tamarind and Burdekin plum, and how to eat mangoes. And it was she who told me of the corroboree on the beach. Torres Strait islanders had come ashore from luggers and were dancing around a huge bonfire. Dolly crept into my room, whispered the exciting news, and together we hurried down to the beach. We must have stayed there for hours gazing in awe at the barbaric scene. Until I fell asleep, and it was Dolly who led me home by the hand, and to bed. And my parents were at first incredulous, then alarmed when next morning I told them of my wonderful night-time adventure. Though Dolly received a scolding, she kept smiling, and remained my closest friend.

◆

A girl named Alma joined the household as a 'general'. She had had scarcely any schooling when she came to us, but she was amazingly intelligent and learnt quickly. Looking back, I now realize she must have had 'photographic memory', a mind capable of registering total recall. My mother was at first dubious about employing Alma, though she had been well recommended; but her unaffected zest for life had an appeal which was irresistible.

Alert brown eyes were the most attractive feature in a plain freckled face. If the house was not run along orderly lines, at least it became for me a much livelier place. And I not only gained another friend, but an escort who could take Dolly and me to the beach and on excursions to Kissing Point, to the Botanic Gardens, and to the park on the Strand in front of Queen's Hotel. What went on 'backstage' was seldom known to my parents, for Alma, Dolly and I had sworn a pact of secrecy: we had our own interests and adventures and confidences, our own lives to live.

Everything was of immense interest to Alma, not only the furnishings, the contents of wardrobes and closets and chests of drawers, and of course the pantry and kitchen, but also the habits of speech and social behaviour of 'town people'. She liked nothing better than to wait at table during dinner parties or afternoon teas, and would stand around listening to the conversation until reminded of her duties.

And she had the odd habit of fully naming things according to the advertisements – of referring to (say) groceries and general commodity goods by their trade names and description. For instance, I would be given a spoonful of 'California syrup of figs for cross, feverish, bilious children'. And once when I suffered an indignity, it was by means of what she said was an 'Arabesque tropical enema syringe specially adapted for the North Queensland climate'.

My father considered the trait highly amusing. If he should laugh, the chances were that Alma would then 'sing' a trade jingle: 'South Townsville has just had a fright/ by an airship's appearance at night/ now the people are learning/ 'twas a smoker returning/ with Bert Brown's best mixture alight'. Mother took an indulgent attitude, and gradually began picking up the habit herself, as I most certainly did. Whenever sausage was served we would all joyously exclaim: 'Found at last – the true pork sausage – Garbutt's special Oxford!' As World War I continued, the litany changed: 'Garbutt Bros. for prime dairy fed pork – 9d. per lb. for fresh, 8d. pickled – no German goods sold.' Later still: 'Are you helping the Belgian fund? Don't forget – by buying Garbutt's Belgian sausage you benefit the Belgians every time,' I came to believe it was our patriotic duty to eat as much pork sausage as possible.

Alma was always surprising us with odd items of news. She would casually remark: 'Stubborn fighting in the Carpathians,' or 'The Kaiser's birthday was celebrated quietly.' She also had an eye for high drama. While removing a tea-tray she would exclaim laconically: 'The Germans torpedoed the Cunard liner *Lusitania* on Friday, May 7th, at 2.30 p.m. Over a thousand lives lost,' or 'Reported Zeppelin raid over London.' Mother would look up, raise her eyebrows, and continue with her writing – she was always sending articles to southern periodicals.

And sometimes Alma, while washing my hair, would suddenly ask: 'Who built the Post Office Hotel at Cloncurry? Rooney's Ltd.' I gained a great respect for Rooney's; and taking my cue would then ask: 'Who paid £15,000 in Townsville for wages last year?' And we would both burst out: 'Rooney's Ltd!' Years later I could still repeat similar items concerning the progress of that enterprising firm.

I liked sitting in her room listening as she read the local newspaper to me. My education rapidly advanced, and I often astonished visitors by telling them they could buy a full upper at the Dental Hospital, that the *Bombala* would sail for Brisbane on 10 April at 5 p.m., and that Warner's rust-proof corsets were best.

HAL PORTER

Hal Porter (1911–84) was born in Melbourne and
educated in Bairnsdale, Gippsland, to which he
returned in later life as librarian. He taught in
Melbourne, Hobart, Adelaide and Japan, managed a
hotel, and wrote novels, poetry, short stories, plays and
an autobiographical trilogy: *The Watcher on the
Cast-Iron Balcony* (1963), *The Paper Chase* (1966) and
The Extra (1975). The use of sophisticated fictional
techniques and a highly self-conscious style make the
trilogy a landmark in Australian autobiography.

◆ ◆ ◆ ◆

◆ *The Watcher on the Cast-Iron Balcony*

In a half-century of living I have seen two corpses, two only. I do not
know if this total is conventional or unconventional for an Australian of my age.

The first corpse is that of a woman of forty. I see its locked and denying face through a lens of tears, and hear, beyond the useless hullabaloo of my début in grief, its unbelievable silence prophesying unbelievable silence for me. It is not until twenty-eight years later that I see, through eyes this time dry and polished as glass, my second corpse, which is that of a seventy-three-year-old man. Tears? No tears, not any, none at all. The silence of this corpse is as credible as my own silence is to be, and no excuse for not lighting another cigarette. I light it, tearless, while the bereaved others scatter their anguish in laments like handbills. I am tearless because twenty-eight years have taught that it is not the dead one should weep for but the living.

Once upon a time, it seems, but in reality on or about the day King Edward VII died, these two corpses have been young, agile and lustful enough to mortise themselves together to make me. Since the dead wear no ears that hear and have no tongues to inform, there can now be no answer, should the question be asked, as to where the mating takes place, how zestfully or grotesquely, under which ceiling, on which kapok mattress – no answer anywhere, ever.

In time, the woman, Mother, is six months large with me, and Dr Crippen is hanged. In time, and missing Edwardian babyhood by nine months, I am born. I am born a good boy, good but not innocent, this two-sided endowment laying me wide open to assaults of evil not only from without but also from within. I am a Thursday's child with far to go, brought forth under the sign of Aquarius, and with a cleft palate. This is skilfully sewn up. In which hospital? When I am how few months old? By whom now dead or nearing death? No one, I think, no one living now knows. Thus secretly mended, and secretly carrying, as it were, my first lie tattooed on the roof of the mouth that is to sound out so many later lies, I grow. I am exactly one week old when the first aeroplane ever to do so flies over my birthplace. On aesthetic grounds or for superstitious reasons I am unvaccinated; I am superstitiously and fashionably uncircumcised, plump, blue-eyed and white-haired. I have a silver rattle, Hindu, in the shape of a rococo elephant hung on a bone ring. I crawl. The *Titanic* sinks. I stand. The Archduke is assassinated at Sarajevo, and I walk at last into my own memories.

These earliest memories are of Kensington, a Melbourne suburb, and one less elegant than that in which I am born between the tray-flat waters of Albert Park Lake and the furrowed and wind-harrowed waters of Port Phillip Bay. The memories are centred in a house then 36 Bellair Street, Kensington. Of this house and of what takes place within it until I am six, I alone can tell. That is, perhaps, why I must tell. No one but I will know if a lie be told, therefore I must try for the truth which is the blood and breath and nerves of the elaborate and unimportant facts.

At the age of six I physically leave Kensington and 36 Bellair Street for ever, lightly picking up and taking with me Kensington and 36 Bellair Street. Until this very point in time a baggage of memories has travelled with me.

The moment of unpacking at hand I am astounded by the size and complexity of this child's luggage. Even now, a middle-aged man, I cannot unpack all: I have not yet the skill to unlade what a happy egocentric little boy skilfully jammed into invisible nothing.

Let me immediately reveal, in my largely visual recollections of this pre-six era, that my father and my mother are not visually alive to me as the young woman and young man they then are. I cannot see them. I remember the face of Father's gold pocket-watch, and the hair-line crack across its enamel, but not his; I remember exactly the pearls and rubies in Mother's crescent brooch but not her eyes. Except for Mother's singing, I cannot hear them; a mere little litter of words blows down the galleries of time, some of it aesthetically haunting, more of it unforgettably trite. I do remember his father-liness and her motherliness, essences informed by their youth and vitality and simplicity in which I have every trust. Fatherliness, motherliness, youth, vitality and simplicity I would not now trust for a moment. Each can destroy. Each helps destroy my parents; each helps them lay waste about them. But, however omniscient the child, he dares not, particularly if he be first born, further blind the parents he has already blinded with his existence by showing that he knows they are dupes not only of himself but of nature. So, my parents, imagining their physical selves as clearly seen as they think they see themselves in looking-glasses, move with blind instinct about me and always towards me and my imperious ego. They play the fool for me. They put on voices. They spend money on rubbish, toys for their toy. They cannot know that they themselves are clouds only, symbolic blurs meaning certainty and warmth and happiness, slaves without faces in a small universe where everything else is exquisitely clear.

The detail!

The colour!

Except in dreams, neither detail nor colour has ever since been so detailed or coloured; the fine edge of seeing for the first time too early wears blunt. But the first seeing is so sure that nothing smudges it.

♦

Eyes half-closed in a simulation of being closed, I make spiral movements above the slate on which Mother has drawn a spiral figure divided into numbered sections. I chant dreamily:

> *Tit-tat-toe, my first go!*
> *Three jolly butcher boys all in a row!*

The kerosene lamp is glowing and breathing like some warm golden animal. Now and then it blinks. It purrs. It almost utters a dim, kind word.

> *Stick one up! Stick one down!*
> *Stick one in the dead man's ground!*

The pencil pecks down softly and bluntly on the slate. My eyes, pretending merely to open, exaggeratedly strain wide open. When Mother adds the figures thus picked out, I win. I always do. I am aware she does not care a rap about winning. Nor, really, do I, but, since I think it will be cruel to her as well as giving myself away to tell her that I know she lets me win, I let her let me win. The fire crumbling apart like incandescent cake, the kettle on the hob droning itself to silence, the lamp exhaling itself and an era towards extinction, I feel, in memory, that Mother's face is never more peaceful. But it is unseen, unrecallable, alas, unrecallable. To be not able to recall that face of peace, at that moment, and yet to recall her face in death and not at peace, is an invitation to regret I dare not accept. Better far to regard the moments of lamp-lit peace as an accidentally charming illustration of mother-and-child indicative of nothing except nothing better to do, and displaying nothing except that mothers cannot help enacting motherhood nor sons sonliness.

Mother is, however, generally too vital and noisy, too young and on the go, to participate often in such scenes of family quietude. She is constantly singing. Years after, heart and head deep in children, her vivacity tampered with, she can still sing. Even on her deathbed she sings.

♦

Victor is my age. Victor is my first playmate and, though scarcely a friend and scarcely loved, is a first reading for the first rehearsal for the first scene of the first act in the long comedy of friends I am still stumbling through.

It is inevitable, it advances autobiography minutely and effortlessly, to come to another and yet another first experience. Even with memory patching what reality must have breached, it is certain that my cocoon is wearing, here and there, thin enough to permit intrusions on a good boy. These intrusions never really more than brush my goodness, though they tear the sheath surrounding it. They do nothing to innocence, for I have never possessed innocence. They give edges to intelligence, they refresh watching eyes. Victor is, for a time, They. Victor is many first experiences.

He is, for example, at eye-level. He is the right size, my size. He is easier to look at than ants and cockchafers. He is much more visible than adults. Whatever Mother and Father, and Aunt Rosa Bona auntishly doting and chirruping under her platter of feathers, may believe, I have never really seen their faces. I have seen no face until Victor's. It is one I can intimately examine for signs of his soul's and emotions' weather. Hitherto, I have caught the climate of people from the rays vibrating out of the space they make animate, from the colours of a voice, from the quality of their silences, even from the manner in which they inhabit the realm of their dark night and their sleep which is, to me, a mere shire in the realm of my dark night and my sleep.

Victor's is the first face to interpose its planes and complexities between me and instinct. This puts instinct on its mettle. We stare face to face at each other. I smell the sap-like scent from his nostrils. What I view, far far back, eternities back, behind the brilliant, curved jellies of his eyes is the future. We know instantly that we have only in common what every human has. Our confrontation is essentially a confrontation of primitive and unashamed warinesses; it could have been the meeting of sophisticated centenarians with nothing to lose and every hope of gaining. Do I gain? I gain indelible information, outside my power, then, to express in words, information on the beauties, surprises, tricks, evasions, lures and lunacies of the mobile mask. I find intimations of his and my and the world's mortality in the pinked edges of his teeth, the wet curling-open or the brutal pressing-together of his lips, the dark grape-like bloom about his eyes, the seeds of yellow wax in his ears, the flushings or wanings of blood under the envelope of skin. Intuitively I know all this will rot like a peach.

Because he is the same marvellously convenient size as I, we understand each other's eases and difficulties of locomotion, and hopes of levitation. We can therefore examine each other's machinery with no more and no less curiosity than we examine our own. We move from the revealed to the concealed.

Peter is the word current then, in our class, for penis. We barter Peters. Since we are similarly pink and white, the only new knowledge I gain is that I am not unique in construction or behaviour, and that Mr and Mrs Richmond, as represented by Victor's penis, are not as civilized as my parents as represented by mine. He has smegma. I have been taught to wash. These exchanges are conducted with directness and busy relish. They are also conducted in what goes for deep secrecy, behind the castor-oil plant in Victor's backyard or the latticed fernery overrun with smilax at the side of our house. Nothing has been said ever to me about the possibility of this sort of amusement occurring but I realize that it is one forbidden to adults. Between each incident I, at least, do not suffer from guilt. Once my trousers are on again my mind is with my body and eyes wherever elsewhere is. Guiltlessness and secrecy avail nothing. When, days or hours later, I am what is called 'playing with Nigger', Mrs Richmond is suddenly there, above me. 'I know,' she says, 'what you and Victor have been doing.' I have met my first dangerous adult. Fathers and mothers rarely seem adult to their children, merely older, distorted by time, and dirty with the soot of years.

♦

I am not the only watcher. The minister performs his last duties, and departs. There are Father, the Matron, a nurse, shadows that stand or come and go. I am not the only watcher until, out of the whisperings, I hear my mother say:

> Tit-tat-toe, my first go!
> Three jolly butcher-boys all in a row . . .

Now, I am the only watcher. I am alone. Mother and I are alone, alone, alone, alone, alone. Her bedtime plait hangs over her shoulder; its end, tied with tape, lies on the furry tablecloth. The Kensington lamp breathes like a warm golden animal. It purrs and stutters. The fire is crumbling apart like incandescent cake, like a world in dissolution.

> Stick one up! Stick one down!
> Stick one in the dead man's ground!

Alone.

I have been punished at last, at long long last.

As my defences of happiness crack within me, they and I begin to make sounds I did not think I could, hard and harsh, bestial and elemental sounds. When I have pillaged my reservoir of tears, when

I have finished my first bout of agony at the marble chimney-piece, when I have done what all humans must do, Matron is saying, 'Ai'm afreed she's gone,' and is wiping with a piece of cotton-wool a disgusting and pathetic occurrence of foam from Mother's lips so that Father and I may kiss what no longer needs kisses.

It is from this thing on the bed I must now flee.

Oh, God, the watcher on the cast-iron balcony screams out within me, Oh, God, put me back on the balcony! One scream within, and one only. There is no one to hear.

God is dead.

Father, undaunted, takes the rings from the fingers, and puts them in his wallet. It is his turn now for agony. I wait until his gruntings and sobbings subside, meantime straightening my tie, combing my hair, and setting my face at nix-nought-nothing.

At that moment I am sure that God is dead, that any love I must have for the world I must make for myself – beginning, at last, after years of happy nothing, at nothing. It has become simple. Mother is dead, God is dead, love is dead, all that I was is dead. So, I think, waiting for Father to make himself publicly possible, waiting to begin watching again those who are watching what they think is me, the dead one.

I do not know that, not only have I not started to die, I have not started to live.

I have not even helped Father across the road to the rectory.

♦   The Paper Chase

When Mother dies in late March 1929, I am newly eighteen. Although I have already blandly participated in, or artfully avoided participating in, enough impure enough or ludicrous enough experiences to be as case-hardened as a stripling can be, Mother's death and the unromantic form of it affront me deeply. No Lady of Shalott she. Writers with their aesthetic inventions about death and death-beds – I *am dying, Egypt, dying* and so on and so on – are, it is too clear to one wading heart-deep in fruitless tears, charlatans.

This latest experience in which I resent participation is startling. The fairy-tale forests of childhood are behind. That blossom-hunt and sun-striped era, at least and at last, is over for ever and ever.

It is not only startling, it is agonizing.

At least that's how, in March 1929, it appears. My knowledge of agony is, however, and to this very today, nearly forty years later, meagre – the dialect of grief is a hard one to learn. My death-side agony may not be authentic agony at all. Agony, grief, sorrow, whatever it is, may be something else yet to accomplish or never to accomplish. Does one – does a writer with his eyes in his heart, and his heart in his brain – ever really get to know? Perhaps, eighteen, and considering myself and the earth cruelly deprived, I am putting, as Westerners are inclined to do, an excessive, maybe an extreme, value on individual life.

As a quick lesson-learner I don't put it for long. By autumnal May the leaves of my sorrow are falling too. Dressed in black like an early Julien Green character I am walking, late at night (midnight?), along the Gellibrand Pier, Williamstown. There is a suitable fog, moveless and rich with chill, and the prehistoric baying of fog-horns. Now and then, far from the lamp before, a pier-lamp appears in its fog-bow. Now and then, below and regularly, the bay water slaps at the pier-piles like swags of cold cold flesh. There is nothing to feel with the eyes but the discernible nothing. Into this salt-spiced lateness and desolation there comes a consoling and informative revelation (doubtless it is canny self-information to self-console) that eternity is what goes on behind one's back, that living is what goes on behind the backs of the dead. Cold fleshy water, blazing flesh, shrivelled flesh, passion and loss, crystals, rocks, barnacles and butterflies, laughter and screams and songs, footsteps on fog-damp pier-planks, all things go on and on and on no matter who – Mother or somebody's mother or Caligula, Mary Queen of Scots or drummer-boy at Waterloo – are filed away among the used-up. Oh yes, the used-up, the blue-pencilled, the dead dead. It is (the revelation continues), it is, however, impossible to kill the dead. Indeed, it is only the dead, salted down for ever, pickled in the vat of time, who illustrate how immortal mortals are, and how unavoidable is resurrection, how immediate and permanent, with no three days required, and no hope necessary – hope, the last and most terrible of all the evils let out of Pandora's box. No need at all for hope: although as dead as mutton, Mother has come upon the earth, a very Tmu from the Book of the Dead, and with her two feet has taken possession of it.

'Clean the *backs* of your shoes,' she says. I obey – 1917, 1923, 1935, yesterday, today, tomorrow, as long as there are shoes and shoe-polish and me.

'Lucifer, Star of the Morning, was a fallen angel,' she says. 'Grace Darling was a brave girl. Those stars – see, there, above the cherry-tree – are the Seven Sisters.' He, Lucifer, is. She, Grace Darling, is. They, the Seven Sisters, are. Mother, therefore, also is because she has her resurrection in them and such unforgotten lessons or legends or lies. She lives in old words to old tunes I catch myself singing in new places and new years which hear thus the errors in word and tune she taught me. She lives in the woodbine and the picotees which have followed the family, sentimental cutting by cutting, from her country garden to this, that and the other garden. She has being in the chipped petals of a white china rose she loved, in an appalling supper-cloth she crocheted, in a Cacao Grootes tin still filled with her blouse-buttons – carved mother-of-pearl, jet, cat's-eye agate, in a silver teapot inherited from her inheriting, in blankets she bought as a young wife over half a century ago and which, threadbare, with faded stripes top and bottom, now lie folded beneath the mattresses of grandchildren she never knew.

Ah Mother, up to your tricks, vital, inexorcizable ghost! As all women are, you are born solitary. You must, as each woman does, mulct a man of his identity. You must, as a mother does, use the subtlest temptations to mulct a son of his identity. A writer son, a marked man, needs particularly to brush aside these temptations. He must round on himself, and bare his unlovable strengths to the bone with the insolence of one baring lovable weaknesses. He must say with finality, 'Listen, you there, *woman* . . . Mother . . . it was a short and merciless happiness, given merely to be taken away. Gifts from Heaven are also gifts from Hell. Be comforted, Mother. Be comforted, immortal. Nature is, after all, not so much cruel as not kind. Now, *now*, I must try to avoid whatever repugnant Utopia you might have wished lovingly or with maternal zeal on your first-born, and defend my right to suffer or not to suffer. Let me find out for

myself if I shall come to regret a desire not to live better and better
but only to live more and more.'

Goodbye, immortal.

Goodbye, Mother.

Eternity will go on behind your back.

♦

I remember, really, little unpleasant about the Depression in
Williamstown, although more than a quarter of its population is out
of work, because I am not punished enough by it to remember: its
cat-o'-nine-tails leaves no mark on my thirty-bob-to-two-quid-a-
week shoulders. I have no wife playing landlady to a mysterious
stranger in the spare room of her belly. I have no brood of children
clamouring like billeted troops for fish and chips, vanilla ice cream
and kola tonic. I keep no mistress, greyhound, saxophone or motor-
bike. It does become necessary to learn to clean and press my own
trousers, and to try to remember to walk on the grass plots, which
do not seem to be called nature strips then, in attempts to save shoe
leather. Beyond that – almost nothing. I am, however, persistently
half-aware, even in the most blinding midsummer high noon, of a
touch of twilight – somewhere – someone else's twilight – somewhere; and, even at moments of absolute cessation, at dawn, say,
with dew-soaked suburban tulips still dead-asleep on their feet, I
feel there is a bleakish wind blowing – but not for me – somewhere
high up, high above a weakened and narrow-gutted world, a streaming, ever-blowing, unheard gale that tears to tatters the unseen
banners of someone's life, of many lives, and showers down no fiery
petals, no bluebird's feather, no warm tears.

During the day, at school, it is impossible not to know that many
of my pupils live on the bread-line, it is impossible not to observe
the home-cobbled shoes, the darned elbows of boys' jumpers –
heather-mixture jumpers just too tight and short of sleeve, the
don't-be-ashamed-of-a-patch trousers and turned shirt collars, the
chapped patent-leather belts and scrubbing-board-dimmed colours
of girls' dresses, their skirts home-made from some obviously adult

material. No one is, however, not neat; there are speckless finger-
nails and polished shoes; no one gets emaciated; all are ebullient and
happy-go-lucky, or undetectedly pretend to be so.

♦

My letter of resignation written, I am immediately no longer Junior
Teacher 26,727 of North Williamstown State School 1409.

What am I?

First of all, I am a twenty-six-year-old male who, between the
extremes of being a restless picker-up and a ruthless pruner, has
acquired a number of habits and convictions nothing will alter.
These particular habits and convictions, chosen after much explo-
ration of other varieties, now serve the purpose of bringing me to
heel when different habits and newly fashionable convictions present themselves along with the unnecessary opportunity to spend
myself in further time-and-spirit-wasting explorations. Old gods
exact fewer dues than new ones. I am wary of being broadminded
because those who profess broadmindedness are, it seems, professing it on behalf of their own appetites. I prefer to keep my inborn
sense of sin unsmothered, and to be narrow-minded about forgiv-
ing myself when I do sin. Self-forgiving is unforgivable.

What else am I?

Out of work. Homeless. Practically penniless and, as it were,
large with child, gravid with the novel which is to have twenty-four
chapters, each covering an hour in a one day's red-hot wedge sliced
from the lives of a number of characters based on Williamstown
people. Each character is to be dealt with in a signature-tune style
which is to involve me in imitations of James Joyce, Conrad, Henry
James, Thomas Mann, Kipling, Evelyn Waugh, Mary Webb,
Proust, and others I forget. The result is, of course, to be the Great
Australian Novel. In short, I have shamelessly – but not for long –
lost my head. I do not lose it long enough to find myself doing a
Thomas Chatterton in an attic. Where, then, am I to take my
Wright's Coal Tar Soap and Euthymol Toothpaste, and hang up

my sponge-bag, while the months of labour drag on? How shall I
buy more soap and toothpaste?

♦

In Victoria Parade the car I am in draws up to disgorge me, outside
St Vincent's Hospital, opposite the flat. I wish them happy drinking, and start across the road laden with what Olivia has bought for
me during the day – a dozen oranges, a dozen lemons, a pineapple, a
ream of foolscap, and a parcel of chemist goods including a bottle of
Aqua Velva, an after-shave lotion. With my library notebooks plus
a bunch of wallflowers given me by one of the actressy young
women in Mario's, my arms are full.

I see headlights coming at me.

Retreat?

Go on?

That minute faltering is dangerous. More dangerous is the fact
that when I do go on, hurling myself forward, I do not throw away
the hampering and balance-impairing parcels. The mudguard of the
car strikes my hip. I feel the ball part of the hipbone plunge through
the socket, feel the bones of the pelvis smash. There I am, flat on my
back on the road, still holding the wallflowers. They have the
wrong smell, and this is the first of a number of disconcerting and
disillusioning things to happen in the next hour. The wrong wall-
flower smell is that of Aqua Velva from the smashed bottle and, this
first problem in a new milieu solved, others present themselves.

The main one is the problem of correct behaviour under the
scrutiny of the hedge of people that has sprung up around me in a
neat oval – one woman has unusual lime-green gloves, one man has
a twinkling fly-button undone.

Shall I say, 'You there, bend down. I want to whisper. You've got
a medal showing.'?

What to say, since I cannot move? A smile? It will, doubtless, be
sickly, and misunderstood.

This is not only an embarrassing situation not experienced
before, it is also one not witnessed before – and not witnessed to

this day – of a human skittled by a piece of heavy machinery. Even the films let me down. And suppose I am dying, what shall I say? My mother's dying words were artless, and are certainly not for me. Plays, novels, films – their death-bed speeches are too high-flown or sloppily long-winded or arch. Only the girl in *The Story of an African Farm* watching herself dying alone on the veldt with a looking-glass in her hand seems authentic. However good an idea, hardly correct, the looking-glass in front of these vertical bystanders who have sprung out of the ground. Anyway, death seems far off. I have never felt so relaxed before. The bitumen could be a goose-feather bed; the stars, I observe, are not sprinkled on the sky's surface at all but embedded in it at various depths; and, disillusionment above all, there is absolutely no pain, nothing for me to centralize an act of manly grit and silent suffering on. It is bewildering. If I could get up and stroll off I should get up and stroll off, but body has told mind, and mind now tells body, 'No!'

Olivia, whose car has not had time to move off before I have spoiled the rest of their evening, is my salvation. She is what I call beautiful, and what Somerset Maugham calls 'exquisitely gowned', will raise my stocks, and is my wife, and knows what to say to me. She makes her perfect entrance among the immediately inferior onlookers. I know she will not let me down. She doesn't.

'Darling,' she says, 'this is too ridiculous. Wallflowers!'

'There were no orchids left.' Ah! I can speak!

'I told you that florist had no morals.'

'Florists don't need morals.'

This absurd exchange, impromptu burlesque of Noël Coward, provides the bracer we need in an absurd contretemps among strangers who, by behaving with human simplicity, seem to put themselves into absurd Alice-in-Wonderland focus. They play their parts with conviction, picking up oranges and lemons and dusting them, helping the woman who has run me down be sick under one of the trees in the central plantation of the road. One has said, 'Stand back and give him air.' One has gone, as into the neighbour's to borrow a cup of salt, to St Vincent's to get an ambulance. It is all very convenient.

I see Olivia's hands being deliberately precise and untrembling as she lights two cigarettes. We are waiting for something to happen. The hedge gets thicker by a tram-load of audience.

'Do men,' I say, 'have pelvises?'

'Certainly not. Only child-bearing women.'

'Well, it's very confusing. I think what men have instead of pelvises is broken.'

'*Pas devant les domestiques!* There is no need to be coarse.'

JUDAH WATEN

Judah Waten (1911–84) was born in Russia into a
Jewish family. In 1914 he arrived in Western Australia
where his father earned a living as a hawker. In 1926
he moved to Melbourne where he became active in
literary and Communist circles. His works have been
widely translated. *Alien Son* (1952), a collection of
semi-autobiographical sketches, first established him as
an authentic migrant voice.

◆ ◆ ◆ ◆

Early next morning I ran into the street while Mother was scrub-
bing one of the rooms. I was impatient to join the children whom I
had seen the previous night. But as soon as they saw me they burst
out laughing and pointed to my buttoned-up shoes and white silk
socks. I was overcome with shame and ran back into the house
where I removed my shoes and socks and threw them into one of
the empty rooms. I would walk barefooted like the other boys. And
when I heard Mother calling to me from the kitchen to play in the
back-yard and not to go into the street, I pretended I didn't
hear.

I tacked myself on to the tail end of a group of boys who were prancing down the street. It was really more a track than a street, petering out a few yards from our gate in a gentle rise that merged with the horizon so that Mother could be pardoned for thinking we lived on the very edge of the world.

I could barely stand the gravel and the hot sand on my bare feet and the short, dry grass of the paddock gave little relief. But I was proud of my own courage and of the attention the boys paid me, though I didn't know a word of what they were saying.

We came to a shed at the back of the general store that was almost directly opposite the railway station and next to a group of wooden, ramshackle buildings that housed a baker, a bootmaker and a newsagent. Farther down the street stood, in solitary splendour, a two-storied wooden hotel with a wide verandah running the width of the building.

I clambered up a high, picket fence with the rest of the boys and held on for dear life while they chattered and screeched like magpies. We were watching a short, elderly man backing a black horse into a cart.

To my surprise the man kept looking at me curiously from under heavy lids which sagged and were covered in a maze of creases. He carried a big leather bag slung over his shoulder like a Sam Browne belt and he wore a marine dealer's badge on his arm. His broad-brimmed hat with its sweat-stained band sat as flat as a pancake on his head. The boys mimicked him in a childish gibberish as he mumbled to his horse in the only language I knew.

But the old man wasn't angry with the boys. He smiled back at them like a deaf and dumb uncle and his eyes lingered a little longer over me. As he jumped up on the cart he nodded his head and stroked his little straggly brown beard and waved his long whip at me. Then with a loud cry he drove out of the yard.

Late that afternoon we were playing on the railway station. It was deserted, although a train was expected within an hour, so that we had the run of some empty trucks. A solitary cart appeared on the horizon and soon we recognized the old man perched on top of a heap of bags. We ran to meet him. He was urging his horse on and the sweaty, velvety hide of the animal quivered as the old man flicked his long whip over its mane. We chased the cart and the boys called loudly, 'Bottle-oh! Bottle-oh! Any bottles today?'

But as soon as we followed him into the yard he jumped off the cart and chased us out, cracking his whip over our heads. Again he was looking closely at me, but this time there was a sly expression in his beady, half-closed eyes that made me feel distinctly uncomfortable. It was as though he had caught me out.

From the high picket fence we watched him unload his cart, stacking bottles in pyramids according to their size and shape. Then he carried a great bundle of bags piled high on his strong shoulders into a shed, where dark doors opened like the mouth of a cave. He curried and brushed his horse and carefully mixed chaff and bran into a bin, gently pushing its soft nose aside. Then he disappeared into the shed and closed the door.

When I returned home Mother complained bitterly that I had run away twice in one day; that I had thrown my shoes and socks away and would catch cold. I would get lost; all her gloomiest premonitions would come true. Father was always blunt-spoken and he said that if I disobeyed Mother again he would take to me in no uncertain way.

It was at that stage that I judged it wise to bring out my bit of news. I said that in the afternoon I had only gone to the shed to find out if the old man was really a Jew. Mother was overwhelmed.

'There you are, you find our people in the farthest corners of the world. Perhaps this place is after all not the end of everything. We might have a community here yet.'

All my misdeeds were forgotten and even Father smiled.

'Bring him home,' he said, cheerfully. 'Let's have a look at him.'

It was not until sundown the next day that I saw the old man again. I was in the street with the neighbour's boy looking into shop windows and watching the men go into the hotel, when I saw the old man pacing up and down on the opposite side of the street outside the railway station. The train had just gone and was climbing into the hills that rose beyond the township. Escaping smoke still hung in grey masses against a purple sky, blotting out the stars which had just appeared.

When he caught sight of me the old man hurried towards me.

Spacing his words slowly he asked me in a wheedling, high-pitched, sing-song voice if I was a Jewish boy. Immediately I spoke in Yiddish his voice changed; every trace of hesitancy disappeared. He pinched my cheeks and rumpled my hair with his strong, calloused palms.

'Why haven't I seen your father and mother? Where are they hiding? I'll have someone to talk to at last. I'll be able to free my heart.'

Then his voice changed and in a wheedling tone, his half-closed eyes blinking innocently, he asked, 'And for instance, what does your father do?'

He seemed relieved when I answered that he was a draper.

From that day old Hirsh was a regular visitor to our house. Mother's hope had been realized and we had the beginnings of a community. Every day at six we would see the old man hastening towards the house, his short body erect and his quick stride soldierly. His appearance never altered except on wet days when he wore a long shabby overcoat over his faded blue waistcoat and the bulging leather bag that he never parted from. He no longer lingered over his horse of an evening; he made the horse comfortable and left without even an affectionate glance.

Even after we had sat down to our meal he remained standing with his back to the fire, often without speaking, his hat still on his head, his eyes almost closed.

GEORGE JOHNSTON

George Henry Johnston (1912–70) was born in
Melbourne. In World War II he achieved fame as a war
correspondent. He later lived for ten years in the
Greek islands with his second wife, Charmian Clift, the
Cressida of the trilogy. His quest for happiness and
self-knowledge forms the theme of his
semi-autobiographical trilogy: *My Brother Jack* (1964),
Clean Straw for Nothing (1969) and *A Cartload of Clay*
(1971). In the first, the contrast between two brothers
dramatises conflicting loyalties to two ideals; the later
volumes explore the situation of the expatriate writer
and the threat of tuberculosis.

♦ ♦ ♦ ♦

♦ *My Brother Jack*

In a sense, of course, I was too young for the war to have had any
direct effect on me, since there was really nothing of it that I could
remember. Yet what is significant to realise now is how every corner

of that little suburban house must have been impregnated for years
with the very essence of some gigantic and sombre experience that
had taken place thousands of miles away, and quite outside the state
of my own being, yet which ultimately had come to invade my mind
and stay there, growing all the time, forming into a shape.

And it went on for years. There was no corner of the house from
the time I was seven until I was twelve or thirteen that was not
littered with the inanimate props of that vast, dark experience, no
room that was not inhabited by the jetsam that the Somme and the
Marne and the salient at Ypres and the Gallipoli beaches had
thrown up. Stubby sitting by a window tearing with his teeth at the
white threads of his doilies; Aleck in another room knitting his
balaclavas or fumbling with quick-tapping insectine fingers for his
tobacco pouch; the bumpy, squeaky sound of someone in a
bedroom testing an artificial leg; the bathroom that everlastingly
smelt of antiseptic and ointment and ether and Condy's crystals:
and even outside, in the backyard sunshine, there would be
Mother's white nursing veils and aprons blowing on the clothes-
line in a smell of yellow soap, and underneath the fig-tree Bert sitting on an upturned packing-case, a long leather bib tied around his
chest and his empty trouser-leg neatly folded up and fastened by a
safety-pin, hammering away at half-soles and heels. There was no
radio then, but we always had 'sing-songs' around the piano on
Sunday nights, with Mother playing, and for years the songs were
always the same – the 'old favourites' of the war years, 'Tipperary'
and 'Over There' and 'Johnny Get Your Gun' and the rest of
them.

It was not until I discovered the big deep drawer at the bottom of
the cedar wardrobe in my parents' bedroom that I began to sense a
form in the shadow that lurked in the wards and the corridors of
the hospital, and to give a shape to the faraway experience which
had moved in behind the privet hedge to occupy every room and
every cranny of our mundane little house. During the years when
Mother and Father were away the drawer must have been the re-
pository for all the souvenirs and things they would send back to
Granny, or the things she had preserved herself for their relationship to 'The Front,' and to this collection Mother and Dad would
have added their own memorabilia when they returned, for there

was a service revolver in the drawer, and a cardboard box full of stubby .45 bullets and clips of .303 ammunition in a leather bandolier and campaign ribbons and various regimental badges and a German Iron Cross and the citation that had gone with my father's Military Medal. But also there were elaborate French silk postcards and innumerable foreign coins and banknotes and, most important of all, the full set of weekly parts of the *Illustrated War News* and a copy of *The Anzac Book* and the three volumes of Louis Raemaker's cartoons about the German atrocities.

I would steal into the bedroom when Dad was away at the tram sheds and Mother on duty in the operating theatre, and I would lock the door and spend hours on the floor in front of the big drawer. The Raemaker cartoons, at first, were the dominant fascination.

One knew nothing then about propaganda, so that the cartoons, in my mind, assumed a horrible reality, the substance of nightmare translated into printed truth. For weeks I was in morbid thrall to these grotesque, hating pictures of brutal infernos, of cloven-footed devils wearing Kaiser Bill hats impaling naked babies and women on their swords, of priests being mutilated and crucified by the Prussians in front of sacked and burning towns, of the grinning skeleton of Death in a Uhlan's helmet wielding a scythe across the shell-pocked desecration of No Man's Land, of the bestial Huns disembowelling starving Belgian children, and mysterious words like *Kultur* and *Gott Mit Uns* written across a ruined world in letters of blood.

But after a time, perhaps because it was essential to reject the horror that the pictures inspired – for I was unable to develop a hatred, which, in fact, was the purpose of their message – I forced myself to realise that these were only drawings, after all, made, I thought, by some vengeful and embittered man who must have suffered frightfully at the hands of the Germans. And as their power to oppress me lessened, I gave greater attention to the copies of the *Illustrated War News*. For these pictures were not imagined and drawn out of wrath and vindictive hatred; these were the *real* photographs of what had taken place.

◆

I was staring in at these photographs one day – really I was only waiting for the signal of the train's whistle on the viaduct, which would be my cue to move on to the second-hand shop window – when a ragged, agate-eyed boy who was at my school but several years older and in the sixth grade, came down the street, kicking a tennis ball before him. He stopped alongside me but said nothing. He just stood there for a long time, right beside me, staring in with me at the pale photographs. Finally, in a flat voice and without even looking at me, he said, 'All them blokes in there is dead, you know.' He stared at the pictures a moment or two longer, then said, 'Well, hoo-roo,' and waved to me and moved off and kicked the tennis ball right down to the end of the street and trotted after it, whistling.

I ran all the way home that day, trying not to cry, because I didn't know what it was I wanted to cry about, but I never after that looked in the window of the photographer's studio or the second-hand shop. From then on, when I went to the Phoebe for the serial matinees or the Harold Lloyd comedies, I would always make a long detour to go the back way.

It was shortly after this that I began to get rid of the contents of the big drawer. I did it quite carefully, a little at a time – I suppose it took me months to complete the job – and after a while I found I could do it with material gain to myself. I sold the books of the Raemaker cartoons and the sets of the *Illustrated War News* to Garcia the greengrocer for wrapping paper, and all the silk post-cards and strange coins and odd souvenirs I either sold to kids at school or swapped for marbles or foreign stamps or toodilumbuks. There was a slight shock one day when we had parsley delivered from Garcia wrapped up in some of the Raemaker cartoons, but Granny didn't even notice it.

I left the revolver there, and the bandolier and Dad's medals and things like that, but my parents never went to the drawer in the wardrobe, and I don't believe they ever knew what I had done with all the other things; perhaps they no longer even remembered that the stuff was there.

It doesn't matter any longer, of course, because all them blokes in there really *are* dead now.

♦

It was like a great river flooding or changing its course, the way the Depression came – the insidious creeping movement of dark, strong, unpredictable forces, the flow of hidden currents, a clod falling and dissolving, a slide of earth, the cave-in of an entire bank, a sudden eddy swirling around a snag, tilting it over, sweeping it off into a black oblivion.

Even when the disaster had spread everywhere and its destructive menace understood, something unfeasible remained. The work trains, to me, going to my job at the same hour on the same days, seemed just as crowded, the same people pushed at the ticket barriers with the same impatient roughness, the shops were as full as ever of their desperate enticements. It was out in the suburbs mostly that one gradually came to see it.

They brought in the dole, and then the dole became 'the sustenance', and around this time they unlocked the Defence Department warehouses and out of the mothballs they took the old surplus greatcoats and tunics and they dyed them a dull black – all that brave khaki of 1914–18 – and against the contingency of a Melbourne winter issued them out as a charity to keep the workless warm. So that as the unemployed grew in number the black army coats became a kind of badge of adversity, a stigma of suffering.

One would see the shabby figures shambling along the suburban streets, carrying a loaf of bread and in a cloth bicycle-bag their meagre handout from the Sustenance Depot of tea and sugar and flour and potatoes, and a wisp of tobacco. Or there would be a queue of men the length of a block, most of them in the ill-fitting, shameful black, in apathetic competition for half a dozen casual jobs. As the situation grew worse desperate attempts were made towards alleviation, and the 'black coats' moved then in the more regimented bands of the 'sustenance-workers' and you would see them with their brooms and picks and shovels and council tip-drays working in slovenly unison on pointless municipal projects. Every now and then one would recognise a familiar figure among them – Dud Bennett, the one-time leader of the Grey Caps gang, driving a council dray laden with gravel, looking small and shrunken now: and Snowy Bretherton in a black greatcoat top-dressing the strip of lawn outside the local town hall. It was a time of a sad and terrible human degradation for which there seemed to be no remedy.

This was the time, too, of the first trickle in from Europe of that
other human flotsam, Jews mostly and refugees from a new malig-
nancy, and this, also, was misleading at first for the trickle had
become a flood almost before one realised what was happening.
Even the language of suffering, of course, had to be Australianised.
The refugees became the 'Reffos', just as the sustenance-workers
had by this time become the 'Sussos'.

Dad by now was depot foreman so he kept his job at the tramways
running-shed, but Bert, who had been 'retrenched' from the Re-
patriation Department, put on his uniform again, although this
time the tunic and the greatcoat were dyed a dull black, so he must
have had a different feeling about it from the time, fourteen years
before, when as a hayseed kid from Corindhap he had gone away
with an assumed name and bright badges and a sense of glorious
adventure to have his leg blown off in France. He went back to
casual snobbing to eke out the sustenance. By this time he had three
children to keep.

In our suburb there was a constant, unnerving movement of
these pathetic and yet somehow oddly sinister figures in their black
tunics and greatcoats. Sometimes they would come to the door
asking for an hour's work to cut the hedge or to mow the lawn or to
stack firewood or even to run errands ... or sometimes more
bluntly just to ask for a handout of food or money. A few of the
more resourceful among them had made themselves crude little
handtrucks which they would push clatteringly around the streets,
collecting old newspapers or scrap-metal or unwanted clothes, or
with coal or kindling-wood to sell.

I remember the evening when Dad came into my room and said:
'I want you to print me up a sign. You do printing at Klebendorf's,
don't you?'

'Lettering things, you mean? Yes.'

He handed me a bevelled oblong of hardwood, and said, 'This is
for the front gate. The carpenter at the sheds fixed it for me. I want
you to paint a sign on it. Can you print this up for me?' He passed
over a crumpled slip of paper on which he had crudely printed out
the words: BEGGARS, HAWKERS, AND CANVASSERS WILL BE
PROSECUTED.

I lettered the sign for him in white on black, but then he made me take it out and screw it to the front gate. I wanted to protest but his face was so stern and implacable that I said nothing. While I was attaching the sign to the gate two middle-aged men in black greatcoats came across and stood there watching me. When in my nervousness and humiliation I dropped one of the screws one of the men stooped over and picked it up and handed it to me, but neither he nor his companion uttered a single word. When the sign was firmly fixed against the gate they just turned away and shuffled off along the street muttering to each other. It was not very long before these signs – or something like them – were on gates all over the suburbs.

At Klebendorf's the terror moved into the big studio in a different way. Advertising appropriations were cut and orders petered out, and there were long slack times when we all worked feverishly on 'spec' designs, but there were very few orders that seemed to come from them. Out in the factory half the machines were silent, and the flatbeds and the big rotaries were covered over with spoiled sheets of double-quad printing paper, like the drapes over furniture in an unoccupied house. Finally there was the surprising day when old Klebendorf came up to the studio. I say surprising, because the old man, whom I had never known to do more than grunt out a gruff sentence, or just grunt, had called the art staff together to hear his careful set speech. That was the only time I remember the two old Germans, Steiner and Richter, coming to the studio together, like two timid mice. Perhaps it was their presence that made old Klebendorf sound more German than ever, or maybe it was only emotion that twisted his speech.

'You vill all know,' he began after a good deal of coughing and throat-clearing, 'that der printing indusstry iss not now in a condition of equitableness. We have been standing off thirty men from the factory already. Thirty goot men! It iss not goot. *Nein!* But' – he clenched his fist – 'it iss not as bad, my frients, as our oppositional firm of McIlwraith *und* Todd, which has its doors closed, *pouf'* – he spread his pudgy hands in a queer little quick gesture – '*und* every man, every goot man at that place is a job without. This iss bad. *Ach!* The times are of great difficulty. Here at Klebendorf und Hardt we have the good company and the good staff. Ve vill act *mit* honour. *Ja!* But the orders they are not, and the overhead is of a cost phen-

omenal, *und* there must be taking place a changement. So! There
will be suffering, but we vill spread the suffering. We will spread it
so that no man he iss hurting too much. *Ja! There is no man here who
iss losing his job. Nein!* Not vun! I have talked together with Mr
Denton, *und* he vill tell you our proposement. Vot ve think iss best
for all of us. Our difficulties ve vill *share*, eh? *Mein Gott! Mein Gott!*
it is of such difficulties the vorld over at this time! I have preoccu-
pational matters very great. *Mein* own land is suffering also, and
many of my own people are coming so far to seek assistance, and
them I must be helping a little also. You understand! It is of great
difficulty. Something bad it happens in this world . . . I do not know
vot it iss. . . .'

As I listened to the old man, his gross, flabby face crumpled in a
mask of concern and anxiety and embarrassment: his thick guttural
accents groping to express some vital message of mercy and loyalty
and consideration and humaneness, my mind turned back to an
image of a child in a locked bedroom rummaging in a wardrobe
drawer. Was this the Hun of the Raemaker cartoons? This ludicrous little fat figure with the heavy gold watch-chain looped across
the burgomaster belly, striving for a 'condition of equitableness' in a
world where economic disaster had sprung out like a beast from the
shadows – was this the hateful figure of German *Kultur*? His voice
had thickened even more as he struggled to get hope and conviction
into his words:

'It vill not last. *Ach Gott*, it cannot last! It is a phase, no more.
There will come another changement, this it iss sure, *und* for the
good. *Ja!* We vill ride it out, eh? We vill all share the difficulties, *und*
so we vill ride it out. . . .'

After he had finished Joe Denton put the situation crisply. 'What
we've worked out is this,' he said. 'There's not enough work here to
keep us *all* busy, we all know that. So instead of chopping staff we'll
try a system of rationing. Each one of us will take it in turns to stand
down for two weeks without pay. *Without* pay, remember. We'll see
how it works out. Everyone will be in this, apprentices and all. If
things continue to get worse it might have to be a month off without
pay, or two blokes off together. We'll have to see about that. It
depends how things go. I don't think I have to tell you that there
aren't any jobs going anywhere else. Here at Klebendorf's we're

probably better off than any other place in the city. One of the apprentices will take his time off with every alternate senior man. I'll be taking the first lay-off myself, beginning to-morrow, and Young Joe here will come with me. You, Paul, will run the studio while I'm away. That's all. Any questions?'

There were no questions.

◆

He was not drawn by causes – I doubt if he ever questioned the rights or the wrongs which were involved: others more qualified, the 'brainy jokers', had decided the justice of the decision (for justice, whether consciously or unconsciously, always *did* concern him): the pull, I am inclined to think, was almost mythic, and dictated by the land in which he lived.

I have thought about this thing very often during the years of my expatriation, and I have concluded that there *is* the substance of myth in the very insistency with which this call towards the distant adventure is repeated to generation after generation of my countrymen. Myths do grow out of the eternal earth, this much is certain: and this Australian myth seems to derive from something primal, an earth-challenge. The continent is cruel and pitiless, four-fifths of it uninhabitable. The vast dry heart of the land is dead, and it is on this intractable central grimness that the teeth of adventure have long since been blunted. Here journeys have ended, the pioneering flame has guttered and failed, hopes and ambitions lie buried beneath the blowing sand. It is the one challenge from which the adventurous Australian has always had to retreat, back to the narrow, safer skin of his coastal holdings, and he has been forced to turn his back, because he must, on the invincible wilderness that lies behind him. So he has been obliged to look elsewhere for the great adventures, the necessary challenges to the flesh and spirit. This is why his wars must be fought for other causes than his own – and often for strange ones – and always in faraway places. He is, because the merciless quality of his own land dictates it to him, the soldier of far fortune. This is why his armies which are sent to these faraway places are always of volunteers, for there is never any lack of young men of eager spirit willing to respond to the far call. I have been with the armies of many races, but I have known no other soldier with such pure and passionate regard for the adventure in itself.

Jack's tragedy was that he was such a one. The myth was lodged and burning deep inside him.

♦ *Clean Straw for Nothing*

SYDNEY, 1968

Today it is quite an odd feeling to be rushing forward to now, whizzing through the last eighteen years as if they had never happened, although something must have happened because the now seems to be so different from the then. Different, that is, until you think about it, because in the crucial and basic things it might not be so different after all. Perhaps nothing really changes that much.

These reflections were sparked by Julian bringing round some of his undergraduate friends from the university. I have kept pretty much to my room because Cressida is due back today and I want to be as fit as possible, but I could hear them in the next room being sure of everything in between playing Bob Dylan records on the pick-up. Dylan, being young, gets considerable homage from them: he is not a god, because all their gods are dead; he seems, rather, to be a kind of high priest of their ideas and rituals. Not just the rituals of protest and dissent and rebellion, which are normal enough with the young, but their ideas of loneliness and aloneness and of being alienated altogether from us of another generation. They talk and listen together as if we would not be able to understand it. As if loneliness and alienation are things they have just discovered for the first time. One of the girl students is Jefferson's daughter Anne: her stepfather, unlike the traditional stepfather of novels, dotes on her and spoils her and is putting her through university, and I found myself wondering whether she could ever realize the awful depths of loneliness and alienation her father suffered before his final collapse. Still, he has been dead now for twelve years, so it doesn't really matter.

There is one of Bob Dylan's songs they keep playing and replaying, a kind of esoteric diatribe against a certain 'Mister Jones' who seems to symbolize the 'oldies' and 'squares' of my generation and the hoarsely reiterated refrain is a taunting, 'Something is happening here, and you don't know what it is – do you, Mr Jones?'

But neither do you, Mr Dylan. Nor they. Not yet.

The early budding is deceptive; these dark, night-flowering hybrids, loneliness and aloneness, take a long time in the growing. Yeats was seventy-two and only two years away from the grave when he said, 'Talk to me of originality and I will turn on you with rage. I am a crowd, I am a lonely man, I am nothing.'

GRAHAM McINNES

Graham McInnes (1912-70), born in England, was
brought to Australia by his mother, the novelist Angela
Thirkell and his stepfather 'Dad'. After graduating from
Melbourne University he left for Canada in 1934 in
search of his father. There he worked as a university
lecturer, journalist and diplomat. His four volumes of
autobiography are The Road to Gundagai (1965),
Humping My Bluey (1966), Finding a Father (1967) and
Goodbye, Melbourne Town (1968).

♦ ♦ ♦ ♦

♦ The Road to Gundagai

One day in class we were asked to stand up in alphabetical order so
that our names could be entered in a nominal roll. When M was
called I unthinkingly stood up. The teacher blinked and said
testily:

'What's the matter with you, Thirkell, your name doesn't begin with M.'

'But my name's really McInnes, sir. At least . . . it used to be.'

'Well, sit down and we'll talk about it later.'

This incident was duly reported to Mother, who summoned me into her bedroom, shut the door and said in a voice deliberately deepened for dramatic effect,

'Don't ever say a thing like that again.'

It dawned on me that she must think there was something shameful, as well as inconvenient, about my name. But I was scared of her when she was angry and so I nodded my head. I kept the promise until I was fourteen, when I asked her where my father was (I hadn't yet found out that he was back in Canada). Her reply was 'I'm not going to talk about him'.

This and similar rebuffs naturally stirred our curiosity the more, but Mother remained adamant. And yet, so curiously complete was her sense of being a world to herself, her belief in 'If I say so, it is so', that she failed to take the most elementary precautions. She never had our name changed by deed-poll so that eventually all that was required of my brother and me was a simple announcement that we were reverting to it. And she kept her diaries and photograph albums in full view for any casual visitor to thumb through. In these albums were scores of photographs of my father in the early years of his brief marriage. In the diary at the time when my brother and I were born, her pretty, rounded Greek handwriting gave way for a few days to his passionate hurried scrawl. Thus, though banished from the house as unclean, James Campbell McInnes continued to lead a shadowy Plutonian existence.

Our step-father's attitude was simplicity itself, relaxed and uncommitted. He was not of course deeply involved; anything that Mother did about her first husband was all right with him. He acquiesced in the arrangement; he never referred to my father at all, who for him just didn't exist. More than that, he lent his name with generosity and invariably introduced me as 'My boy Graham'. When he came to have a son of his own he treated us all exactly the same. If young Lance was a favourite it was because he was the baby, not because he was Dad's own son. Lance never had a favoured place and there was no discrimination against us older boys. Dad's genial off-handed goodnature flopped about impartially and his occasional rages never chilled us as much as Mother's, for they were unpremeditated. It was an absent-minded affection exercised by fits and starts, but what there was of it, all three boys shared alike.

Perhaps the greatest practical disadvantage was that of being known throughout my Australian boyhood by my stepfather's name, which I discarded as soon as I was twenty-one and able to find my own father in Canada. This had the effect of isolating my Australian experience under a false label. It meant for years afterwards, redrafted documents, lawyers' certifications, assurances to friends that I was the same old fellow, and of course endless, tedious explanations to them and to others of what had happened. In attempting to take away my own name, Mother succeeded in transferring from herself to me and my brother the burden of explanation and embarrassment which she herself was unwilling to assume.

♦

It is time now to take the lid off this Family Antipodean Peyton Place and see what it was like inside. We enter the house from the back since this is invariably the route chosen by the boys and their friends whenever they come in for a drink of cocoa after Wolf Cubs, sneak in late at night through the casement window into their bedroom, or rush banging in after school. First then, round the corner of the feeble lawn which is forever being trampled down because it lies across the short cut from the house to the outside lavatory, and as constantly rebuilt and refenced by Mother's tenacity. At the centre of the house is the back porch or 'sleep-out' where I've spent many a cold winter's night, first with a teddy bear and later with Smut, our cat – if I could get him from my brother – crammed down below my buttocks. The 'sleep-out' is asphalt floored and lying in bed I can see above the rafters from the underside of the terra-cotta tiles that they were made in Marseille.

Up one step, bang the screen door and you're in the dining room, surely the most inconvenient ever designed with no less than five doors leading off it. It has one window giving onto the rear 'sleep-out' with a view of my bed covered with Dad's old military ground-sheet, a couple of clotheslines with skinned stringy-bark props, and the yellow jasmine trellis outside the toolshed. In one corner of the room is the linen press, effectively clamorous and eccentric with its sheet of William Morris wallpaper pasted over one end. The walls are surrounded by low bookcases crammed with boys' books, perhaps six to seven hundred: R. M. Ballantyne, Jules Verne, Captain Marryat, Hugh Lofting of Dr Doolittle fame, John Masefield (the totally unreadable *Sard Harker*), cheap sets of Dickens and Scott, *The Parents' Book: Answers to Children's Questions*, Judge Parry's *Butterscotia*, the fairy tales of Mrs de Morgan and a few school prizes and family albums. In these latter are photographs of my father, dark, rascally, and moustachioed, which embarrass me horribly but don't seem to affect Mother at all. Against the vacant wall is the 'dumb waiter' or 'traymobile' on which food and crockery come in from the kitchen next door; behind it the damp creeps splotchily up the white plaster wall each successive winter. Wonderful patterns here, forestalling non-objective art of the 50's and 60's. The five doors lead to the back garden, the kitchen, the boys' bedroom, the bathroom, and (up another single inconvenient step) the passage off which lie the other rooms. In the middle of this strange sunken area (hardly a room) stands a round table of stained and well worn mahogany-veneer at which we have eaten some thousands of meals beneath the single overhead light hanging from its inverted china saucer.

Mother presided and carved; Dad, who was rarely in on time, ate and talked. Once he brought an office friend home to dinner late and without notification. Mother was in a grim mood and hardly civil as she wielded the knife at the 'head' of the table, while the poor fellow found the evening hanging pretty soggy on his hands. In walked the Lady Help with the all too familiar spotted-dog, and laid it steaming darkly before my Mum.

'Would you care for some suet pudding?' she asked in icy tones, flourishing the knife.

'Well, I don't mind if I do,' said the well-meaning but luckless guest.

'In that case,' said Mother, 'you don't mind if you don't.'

The quiet that followed was so awful that I rose without permission in order to draw on my head the inevitable reproof that would at least break the paralysing silence.

Another crisis occurred on one of the many occasions on which Mother valiantly strove to impart an air of Oxbridge distinction to suburbia by arranging, single-handed, a scholarly black-tie dinner for eight to which my brother and I were necessary adjuncts in the form of serving boys. Dressed in carefully brushed blue serge and school ties we served the food and cleared away the empty plates into the kitchen where we were allowed to eat the scraps with the Lady Help – banished below the salt for this high powered occasion and resenting it visibly. No doubt our innocent faces, well scrubbed under maternal supervision, were designed, along with our amateur but patently eager performance, as a 'talking point' on which to hang what was inevitably an off-beat evening for the guests, redeemed by Mother's relentless, crackling literary conversation.

It was the era of aigrettes, black sequins and velvet bandeaux and we asked if we could 'see the guests'. Mother, harassed beyond endurance as she endeavoured to cope with a dinner for eight on a gas stove with two burners, snappishly refused, ripped off her apron, wiped her steaming visage and rushed off to 'put on her face'. When our fury was added to that of the despised Lady Help, a plot was soon brewing to make their meal memorable.

Solemnly, carefully – and liberally – we spat on all the half cantaloups, mixed in the sugar and sprinkled lightly with ginger. Then with angelic faces we bore in the lethal loads and set them gently before each guest to the accompaniment of beaming smiles. We retired into the kitchen and observed proceedings through the keyhole.

'They're eating them! Professor Scott has taken a huge bite! Now Dr Busing! Oh, Mrs Streeton has an enormous mouthful . . .'

The bell rang. We walked blandly in, removed the empty rinds and began to serve the next course. No matter what the guests might think the evening was now a triumph for the servants.

◆ *Humping My Bluey*

So much – and so much more horrific – has happened in the world of sport (to say nothing of the world at large) since 1932, that the furious storm of anger and abuse stirred up by 'body-line bowling' seems to belong to the distant days of gunboats and Jenkins' Ear. But it was real and terrifying enough to those who were in the middle of it; and because the Shoobridges had cast me in the role of ersatz Englishman there I was – right in the middle of it.

The initial performances by the English were distasteful and disconcerting, but not alarming or dangerous. They bowled on the leg side, yes; they tended to pitch the ball short, yes; so that it bounced a bit – flew, some might say – but was manageable. Clearly we'd been getting drunk on the great run-getting period of our history. Cricket had become a batsman's game. Individual scores of 300 or even 400 were not uncommon. The English aimed to correct the balance, to make it a bowler's game. Well, nothing wrong with that.

But at Melbourne it was noticed that our batsmen were starting to duck. The balls seemed to be not only fast, vicious and on the leg side; they seemed to be being pitched shorter and ever shorter, to fly up higher and ever higher. The batsman appeared to be not so much playing the ball, or even a game, as defending himself against a missile. And Jardine had a regular battery of fielders round the leg side. Did the batsman duck or snick a ball or simply raise his bat, then he'd be caught out. This isn't leg bowling; this is bowling – not at the leg, but at the body – why it's, it's *body-line bowling!*

At the Melbourne ground it was observed, not once nor twice but several times, that when a batsman missed one of Larwood's balls it would sail over the heads of the wicket keeper and the longstop and hit the boundary fence on the full. A low growl of disapproval came from the crowd and from the sports writers. This wasn't cricket, this was murder. Jardine kept his arrogant aquiline calm. He would give no interview to newsmen. The balls kept getting higher, harder and faster. Aussie batsmen fell like ninepins.

Aussie tempers rose. Hey, someone said, as if suddenly realizing the danger, we might lose the Ashes! Cries of 'unfair' were countered by cries of 'Keep calm, Australia; be sports.' All's fair in love and war; and if cricket wasn't war what was it? Conversation round the Shoobridge loudspeaker was excited and loud though not yet harsh or strident. But I couldn't help feeling uncomfortable, defending these fellows.

At Adelaide one memorable day the blow fell, and in a trice Aussies and Pommies were at each other's throats. It was the Third Test. The English had already won two (by their unfair body-line bowling of course) and the atmosphere was tense with a big crowd at the Adelaide Oval. The Australians were batting and Jardine was alternating Larwood and Voce, with his usual battery on the leg side. Balls were flying viciously high and the crowd, very hostile, had started barracking. Jardine in crisp flannels appeared entirely unperturbed. His whole attitude and the cut of his jib suggested 'You just can't take it, you poor miserable Aussie bastards.' Our Captain, W. M. Woodfull, had already been hit painfully over the heart. Then in to bat went the beloved W. A. Oldfield, the greatest Aussie wicket keeper of all time; and also a sturdy tail end batsman. Bill Oldfield shaped up at the wicket and Larwood started his long express-train run. The ball left his hand like a sizzling rocket, the next moment there was a hideous thud and Bill Oldfield, hit on the head, dropped like a stone.

A great roar of anger burst from the crowd. The boundary fences went down like matchwood, and in a few seconds thousands of enraged Australian cricket fans were starting to stream across the ground. It looked as if Jardine and his team would be lynched then and there. But police, groundsmen and officials went tearing across to the pitch and strained with linked arms to hold the mob in check. Even they mightn't have succeeded if, Oldfield, still severely shaken, hadn't begged the crowd to return to the stands. For him they went, with menacing growls; for no one else would they have gone.

After a break the match was resumed but no one's heart was in it. Or in the rest of the series, for that matter. Victory had become meaningless. Let England take the bloody Ashes if that's the way they want to play. This wasn't cricket, this was legalized murder.

Around the Shoobridge loudspeaker the wrath and resentment turned on me. Me and my bloody Englishman! Bastards they were! No hopers! Bludgers! In vain I protested. But you made me . . . ! I'd been born there, hadn't I? Bunch of bloody narks. I felt extremely miserable. I didn't think I ought to accept the Shoobridges' hospitality any more. Pat wouldn't even speak to me, let alone play Russian pool. Jim and Fergus were stormy-eyed; even Mollie and Norah were cool and correct. I went up to my big glorious room under the eaves, looking out on to the hopfields and the soldierly Lombardy poplars along the river, and the heavy-laden apple trees and the tawny hill-pasture and the purply blue mountains in the distance. I started to pack my suitcase. Exiled by body-line bowling.

While engaged in this melancholy rite, the door opened and in came Mrs Shoobridge. She put her arm round my shoulder and told me not to be a fool, and that they all liked me and all wanted me to stay. I found myself blubbing like an idiot. After a while I went downstairs, and everyone was very kind and solicitous. Pat poured me a big tankard of beer. But the pretence that I was English was dropped and when the next Test came up we all concentrated on hating the Englishmen together. Much more satisfactory.

Cricket didn't recover for several years from the bitterness engendered by the body-line controversy. It united Australians as never before. But what was played – and discussed – wasn't cricket; but a kind of desperate internecine civil war with slit throats, knees in the groin and jabs to the kidneys. Well, if that was the kind of cricket they wanted, I knew where I stood. In the golden glorious Valley we were all Dinkum Aussies together; there was no room for a Pommie.

◆ *Goodbye, Melbourne Town*

Anyway, Tiger and I were bosom friends, and I think about the only time we came near to completely getting our wires crossed was when he tried to make a professional birdnester out of me, and I tried to make a professional concert-goer out of him; or when we both made the mistake of breaking and entering the weekend shacks.

Tiger had started a small collection of birds' eggs and invited me over to his house after school one day to inspect them. My tremendous enthusiasm took him aback to the extent of his giving me a mynah's egg to start off with on my own. Thereafter we lived a semi-arboreal existence, principally in the extensive grounds of our school which stood in sixty acres of hilly parkland in the suburbs, plentifully dotted with *pinis insignis*, oak, blue gum, red gum and stringybark. Each lunch hour and every evening for at least three weeks we 'bunked each other up' into convenient tree crotches and clambered towards the squawking nests. Our take was usually mynahs' and sparrows' eggs but we also got the eggs of the rosella parrot, the wattlebird, and one rare sparrowhawk.

Our marauding came to an abrupt end with a bold attempt to filch a magpie's eggs. Australians used to argue whether this large black and white bird was a magpie or a shrike. Certainly it was larger than the English magpie and its song, when at rest, and especially at dawn and sunset was the most unforgettable and hauntingly lovely bird music. On the wing the magpie might utter a hoarse brief cry, ugly and strident; but perched on a ring-barked tree at sunet or in a grove of tall white gums at dawn, the bird produced a wonderful golden warbling sound like bells ringing and piano strings being plucked underwater. It would glow for minutes at a stretch and seemed to speak of an age when the world was young and the sun raked the tips of high hills with a golden light. If the Kookaburra was the laughing jackass and red-nosed comedian of the bush, the magpie was its Emperor Concerto.

But the magpie could also be fierce and combative especially in defence of its nest. Spying a marauder from afar it would swoop on him in a treacherously silent dive-bombing action, sometimes grazing the intruder with beak or wing. On the nest the female was equally fierce. The woods of *pinis insignis* on the hill above the school were full of magpies' nests and Tiger and I determined to assault one that struck us as particularly vulnerable because it hung on a large, low needle-less branch within easy distance of the ground. This was going to be easy.

Never were we more mistaken. As we approached the tree –
Tiger walking in front and I following slowly on the bicycle – there
was a sudden darkening from a clear sky, a rasping, flapping flurry
of wings in my face, and with a harsh cry a magpie flew skyward. I
fell off the bicycle and while picking it up the magpie made a second
attack, this time on Tiger. I cried out to him but as he craned his
neck, the bird dropped silently and cunningly from the sky right on
top of his head like the seagulls in L. A. G. Strong's *The Brothers*.
Tiger crouched and covered his face with his hands. There was
another roaring flap as the magpie soared upward and then Tiger
was running back towards me, his face oozing blood. The magpie,
with beak or claw, had made a long scratch across the length of his
cheekbone. 'Let's clear out,' he said in a shaky voice. It was the only
time I ever saw him scared. He hitched himself up on to the bar of
my bike and we pedalled away for dear life before there would be
another attack. That was the end of our bird-nesting; but, we re-
assured each other, we were going to give it up anyway. We were
going to fish for yabbies and explore the week-end shacks instead.
That would be real excitement, not kid stuff like bird-nesting.

ROLAND ROBINSON

Roland Robinson (1912–) was born in Ireland and
came to Australia when he was nine. His many jobs
have included rouseabout, boundary-rider, fettler,
ballet-dancer, factory worker and groundsman. He has
celebrated his feeling for the land and its original
inhabitants in numerous volumes of verse. His
autobiographical trilogy consists of *The Drift of Things*
(1973), *The Shift of Sands* (1976) and *A Letter to Joan*
(1978).

♦ ♦ ♦ ♦

We are staying in a terrace of houses in a suburb not far from the
city. Across the street, the terrace looks on to a park. We are living
upstairs. The street and the park are filled with strong sunlight.
From the street below us comes the voice of a man selling honey. He
must be in a cart, driving slowly along the street. He is singing about
the honey. He has a tenor voice and he sings over and over again,
with a trill 'Honey, today, a-li-ah-ti'. Mother is delighted, transported. She runs to the balcony, leans over, and calls out to the
man. I distinctly remember mother calling out to the man that he
was like Caruso. Mother felt, and I did too, that a man with a beauti-

ful voice like that should not just be wasting it selling honey on the streets. Something was wrong somewhere.

Bill and I are in the park opposite the terrace. We are being questioned and 'tried out' by a group of other boys from the neighbourhood. Most of the boys are older. Bill and I discover that we are 'Pommies'. The other boys are 'Aussies'. They question us and laugh at and imitate our broad, deep, English Midlands speech and accent. We say 'butter' with a deep, heavy pronunciation as in 'butcher'. But when we try to lighten our pronunciation in the Aussie way and say 'butcher', we say the word as the Aussies say 'gutter' or 'butter'. We bring peals of derisive laughter from the Aussie boys. They say 'laugh' and we say 'laff'. We try to say 'grass' as they do and discover that we must say 'grarse'. Bill and I think that we will never get the Pommie accent out of our voices.

Now the Aussie boys are trying us out to see what Pommies are like at running, wrestling and jumping. Bill and I were a pretty good pair of wrestlers for our ages. We were always at it together. I had to have a contest with an Aussie about my own age. We had to see who could climb the fastest to the top of one of the swing chains in the park. I must have shot up the swing chain hand over hand like a monkey because I easily beat the Aussie boy to the top of my chain. No doubt this was due to my playing about in the rigging of the *Sophocles* – we were always climbing ropes, rigging, anywhere where we could frighten our parents or bring the old sailor along to threaten us with a 'rope's ending'. The Aussie boys were not cruel to Bill and me. After my chain climbing effort, one of the big Aussies said 'Well, at least that's one thing that Pommies are good at – climbing chains'.

Father wasn't going to be a farmer after all. Apparently you needed a lot of money to be a farmer, a lot more than father had.

◆

My duties included keeping up a good stack of firewood for the cook. Outside the kitchen was the wood-heap – a great tangled mass of bush timber on a huge mound of chips. This was one of my main jobs for the cook, provided I kept up a good stack of firewood, I was on the right side of Charlie. Charlie showed me how to save time and energy on the wood-heap. You rarely cut logs into lengths. You split them and then broke up the split lengths with the back of the axe. This was a secret of Charlie's. The boss said that he could never hear me cutting wood and yet I always had a good stack of firewood outside the kitchen.

The men were good to me. They told me to have the 'killers', the sheep, in the yard in the afternoon, and to have the knives sharpened ready. I remember one of the men cantering up to the yard a bit earlier than usual. Now I was to be shown how to kill, skin and dress a sheep. The homestead needed about two sheep a day, sometimes three.

The station-hand got off his horse, threw the reins over a fence post. 'Got the knives and steel?' he asked. He went into the sheep pen, dragged out a sheep by a back leg, and threw it on its side on a wooden slab covered with flat, galvanized iron. He knelt on the sheep's side, and pulled its head well back by the jaw. 'Now, watch me son' he said, 'you've got to be quick with this.' He felt in the neck wool for the wind pipe. He held a pointed knife in his hand. He pushed the knife in, cutting the sheep's throat outwards from behind the wind pipe. The sheep kicked and struggled but the station-hand knelt on it hard. He bent the head further back, cutting the white sinew in the jointed neck bone, then cutting the neck right through at a joint. Blood gushed from the sheep's throat as it was held, kicking on the slab. 'Cut his throat like this' said the station-hand. 'Otherwise, the sheep'll get away from you and rush off down the paddock with your knife in his throat.' I nodded, then, suddenly, I vomited at the sight of all the life blood of the sheep still pouring out of its throat. 'Ah, you'll soon get over that' said the station-hand. 'In no time, it'll be nothing to you.'

'Now I'll show you how to skin him' said the station-hand. A back leg held between his knees, a pinch of skin cut off at the inside of the leg joint, the knife slid down under the skin across the crutch, the same process with the other back leg, the skin slit up the belly, through the hard, fatty chest pad and out at the throat. Then the forelegs. 'You can start the skinning with the knife' said the station-hand, 'but you want to "punch" the skin off.' He used his fist, punching away the skin without breaking the red underskin to the carcass.

Now the clean, white skin lay out from the carcass but still attached to the back. A cut at the right spot of each leg joint, and the joint was bent back and the leg cut off. 'Now the gamble' said the station-hand. The bow-shaped gamble, with a hook at each end, was hooked between the sinew and bone of each hind leg, spreading them. The gamble was hooked to the gallows, which was just a pole between an upright, forked post. The long end of the pole was pressed down and secured to a wire loop on a peg in the ground, and the carcass was hung up for disembowelling, and the final removal of the skin. If the skin had been punched off properly, the skin would strip right down the back without bringing away any fat or flesh. The stomach was opened with two fingers between the outer skin and the paunch with the knife running down between the two fingers. The viscera removed, a knife placed right at the pelvic joint split this joint. The brisket was split with a knife, and then a chaff-bag was then drawn up over the carcass.

You took the carcass on your shoulder and carried it down to the butcher's shop outside the kitchen. There, hung up, it would set by morning and be ready to cut up.

Next evening I was faced with killing the sheep by myself. I could not bring myself to cut their throats so I got my .22 rifle, rested it on the rails of the sheep pen and shot the sheep I wanted through the head. I then dragged it out and cut its throat. The first sheep I skinned brought some caustic comments from Charlie the cook. The skin, hung on the wire fence, was a pretty cut about and fleshy job. Although I vomited when I first saw a sheep slaughtered, and although when I first actually cut a sheep's throat without shooting it I had to steel myself to drive in the knife, I ended up, as the station-hand said, in thinking nothing of it. I actually took a clock to the pen with me to find out how fast I could do the job. From the time of cutting the sheep's throat to the time when it.was skinned and dressed, was five minutes. This was, of course, after a good deal of killing.

◆

It must have been Frank who first put into my hands a copy of Palgrave's *Golden Treasury of the Best Songs and Lyrical Poems in the English Language*. This was the little Oxford edition which began with Nash's 'Spring, the sweet Spring, . . .' and ended with Shelley's 'Music, when soft voices die, . . .' For years this volume never left my pocket. It became my 'bible'. It was a constant delight, and a comfort to me through all the years during which I worked in that underground of a factory which was Lustre Hosiery. The little book was the foundation of my literary education. The poet I admired most in it was Shelley. For me, he possessed a supernatural magic. His 'Ode to the West Wind' hypnotized, swept me away like a leaf, a winged seed. His sustained flight, his imagery, his fierce, shrill, now deepening tone, his voice haunted me. I though his 'Ode to the West Wind' was the greatest poem in the English language, and I guess I still do.

A few years ago I was travelling round Australia writing a travel book. I was mentally tormented, as I always have been, and was camped at the Barron Falls in northern Queensland. In the rainforest, jungle country of the coast, I found myself walking among the ruins of a stone temple. Flagstones were under my feet, and a circle of broken columns stood round me tangled with vines and foliage. I was striding across the flagstones and reciting the 'Ode to the West Wind'. I knew that I was invoking the full moon to rise behind the jungle and the broken columns. But it was not the moon I was invoking, it was a goddess. When she rose, in the form of the moon, I knew that her beauty would be so terrible that it would kill me. And yet, I was running across the flagstones, reciting on and on. I thought I could see the first light of the moon beginning to appear behind the jungle and the broken columns . . .

Yes. It was a dream. I told this dream to Sadie Herbert, the wife of the novelist Xavier Herbert, whom I later met at Redlynch near the Barron Falls. Sadie seemed to fully understand this dream, which is still more vivid than many experiences I had on that round Australia expedition. This is my attempt to explain the supernatural magic which Shelley had for me. Of course this magic is in so many of his poems – 'Swiftly walk over the western wave . . .', 'The Poet's Dream', 'One word is too often profaned', 'The Recollection', 'The Euganean Hills' and so on. Scott had this magic, Byron had it –

'When we two parted'; Herrick's verse had the dew on it, or it was a jewelled darkness – 'Her eyes the glow-worm lend thee . . .'. And then there was Keats's 'The Mermaid Tavern', 'Happy Insensibility', and of course, '. . . And haply the Queen-Moon is on her throne, clustered around by all her starry Fays . . .'; Wordsworth could be pedestrian and didactic – compare his skylark to Shelley's outpouring. The Augustans I couldn't stand, they were flat versifiers. I liked the rich, slashed colour of the Elizabethans, and still remember the magic of Webster's 'Call for the robin and the wren, since over shady graves they hover . . .' Shakespeare had been spoilt for me at school, and Milton was a glassy, unscalable cliff.

♦

I found an advertisement in the local paper for a full-time gardener. The situation was in Kent Road, just across the Cranbrook School playing field at the back of our flat. It was a big, double-storied house overlooking Royal Sydney Golf Course. From the entrance in the stone wall outside the grounds, a gravel drive curved round through the grounds to the pillared porch of the house. I remember being interviewed by a rather small, slight man. We stood on the lawn which sloped steeply down to a grass tennis court. The man was asking me about the state of his lawns, his tennis court, and what should be done to them. Of course, I had the experience of my work as a groundsman at the Rose Bay Convent behind me and I spoke out forthrightly to the man, telling him what was wrong with his grounds and his grass. The man turned to me as we stood on the lawn and said 'I don't think you're aware to whom you're speaking.' 'No, I'm not' I replied. 'I take you for a man like myself. I suppose you know your particular job, whatever it is, as I hope to be able to show you that I know what I'm talking about.' I was not being cheeky. I was just a labourer, a battler, but I was a man of independent mind. I had to bow and scrape to no man.

The small, slight man turned and faced me at this. 'I'll have you know,' he told me, as he seemed to draw himself up, 'that I'm Lieutenant-General Morshead.' I had not heard of the famous General. 'Well,' I replied, 'I'm pleased to meet you. My name's Robinson.' I held out my hand. The General took it. 'You seem to know your job' he told me. 'You can start this morning, if you like.' 'Thanks,' I said, 'you'll soon find out if I fill the bill or not.'

There should be no need to tell anyone who Lieutenant-General Sir Leslie Morshead is. I found out later that he had a string of military decorations as long as your arm. He had served with distinction in all the wars since, and including, the first World War. For Australians, it is enough to say that he commanded the 'Rats of Tobruk' against Rommel.

I was raking the gravel drive when a black limousine drove up to the porch of the house. It passed me again with the General sitting in the back behind his chauffeur. The General was in a black business suit. He raised his walking stick, or furled umbrella, to me as the car passed.

Without being in any way familiar, the General and I became friends. He was a director or something of a shipping company in the city. On days when he did not have to go into the office, he used to come and help me plant out garden beds of flowers. I thought him a gentle man. Strange, isn't it, that such a man should have commanded the 9th Australian Division in the African desert against Rommel. I could see that the General liked gardening, getting his hands in the soil. He always used to ask my opinion about top-dressing the lawns, or anything he needed done to the grounds. He even showed me how to mow the lawn tennis court in strips instead of in my way of two halves. Apart from our first encounter, the General never came the military act with me. I hope that I can assert, with respect, that we were two mates. When, eventually, I left the job, the General gave me a beaut reference. Somewhere, in my travels, that reference has disappeared.

This incident belongs to a pattern which has been repeated throughout my life. Today, on the labour market, I'm still really only a labourer, although they tell me at the Woollahra Golf Club that I'm on their books as a 'Senior Groundsman' or 'Greenkeeper's Assistant'. But the pattern, throw me into the meanest situation and, somehow, somewhere, someone of importance and accomplishment will discover and 'salute' me. I'm not boasting. You see, I told you that I'd 'wing' you. I was like Billarni the Battler.

When the Irish farm people found out that he was a poet, they dusted the chair for him before he sat down.

During the time I worked for the General, I edited the 1948 Jindyworobak Anthology for Rex Ingamells. I was reading the proofs during my lunch hour. The General came along and I showed him the proofs. Did you know that Generals like poetry? They should do. Poets are the trumpets that sing to battle. Like the war-horses, they sayeth 'Hah-hah' among the trumpets. Their necks are clothed with thunder. At least, the old, oral poets were like that.

KYLIE TENNANT

Kylie Tennant (1912–) was born at Manly New South Wales, worked briefly for the ABC and then took an assortment of jobs to acquire first-hand experience for her novels, the best known of which are *The Battlers* (1941) and *Ride On Stranger* (1943). Throughout her autobiography, *The Missing Heir* (1986), she refers to her strong-willed, dominating father as 'The Parent'.

♦ ♦ ♦ ♦

When I was a child I detested the Tennant family. The Parent's pompous references to his cousin Margot, who had married Prime Minister Asquith, his side glances at Lord Glenconner and so forth sickened me. I became a terrible little anti-snob and decided to join the Communist Party when I grew up, having heard the Parent speak of the Communist Party.

As a handsome young man living in Artarmon where his mother had a roomy house of ugly brick – she also owned two houses in nearby Chatswood – the Parent was set to follow his father into the Presbyterian ministry. He became a lay preacher. However, he told my husband, he was seduced, in a hammock, by the lady organist. This made him lose faith in the Presbyterian Church. He should have been warned against lady organists because my mother was one.

He also had dreams of military glory when World War I broke out. Had not his father, Dr Tennant, formed a regiment at Tenterfield which was, according to the Parent, known as Tennant's Own? On one occasion this regiment of horse was to be reviewed by some notable – the Parent said it was the Duke of Edinburgh. To present a more uniform appearance it was decided to dye the horses brown. One can imagine that this may have been some ploy of the shadowy Cracky the Coachman. The horses were dyed with Condy's crystals, but it came on to rain and they all turned green. I can imagine the vast laughter of the local horsemen as they spoke of Tennant's Own.

I still have my grandfather's cavalry sword – a heavy long blade, a metal scabbard, a twisted metal hand protector. I don't quite know how I came by it but my mother was in the habit of foisting anything she didn't want on me. She certainly wouldn't have wanted the sword around the house. Nevertheless, my father had a photograph of himself as a handsome cadet in the cadet corps of Shore where he won the King's Medal for marksmanship. Yes, the World War must have offered opportunities. I was two years old in 1914 and my sister a small baby – that would not have held him back. But he contracted appendicitis – or peritonitis – and lay in hospital with a large jagged wound across his stomach while other men were enjoying that masculine mateship of muck and danger. He lay at death's door once again without firing a shot.

I remember visiting him in hospital when my sister was a baby. He was, of course, the life and soul of the ward, making friends, learning the life history of every one of his ward mates. Limping out of hospital he attained importance in the collecting of funds for the troops in an organisation known as the War Chest. He mingled with the great, leaving my mother in a pokey terrace house with two tiny daughters, while he attended functions and banquets.

I remember being taken to see lines of khaki-clad soldiers marched down Macquarie Street to the troopships. Some kind of road repairs were going on and we stood on the edge of a ditch of yellow clay as though it were an open grave. The nurses in their white uniforms passed, the men in khaki went by with a squeak of leather boots, a pounding of a huge drum that filled my heart with terror. There were cheers but below the cheers, the blare of the bands, I felt a terrible silence with the ominous drum thudding over all. I hated the procession – I hate all processions because they are a false showing, changing individual worth to a fused blind clamouring of power. I always weep at processions and circuses – the circuses because little children are being asked to applaud the cruelly trained animals and the stupidities of clowns. They are trained to think circuses – the remnants of the old arenas – wonderful.

My father was in his element. Recovering from his stitches he even took us for a holiday to Stanmore Park, a beach on the South Coast where my parents spent their honeymoon. There on the verandah of the boarding house, an officer in uniform, who was trying to flirt with my pretty mother, picked me up and teased me. I screamed at him. To me he represented all that masculine arrogance which later made me a pacifist. The World War I period had an hysteria of a hateful falsity that a child could sense. But, as I said, in the fund-raising festivities my father shone.

My distaste for masculine violence spread to a wider social field when as a half-grown girl I made the acquaintance of a certain Major Jacobs who lived next to my grandmother Tennant at Artarmon.

'You ought to go and have a yarn with Jacobs,' the Parent advised, 'Went all through the Gallipoli campaign. I think he's a bit cracked about it. Never stops talking.' On one of the family's rare visits to Grandma Tennant I was reaching for one of the half-wild lemons with thick skins which grew along her fence when I made the acquaintance of the famous major. I mentioned politely that my father told me he had fought at Gallipoli. I was invited through the crack in the fence and the major – a thin dark man – brought out album after album of scenes in the trenches and launched out on a description of what had happened from the landing on the beach until the survivors were evacuated. I hope those albums are now somewhere in the War Memorial at Canberra and that no busy relative loaded them on to a bonfire. I listened to the major for several hours – until, in fact, my mother, with her sweetest falsest smile came peering at the fence to ask whether I shouldn't come inside as the major must be very tired of talking to me. The major relinquished me – wistfully. He would seldom have found a better listener. I should, when I grew older, have gone back to take notes but by that time the major had died.

To say that he made an impression would be an understatement. He was recounting the period of life when he had lived at peak but to a stern-faced little girl his narrative reinforced my lurking suspicion that there was something very wrong with the society into which I was born. I resolved that I would not only never do anything to assist any war effort whatever but I would do everything within my weak power to oppose, resist, defeat, thwart, any of the glory boys, the diplomats, the rich, the army heads who sent men to become lumps of mud and blood in some far corner of the world. I knew about the splendid horses sent to Flanders because the old men still thought World War I would be won by cavalry charges. The horses died of pneumonia and poor feeding, standing in the rain behind the front lines. The Australians who went with them and loved those horses also died of pneumonia – some of them – waiting hour after hour and day after day in the lashing downpour while officers conferred about more important matters.

The Turks and the Australians at Gallipoli had no particular quarrel but they killed each other on orders from England in the biggest fiasco of a long line of military fiascos. And in Australia on Anzac Day people marched with bands to war memorials to celebrate a hopeless defeat. It didn't make sense. Many years later when I was on some panel on the radio I was asked: 'What are your views on Anzac Day?' 'It is on a level with the Japanese shinto – the worship of the ancestors –' I responded. 'It should be abolished.' Naturally, I was never again asked to speak on that program.

PATRICK WHITE

Patrick Victor Martindale White (1912–) was born in
London when his wealthy grazier parents were on an
extended honeymoon. After attending private schools
in New South Wales, he was educated at Cheltenham
College, England, and at Cambridge University. He did
not return to live in Australia until 1948. Author of
numerous novels, plays, and two collections of short
stories, he was awarded a Nobel Prize in 1973. In all his
works childhood experiences, family tensions and
private symbols play a crucial part. His autobiography
Flaws in the Glass: a Self-Portrait (1981) throws fresh
light on all three.

♦ ♦ ♦ ♦

I was approaching old age when I met the poet R. D. Fitzgerald,
who recalled an incident from my childhood. His brother had married one of my distant cousins. The poet ran into the couple on a
day when they were expected by my parents at our house at Rushcutters Bay. On next seeing his relations he asked how the visit had
gone. 'Oh, all right . . .' my cousin sighed, 'but that dreadful little
boy was there.'

Visitors were always charmed till my sister, a pretty, dimpled
child, told what I had been saying about them. I was this green,
sickly boy, who saw and knew too much. If I was shy and with-
drawn, it was only till provoked. Then I could answer back.

My parents were very disturbed by having a delicate son on their hands. I was kept out of draughts and protected by woollen combies. They needed me to give them a sense of their own continuity by inheriting my share in a considerable sheep-and-cattle station. A grazier's heir should have been sturdy, but nobody would insure the life of the one they had got. If I half-realised that my languor and breathlessness were causing a serious situation, I was not worried by it. All that I saw, all that was happening around me, was far too vivid for me to believe in the event which carried off old people and pets.

We cried for the cats and dogs we buried under crosses made from the spines of palm leaves, in graves stuck with wilting marigolds. The deaths of old people were casually mentioned. They hardly concerned us.

Thunderstorms were more frightening than death, and the Mad Woman, and the remark overhead in a discussion between other people's mothers '. . . can't help feeling he's a little changeling . . .' Nor did the laughter which followed help explain what I was or what I had done to my evidently unfortunate parents.

It was only a brief flicker of fear, like the lightning in the purple thunderstorms. There were the steamy mornings, the walk home from the baths, and watermelon at the end.

It was on the walk home from the baths, around the age of seven, that I had the first erection I remember. While looking down I suggested to my father that something unusual was happening. He became prim and embarrassed, shifted his wet bathers from one shoulder to the other, and told me to step out. At the same time there was the passing glimmer of a smile.

It was around this same age, after the baths, that I met my first poet, without knowing or caring much what a poet was. Sue and I had got stuck into the watermelon in what for me was the best part of the garden, all shade and spangles, under the custard apples and the guavas, outside the latticed summer-house, when our father came down the stone steps bringing some friend I had not seen before. He was dressed like any other gentleman, in a tobacco-coloured suit with a gold watch-chain strung across the waistcoat, trilby hat, and one of those stiff collars which grew grubby at the edges soon after contact with the cleanest skins. This was the driest kind of gentleman, his face like a wrinkled, sooty lemon. My father introduced his children to Mr 'Banjo' Paterson. Whether the stranger spoke to a child whose face was buried in a slice of melon I can't remember. My father seemed proud of the acquaintanceship. I've wondered since what they talked about. They could have got together over horses, sheep, and cattle, and of course the poetry was of a kind no self-respecting White need feel ashamed of.

On those steamy Sydney mornings, my first erection and my first poet: first ripples on the tide of passion . . .

♦

I wrote to 'Nursie' too. All the genuine love in me was directed at this substitute for a mother. Lizzie Clark came to us shortly after Sue's birth, when I was three. I hated her at first because she brought change. What with the baby and the new nurse it was a time of upheaval. I was hateful and destructive. I stamped on her toothpaste as she unpacked. I let the water out of the hotplate as we sat at our dinner of boiled brains. Nanny had always fed the animals on the mantelpiece before I would accept a mouthful. Nursie refused to take on the animals. She even made me feed myself. I suspected her dark face, the curved nose with a distinct hole or single pockmark on one side, the glossy black hair, the Scots accent. I don't know how she won me over, perhaps by the wet kisses she planted on my unyielding mouth, drawing me out of myself until we were united in a common wet.

I loved her. We both did. We nearly cried our heads off when, on one of her afternoons off, silly Eliza told us Lizzie had gone for ever. Lizzie never had a child of her own, except a stillborn one late in life. She considered we were hers, as in fact we were.

Ruth, the titular mother, bound us to her by a series of surprises such as changes of dress, presents, tantrums, powers of organisation, and bursts of general knowledge. But she wasn't always there, what with the committees, the fittings, the luncheon and dinner parties, or else she was lying down with a headache or falling arches. Except when a little child, I don't think I loved, I only admired her after a fashion, until I pitied an old bedridden, half-blind senile woman, and pity is a pinchbeck substitute for love.

◆

Till well into my life, houses, places, landscape meant more to me than people. I was more a cat than a dog. It was landscape which made me long to return to Australia while at school in England. It was landscape more than anything which drew me back when Hitler's War was over. As a child at Mount Wilson and Rushcutters Bay, relationships with even cherished friends were inclined to come apart when I was faced with sharing surroundings associated with my own private mysteries, some corner where moss-upholstered steps swept down beside the monstera deliciosa, a rich mattress of slater-infested humus under the custard apples, or gullies crackling with smoky silence, rocks threatening to explode, pools so cold that the breath was cut off inside your ribs as you hung suspended like the corpse of a pale frog.

On the mountain there were always threats of explosion, whether natural or human: a telephone torn from the wall by lightning, the eruption of a bush fire with scrolls of smoke and pennants of dirty flame advancing through shaggy scrub. I often flung stones at human beings I felt were invading my spiritual territory. Once I set fire to a gunyah to show that it couldn't be shared with strangers. Years later I persuaded myself that I hadn't been acting merely as a selfish child, but that an avatar of those from whom the land had been taken had invested one of the unwanted whites.

My decent parents were disgusted, never more than when I ran away and hid in the bush to avoid a Christmas service held in the asbestos church. Ruth despised the Mount Wilson church for aesthetic reasons: 'I'd burn it down if it would burn.' If she were alive today she might have got some satisfaction from reading that we are being poisoned by asbestos. But on Christmas Day 1923 the asbestos church, erect amongst the tree ferns she rooted out methodi-

cally in establishing her English garden, was accepted as a spiritual
ally in accusing her infernal child.

◆

Theatre and magic, whether my misfired attempt at finishing off the
master who took us for Latin Unseen by sticking pins in a wax
image, or the vision of the child-fairy emerging from an enormous
panto rose to swing above our heads on a wire in what used to be
known as the Grand Opera House near Central Station, made me
vaguely conscious that I was in some way involved with a world of
illusion, half terror half delight, like those orgasms in a hot bath and
the near ejaculations of fear which accompanied my encounters
with the Mad Woman.

The Mad Woman was real enough because I first came across her
by broad daylight in our back and rootling through the garbage
bins. But even by daylight she seemed to belong to some nether
world rather than the realities of poverty and hunger. I could con-
nect her blotched, alcoholic skin and munching gums with the
frosted glass of pubs I hurried past at the Cross, but the stinking fish
skeletons and heads she was sorting and wrapping in greasy paper
had undergone some magic change. I would recognise them years
later as paraphernalia of the illusion referred to as art.

By day, above the garbage bins, the great hat she always wore
looked insignificant, extinct. Dusk was when it flowered, becoming
for me the distinctive symbol of the Mad Woman, its huge targe
apparently constructed out of the trumpets of grubby, wrinkled
arums. Although she appeared to me in dreams and waking fantasies I can't have met the Mad Woman more than three times in the
flesh. There was the occasion at the garbage bins when the fish
skeletons and heads dangling from her fingers took on a significance above daylight and reality. There was the evening when
walking with my dog through my private territory the lower garden,
in a gloom of hydrangeas, guavas and custard apples, she loomed at
us, swaying in a stately manner I didn't associate with drink while
knowing from what I had observed that she must be drunk. She

gave us a green, dreamy smile. The strange thing was she took it for granted that this part of the garden, which I considered mine and resented other children entering, was hers as well, perhaps even more essentially hers. The terrier seemed to accept it. He didn't bark or attempt to attack. When we went up to the house to tell them the Mad Woman was down in the garden, then he began to bark and skirmish. I stayed behind when he ran down with them to chase the intruder, but by then she had disappeared, except from my mind.

The third occasion, more frightening because more violent, was also at dusk. It was during the season of guelder roses, and I came across her tearing them by handfuls, stuffing them into a carrier bag, their bracts fluttering and falling amongst the privet. My mother was not far behind me. She ordered the Mad Woman to stop destroying her guelder roses. She was not obeyed of course. So she called for Solomon Rakooka, the Solomon Islander who had worked for the Withycombes at 'Piercefield' while 'Miss Root' was a girl. Sol came down the drive looking very black in the dusk, laughing for this big joke, squelching in his badly fitting boots (he never walked happily in boots; he had bunions and his arches were gone.) Sol grappled the Mad Woman in the shadow of the guelder roses, just beyond the bunya-bunya where, at another time, Mrs Bonner ordered the carriage to stop and they picked up Voss. Now Sol and the Mad Woman were wrestling and spinning in the dusk, she hissing, Sol shouting through his ragged moustache and brown stumps of teeth. Then the Mad Woman's skirt fell off. I did not see what happened after that. I ran away. I ran upstairs. I lay on my bed. The glass above the dressing-table showed me palpitating in green waves. My heart was beating, a wooden, irregular time, as in another situation the hooves of Voss's calvalcade drummed their way down the stairs in this same house.

They came and told me Sol had sent the old thing packing and I must get myself ready because we were going to the theatre. It was a popular musical comedy. As the heroine sang about the silver linings she saw while washing up the dishes I could only see the Mad Woman, the snowy bracts of guelder roses falling in a storm as she wrestled with Sol. All round me in the plush tiers of the theatre, families were offering one another chocolates and smiles and enjoy-

ing the predicaments and final metamorphosis of a waif-heroine
into the wife of a millionaire. For the first time I was a skeleton at
the Australian feast. I could not have told about it, and went out of
my way to present the normality and smiles expected of me, while
drawn back into the dusk, and storm of shattered guelder roses
enveloping the Mad Woman and myself.

♦

One of the duties of the I.O. was to censor the letters the airmen
wrote. While part of a somewhat redundant Air Force-Army
Liaison Wing stationed at Maaten Bagush during a lull in desert
warfare, I became obsessed by my role as censor. It seemed as
though the scruffy, crumpled letters left in my tray, together with
the letters to and from Manoly, were my only connection with real
life. There were the bawdy effusions such as the letter from the
Corporal i/c Latrines enclosing for his wife the outline of his erection on a scroll of lavatory paper. On the other hand, there were the
doors opening, by degrees, week after week, on the tragedy of relationships falling apart. All the while, knowing that I knew, the
writers had to face me. I would have liked to share our condition,
but this was never possible. I had to remain the officer, the censor,
an anonymous figure, guarding the common good against any
excesses of human emotion.

As a result, isolation, desert, repressed sexuality, the voice of
Vera Lynn on the Orderly Tent wireless, the letters which might
never reach their destination or, if they did, convey an uncommu-
nicative message, preyed on me to the extent that my present
circumstances began to coalesce with memories of nights in my
Ebury Street bedsitter reading Eyre's Journal as the bombs fell on
London. A seed was sown in what had the appearance of barren
ground. It germinated years later in a public ward of a Sydney hospital where I had been brought from Castle Hill during one of my
most violent asthma attacks. In my half-drugged state the figures
began moving in the desert landscape. I could hear snatches of
conversation, I became in turn Voss and his anima Laura

Trevelyan. On a night of crisis, with the asthma turning to pneumonia, I took hold of the hand of a resident doctor standing by my bed. He withdrew as though he had been burnt. While recovering, though still in hospital, I sketched the skeleton of the book I now knew I would write. It was only after returning to Australia and reading a school textbook that I saw the connection between Voss and Leichhardt. This led to research and my borrowing details of the actual expeditions from the writings of those who found themselves enduring the German's leadership. The real Voss, as opposed to the actual Leichhardt, was a creature of the Egyptian desert, conceived by the perverse side of my nature at a time when all our lives were dominated by that greater German megalomaniac.

Voss's controversial origins led to strife with Leichhardt's academic guardians and confusion amongst the thesis writers. All demanded facts rather than a creative act. In time I was forgiven, Voss canonised, and it became my turn to resent the misappropriation of a vision of flesh, blood, and spirit, for translation according to taste, into a mummy for the museum, or the terms of sentimental costume romance. Half those professing to admire *Voss* did so because they saw no connection between themselves and the Nineteenth Century society portrayed in the novel. As child-adults many Australians grow resentful on being forced to recognise themselves divorced from their dubious antiques, surrounded by the plastic garbage littering their back yards; they shy away from the deep end of the unconscious. So they cannot accept much of what I have written about the century in which we are living, as I turn my back on their gush about *Voss*. (If there is less gush about that other so-called 'historical' novel *A Fringe of Leaves* it is perhaps because they sense in its images and narrative the reasons why we have become what we are today.)

♦

Until painting this self-portrait I had never tried to draw the graph of my religious faith. There were the Gentle Jesus prayers gabbled from behind Gothic hands to Mummy or Nursie in the days when we were Pretty Baa-Lambs. My pagan moment chanting a home-made hymn in the latticed summerhouse in the lower garden at 'Lulworth' which so shocked my worthy areligious dad. The services at St James's in the city under the spell of Mr Micklem's ascetic icon and the fainting ladies carried out by vergers and propped on chairs in the porch, at the same period Una de Burgh (the Bad Fairy) who wanted my voice for the choir. Confirmation at Cheltenham and waiting for the miracle which didn't happen.

I threw it all off in my late teens. Then, and in my early manhood, I was too egotistical, too sensual, to consider spiritual matters. As an Australian, perhaps too materialistic – though God knows, many of the more enthusiastic Australian evangelists, Methodist and C. of E., are materialistic enough.

Greek Orthodoxy's straitjacket prevented Manoly ever losing his religious faith. During the brash barren years of what I saw as intellectual and sexual freedom he was my ethical if not my spiritual guide. Because I loved him and was grateful to him, perhaps in the end he influenced me spiritually too. Looking back it is difficult to tell. I can only recall my disillusionment and despair for the wrong turning I felt my life had taken when I came back to Australia.

My work as a writer has always been what I understood as an offering in the absence of other gifts. *The Aunt's Story*, my first published work after settling at Castle Hill, was considered freakish, unintelligible – a nothing. You only had to pick up a library copy to see where the honest Australian reader had given it up as a bad job. I brooded after that. I considered giving up writing altogether, before starting on what was in some ways the even more calamitous *Tree of Man*. Living amongst our weeds, in what was an asthmatic hell, dragging the milk out of a couple of cows and selling their thick, illicit cream, I believed in nothing but Manoly, whom I had brought on a wild goosechase to the other side of the world. When our funds were at their lowest, he went out mowing lawns and stripping schnauzers. Members of 'old families' and a lady whose husband had made money out of saucepans treated him with condescension. On the other hand a widow fell in love, and bicycled down regularly for cream and conversation.

The seasons we experienced ran through every cliché in the Australian climatic calendar: drought, fire, gales, floods along the road at Windsor and Richmond. During what seemed like months of rain I was carrying a trayload of food to a wormy litter of pups down at the kennels when I slipped and fell on my back, dog dishes shooting in all directions. I lay where I had fallen, half-blinded by rain, under a pale sky, cursing through watery lips a God in whom I did not believe. I began laughing finally, at my own helplessness and hopelessness, in the mud and the stench from my filthy old oil-skin.

It was the turning point. My disbelief appeared as farcical as my fall. At that moment I was truly humbled.

We both began an exercise in organised humility. There is nothing remoter from Greek Orthodoxy than Sydney Evangelical C. of E., but in its hatred of Rome the Eastern Church had accepted Protestant overtures. A Greek living at a distance from a church of his own faith might attend the local C. of E., as Manoly did during our years of trial and error.

Every Sunday we set out for early communion as it did not interfere with our activities about the 'farm'. Built in the early days, the church at Castle Hill had accumulated the kind of Victorian and Edwardian bric-à-brac with which prosperous Australians express their gratitude for God's recognition. Kneeling in this church, under a succession of worthy and not so worthy rectors, in winter frost or the cool before a summer blaze, perhaps I was awaiting unconsciously one of the miracles which had not occurred after confirmation. Secure in a more elaborate tradition Manoly was less expectant or more sceptical. Like any expatriate he was not responsible for the farce he had dropped into. I could not protect myself as he did from the bigotry we found. We withdrew after the rector of the day declared it sinful to guess the number of beans in a jar at the annual church fête.

For a brief space we tried driving to Sydney to the service at Christchurch St Lawrence, unintelligible to both of us, though there were some nice moments of theatre as the acolytes, including a young Chinese, strolled among the faithful weaving veils of incense. Surprisingly, it was the esoteric element which caused our withdrawal – and the presence of the Bad Fairy from my childhood at St James's, now in charge of vestments at Christchurch. So each of us retreated into his private faith, and there we have remained.

Each respects what the other believes, though Manoly, I think, disapproves of my erratic spirit, chafing free, rejecting tradition. Is it ever possible to believe entirely in somebody one knows by heart, who is, at the same time, the one it is impossible to know?

My inklings of God's presence are interwoven with my love of the one human being who never fails me. This is why I fall short in my love of human beings in general. There are too many travesties of an ideal I am still foolish enough to expect after a lifetime's experience, and knowledge of myself.

In my own opinion my three best novels are *The Solid Mandala*, *The Aunt's Story*, and *The Twyborn Affair*. All three say something more than what is sacred to Aust. Lit. For this reason some of them were ignored in the beginning, some reviled and dismissed as pornography. After years two of them were accepted; it remains to be seen what will become of *The Twyborn Affair*.

Strange to think *The Solid Mandala* was ever considered pornographic, yet an Australian professor told a friend it was the most pornographic novel he? she? had ever read. One wonders where he or she spent his or her literary life before *The Solid Mandala* appeared.

♦

I sometimes wonder how I would have turned out had I been born a so-called normal heterosexual male. If an artist, probably a pompous one, preening myself in the psychic mirror for being a success, as did the intolerable Goethe, inferior to his self-abnegating disciple Eckermann. My unequivocal male genes would have allowed me to exploit sexuality to the full. As a father I would have been intolerant of my children, who would have hated and despised me, seeing through the great man I wasn't. I would have accepted titles, orders, and expected a state funeral in accordance with a deep-seated hypocrisy I had refused to let myself recognise.

As a woman, I might have been an earth-mother, churning out

the children I wanted of my husband, passionate, jealous, resentful of the cause and the result, always swallowing the bile of some insoluble frustration. Or I might have chosen a whore's life for its geater range in role-playing, greater than that offered an actress, deluding my male audience of one into thinking I was at his service, then flinging back at him the shreds of his self-importance as he buttoned up. Or else a nun, of milky complexion and sliced-bread smile, dedicated to her quasi-spiritual marriage with the most demanding spouse of all.

Instead, ambivalence has given me insights into human nature, denied, I believe, to those who are unequivocally male or female – and Professor Leonie Kramer. I would not trade my halfway house, frail though it be, for any of the entrenchments of those who like to think themselves unequivocal.

In fact sexuality refreshes and strengthens through its ambivalence, if unconsciously – even in Australia – and defines a nation's temperament. As I see it, the little that is subtle in the Australian character comes from the masculine principle in its women, the feminine in its men. Hence the reason Australian women generally appear stronger than their men. Alas, the feminine element in the men is not strong enough to make them more interesting.

One English critic finds it a serious flaw in my novels that my women are stronger than my men. I see nothing anomalous in this imbalance; it arises from a lifetime of observing my fellow Australians, in closest detail my own parents when I was young.

Where I have gone wrong in life is in believing that total sincerity is compatible with human intercourse. Manoly, I think, believes sincerity must yield to circumstance without necessarily becoming tainted with cynicism. His sense of reality is governed by a pureness of heart which I lack. My pursuit of that razor-blade truth has made me a slasher. Not that I don't love and venerate in several senses – before all, pureness of heart and trustfulness.

BERNARD SMITH

Bernard Smith (1916-) was born in Sydney and
brought up as a State Ward by good foster parents,
'Mum Keen' and 'Old Dad'. He showed early artistic
talent. After teaching, becoming a Communist, and
working in the New South Wales Art Gallery, he
joined the Fine Arts Department of Melbourne
University. From 1967 to 1977 he was Professor and
Director of the Power Institute of Fine Arts at Sydney
University. As critic and art historian, he has had a
profound effect on Australian cultural history. In *The
Boy Adeodatus: The Portrait of a Lucky Young Bastard*
(1984) he combines the skills of historian, biographer
(in his affectionate portraits of his mother Rose Anne
and foster mother), art critic and autobiographer.
Adeodatus was the name of St Augustine's illegitimate
son. Italicised quotations from *The Confessions of
St Augustine* universalise Smith's themes.

♦ ♦ ♦ ♦

'I love coming here,' said the insurance man to Mum Keen one day,
as he stood under the tall loquat by the back door. 'So cool and
restful. You've made it look so beautiful. It's like the garden of
Eden. All you need is Adam and Eve.' And gave young Bertha a sly
look.

Little Bennie didn't like him. A bit of a flash Jack. Each week he
picked up the sixpences on the industrial policies that Mum Keen
had taken out on Bertha's life and then on Ben's.

He never forgot that day.

'What's his name?' the insurance man said to Bertha, who was standing shyly by the back door, her long hair hanging down to her waist. She loved her hair.

'Bernard William Smith,' she said.

'Then he's not one of the family,' he said.

'No,' she said.

'He's not one of yours,' he said with a sly smile.

'Of course not,' she said blushing. 'His mother's gone to Queensland.'

'Oh, he's one of those,' he said.

Bertha, still blushing, said nothing. But little Bennie knew what the man meant. He had always seemed to know; and to know was to know the world. To know everything. *And now behold, my infancy is dead . . . yet I live still.*

◆

'How many times have you been saved now, Val?' young Ben asked one morning as he was recovering from the effects of a powerful missioner. 'I've been saved six times, I think.'

'I've been saved eight times,' she said. 'But Enid thinks it best to get saved whenever you can. She's lost count.'

They thought that was overdoing it.

Yet the Salvation Army gave them both a sense of purpose in life; a belief that it should not be lived for oneself, but for others. It gave Val a faith she came back to later in life. It gave Ben some good friends. That was particularly important for State wards. Because they were different. Although Braeside was a good home, as the Child Welfare inspectors said in their regular reports, all the wards were well aware of the difference between their home and those of their school playmates. Braeside was as clean and tidy as theirs, had a better garden than most. They were never allowed to go barefoot to school as some of their friends did. But the easy give and take, the normal transactions of the legitimate, the chatter about one's parents were not for them, and they knew it. They never invited friends to come and play in their yard and Mum Keen did not encourage it, though she did not prevent it. It was much easier to play in a friend's yard. Awkward questions that cropped up all too easily were avoided more readily away from one's home. For why should a boy called Smith and a girl called Welsh live with a mother called Keen? Was she really their mother? For the curious minds of little friends, who might turn and show their fangs in a moment, the most enticing mysteries lay upon the threshold of that discourse. So such questions were better avoided, if possible.

The extended family at Braeside became a self-supporting world, an enclosed garden for their self-esteem, which was so easily pricked and penetrated. They didn't want to be pestered by silly kids who didn't understand. But somehow Salvation Army children, the best of them at any rate, were different. They didn't bother the kids at Braeside with questions about their parents. If the questions were not asked, friendship became a possibility; the children of nature were prepared to accept those others, the children of the law, as their equals. But not otherwise. It opened up for young Ben the possibility of boyhood friendships.

♦

Because what he enjoyed most was drawing and painting in water-colour, in the cool of the morning, the deep reflections in the quiet water of the river, as seen from Paddy's deep, shady verandah. He tried to keep the washes of colour as broad and transparent as he could. Washes that made you feel the limpid, watery depths. He had seen how John Nash did it. What effortless skill it was! To suggest so much, so simply. That was what he really wanted to be. An artist. Not a teacher. But in order to be an artist you had to have someone who could support you through art school. It seemed, like being a lawyer, quite out of his reach.

Sketching, drawing, painting were activities, he found, that could sustain him; by which he could return into himself and find a kind of peace. For despite the comforts and kindnesses of Paddy's home he continued to feel strangely out of place. His existence was, he knew, a problem to them. And they acted, despite all their efforts at kindness, as if they were holding something back from him. It was to be assumed, of course, that any son of Rose Anne's, indeed any Tierney, was a good Catholic, or was at least doing his best to be. They assumed, but with a certain uneasiness, he knew, that he would not disgrace them. That he would play along with their own self-protective assumptions. That he would go to Mass. That he would place his sixpence in the offertory like all the others. That he would follow the service as best he could. And all this he did, out of deference to his mother, and his mother's feelings. Nor was the name Smith to be used unnecessarily. He began to become fairly skilled in the game that he was playing for them. But he had to ask himself, increasingly, what kind of game it was that he had begun to play with himself. He had already rejected one great set of traditional loyalties, or thought that he had, in an effort to find a place for himself in the world. Was it then for this other family that he had rejected old Dad's heavenly kingdom? *I became a great riddle to myself.*

♦

It was the first week of November 1936; the year Wotan won the Melbourne Cup. The new leaves on the tall young poplars in Wagga Park were as green as the spring lettuces in the Braeside garden. These were the trees of culture, not the trees of nature. Living tokens, they attracted him irresistibly and he spent most of the weekend – for he'd arrived early on Saturday morning – rendering them in pen and ink, seeking to endow them with something of the aching and timeless melancholy of the gardens of Watteau. How comforting it was to respond to the familiar signs when the signs were there; but to reduce the scraggy gums that grew around the schoolhouse to some kind of order, that was much more difficult.

The traditional patterns that the poplars imposed still exercised a power over him that he little understood. He left the gardens by the shady lagoon and walked along the Esplanade, coming into Fox Street, which was full of well-tended and homely suburban gardens; the day itself fresh and radiant, almost dream-like.

As he ascended the hill towards the railway line sacred music suddenly filled the air, though there was not a soul in sight. It drew him towards it like the force of a powerful magnet, and he hurried to the top of the hill where he saw, as he came over the bridge, a great concourse of people. They were watching an ecclesiastical procession as it began to wind its way into the gardens of a convent. It had all happened so suddenly: the music and then the brilliant colour. He felt like one transported into another realm, and in a daze walked into the convent grounds and joined the crowd. The procession had moved into the garden and was winding slowly around the broad rust-red paths. He stood there among the crowd, to one side of the path, and watched the procession coming towards him: the young, pink-faced acolytes in front, in their red frocks and broad white lace collars, swinging incense-burners from side to side, then a tall man carrying a great brass cross with the bronze serpent entwined, and behind him the candle-bearers and then the line of clergy.

As they neared him he was suddenly seized, as he had never been seized in his life before, with a sensation, highly physical, of abject humility, a sense of utter abasement. An ocean of emptiness opened within his bowels, and he felt as though half his body was dead. His legs did not belong to him. His knees trembled and became weak, as though he were looking down from a great height. But he felt he was sinking into a great depth. He sank on his knees as the Cross passed and tried to pray. But no words came because there was nothing to say. He knew that he desperately craved spiritual nourishment; hungering not for food but a sign. *How did I burn then, my God, how did I burn to fly from earthly delights towards thee, and yet I knew not what thou meanedst to do with me.*

◆

Shortly after he returned to Sydney in May 1940, Bernard joined the Teachers' Branch of the Australian Communist Party. It had not been a sudden decision. He had been preparing himself for it, he realised, for over twelve months: by his reading, the continuing correspondence and conversations with Lindsay, the unrelieved pressure of international events.

It was a simple enough decision in the end. He possessed the kind of temperament that needed to relate action to belief; belief to action. He needed, he felt, a coherent vision of life in order to stabilise his own sense of identity and gain a measure of self-respect. That is what he had sought through his childhood and adolescence in Christianity; and it had failed him. Neither intellectually nor emotionally was it for him; though he respected those who believed the great myths and acted as members of the Church militant. They were real people. It was possible, he found, to respect and dislike people at the same time; but he came to hold in supreme contempt the nominal Christians; those who had lost all belief and were prepared to exist in a kind of half-life, maintaining the forms. So far as he was concerned being a Christian meant that Christ really was born of the Virgin, as the Creed said, and that one did indeed eat the body of Christ in the Sacrament. All talk of the high mysteries of the faith, or of ritual as a symbolic discourse, was to him a mockery; the hypocrisy of the faint-hearted.

He had not come to believe that the communists possessed all the answers. He knew they had not. But they could at least, through Marx, provide a reasonably coherent picture of the course of human history that was not an affront to his intelligence. And they did propose a coherent course of action for the improvement of society.

For he had come to the conclusion that human society had been, and could be, improved by those who took action; believed that a line of progress could be seen in the complex pattern of human history, in the way that the theory of evolution implied. It had been a long haul, and a painful one, in which individuals had counted for little and there had been long periods of regression. But yes, there had been progress. There was a difference between a community of microbes and a community of human beings. And the difference was more than one of physiological complexity. There had been moral progress as well. For what great acts of moral grandeur had the microbes performed? None, so far as he knew. But he knew of a few on the human side. If that was faith, then it was the kind of faith that he could live with.

For he had listened to the sceptics and the cynics. There was a fellow up at the university called Anderson who played Socrates to a crowd of his admiring disciples. Clever bastards, all of them! But not real ones. All born on the right side of the sheet, all knowing on which side their professional bread had been buttered; all hiding a colossal sense of guilt behind those brightly questing facial facades. Perhaps their own sense of impotence was well merited. For neither Adam nor Christ had been born in holy wedlock; neither the fall of man nor his redemption seemed to depend very much upon honest madam's issue. The very illegitimacy of communism within the tainted legitimacy of Australian society gave it for him a certain sanctity.

♦

The attitude of his opponents he could understand and perhaps cope with. But he began to find to his dismay that even his closest friends had little sympathy for his new work. Lindsay Gordon seemed to be nonplussed. Sam Lewis told him that he just could not understand the work. In Sam's opinion painting from the Left should be much more accessible, more concerned with the lives of the workers; with the daily struggle. Bernie could see the logic of all that; clearly. Realism could add an important new dimension to Australian painting. Heaven knows, it was all so narrow in its interests. But he could not, he knew, paint in a socially realist manner. He was not personally interested in the depiction of work, poverty, suffering or the expression of compassionate attitudes – though he recognised their value. His interest as an artist lay in the creation of a secular and political iconography that might give visual expression to a Marxist view of history, and invoke an objective and critical perception of the contradictions of contemporary life.

His problem, though he did not fully realise it at the time, was similar to that which had faced Bertolt Brecht in the 1920s; to develop out of the new experimental forms of modernism, out of surrealism and expressionism, a politically conscious art. He knew little of Brecht's theory of *episches theater*, though he had read of Brecht in Peter Thoene's little book and learnt more about him from the British *Left Review* and the American *New Masses*, to which he had begun to subscribe through the Anvil Bookshop in Hay Street. It did seem to him, though, in his sharp rejection of naturalism at that time, that it was both sensible and logical to expect that the most politically conscious art could only be developed from the most advanced contemporary styles and techniques. But such an enterprise would involve a critique of modernism itself so that that which could be shown to be escapist, narcissistic, individualistic and opportunistic, that which used the new forms to indulge the old ambitions, could be distinguished from an art which both in its form and its content undertook to generate a real critique of contemporary society. So in his own new style he introduced elements of narrative, parody, allegory and distancing devices that were comparable in painting to Brecht's theatre.

But Sydney in 1940 was not Berlin in the 1920s. The last thing that the cosy, hedonistic society of Sydney wanted, even in wartime, was a politically conscious art derived from modernism. Not even the Left wanted it. To produce paintings like *Lot* and *Pompeii* was to invite charges of obscurantism and elitism.

So towards the end of 1940 he began to arrive at a decision – though, like all deliverances from old and cherished habits, it took some months to assert itself. He would give up painting. Entirely. There were many artists in Australia. There were even artists in Melbourne, so he had heard, though he had not seen their work, who were attempting to relate modern art to contemporary political realities. What Australia lacked was not artists but an informed audience for art. There was a complete lack of intelligent criticism; no interest in the theory of criticism; and an abysmal ignorance of the history and development of art within Australia. A truly advanced art, a committed art, could not possibly exist in such a cultural vacuum. He began to feel that his own role might lie not in being another artist but in helping to create an educated audience for art in Australia. This would involve developing a critique of modernism that would expose its strengths and weaknesses, and some knowledge of the history of Australian art – about which he, like everyone else, knew little or nothing. How could a serious art ever develop in Australia if its artists possessed no interest in or understanding of their own origins?

Other external factors contributed to his decision to abandon painting. For one thing it was not a propitious year, 1940, in which to paint pictures that were sympathetic to communism, even in a distanced, allegorical or parodic manner. On 15 June the Party had been declared illegal; police raids on offices and houses that took place early the next morning impounded a great quantity of books and journals that were claimed to be seditious or were on the banned list. He had hidden his own books for months; but he was not well enough known as a political activist to be so honoured. Furthermore his own creative interests had for some time been delicately balanced between poetry and painting, between word and image; and for both arts there seemed to be a compelling need to relate the whole history of art and aesthetics to Marxist thought. That too was an important undertaking for Australia. So he threw a lot of his energies in that direction, and began to give the organisation of the Teachers' Federation Art Society's fortnightly lectures a high priority. They came to range during 1940 and 1941 over the whole history of art and attracted a well-informed audience. The lecturers included people from Sydney University interested in the visual arts, such as Professor A. D. Trendall, the classical archaeologist, Dr A. H. MacDonald, historian and classicist, and R. Keith Harris, Lecturer in Town Planning. Equally important were the lectures given by European scholars who had recently emigrated to Australia to escape the Nazi persecution, such as Dr G. M. Berger, Dr Heidy Spiegel, Stephan Palyak and others. And to these were added lectures from practising artists such as Margaret Preston, James Gleeson, Rah Fizelle, Eleonore Lange, and Arthur Fleischmann. The range of subjects was comprehensive, the variety of approach diverse; and the series attracted a critical audience. It was at one of the lectures, in July 1940, that Bernard met the young English woman whom he would marry a few months later.

Once he had finally decided to give up the ambition to be an artist, he felt he must make some kind of symbolic gesture. He took all his smaller works of 1940 and burnt them. And when the Sydney showing of the Contemporary Art Society's exhibition ended late in October 1940 he decided not to collect his picture *Lot* from

S. A. Parker's, the framers in George Street, as he should have done. Another ritual gesture of dismissal. The painting had meant nothing to any of them. So he would abandon it too. He did not see it again for over thirty years.

JOYCE NICHOLSON

Joyce Nicholson (1919–) was born and educated in
Melbourne. She is a feminist, publisher and author of
numerous books. 'Destination Uncertain', from which
the extract is taken, appeared in the collection *The
Half-Open Door* (1982).

◆ ◆ ◆

For most of my life I have been dominated by men, often to my
ultimate advantage and the cause of much happiness, but probably
the reason why I am now a committed feminist.

First, there were my father and elder brother, then my husband
and then a managing director of the family business. Also there was
the Methodist Church, male dominated, which contributed to a
strict upbringing. I did not touch alcohol until I left the university,
something for which I am thankful to Methodism. Discovering
after marriage that I was a very sexual being, I am sure that had I not
been a teetotaller during my adolescence I would soon have become
pregnant and married.

It was not until fifteen years ago that I began to think for myself, but it was a long, slow process, often one step forward and two steps backward, and it is only in the last two or three years that I have won my freedom, and no longer do what men suggest, if I do not see a good reason for it. In fact, after a life of good natured and often stupid co-operation with my contemporaries, regularly finding myself conscientiously plodding along completing tasks I disliked, I now refuse to do what anyone urges, unless the request seems reasonable. Sometimes I forget, and find myself again in the be-kind-to-everyone syndrome, but I have become surprisingly mentally tough. The only men who can occasionally catch me out are my two sons, and I am learning even to resist them.

◆

As so often happens, one day a quite trivial matter of disagreement released this dam, and it resulted in a massive confrontation between the MD and myself. Still very angry, I then went to my father, confronted him also, and said I could not continue. Confrontation is against my nature, and I was left sick and shaking for days, but it had its effect. An outside person was brought in to investigate and report on the business and at the next Directors' Meeting the MD was dismissed.

At that meeting my father then said to me, 'Well, you had better take over the business now'.

With my female upbringing and lack of confidence, I was still stupid enough to say, 'But I don't know anything about the book trade'. Fortunately, I was easily persuaded, and I did feel I may as well have a try at it. I could not do worse than my predecessor. But I still was unable to reconcile myself to the magnificence of the position.

'You had better call me managing editor,' I said. 'I could not be Managing Director.'

My husband, a solicitor, was at the meeting, and had been a tower of strength in the crisis, sorting out the legal side. At this stage my husband made the one really constructive remark I can remember from him in my long and muddled progress towards a career. Usually he had been either passive or negative. Now he said, 'Don't be bloody stupid. You have to be Managing Director. The Articles of the Association say so. Anyway, you know you can do it, if you set your mind to it.'

So, at the age of forty-nine, I found myself in the extraordinary position of being Managing Director of a small, run-down publishing business, situated in a seedy, equally run-down terrace house, a business which I had always believed was by its nature struggling, but which I gradually discovered had great potential for both profit and power.

The other strange discovery was that when one occupies a certain position the knowledge I had feared I lacked automatically comes with that position. The mail and literature that arrive on one's desk every morning are full of information about the areas of greatest concern to the business and the trade, the politics of it, the people in it, trends in bookselling, publishing, writing, copyright, markets, and management, both in Australia and overseas.

With the utmost conviction, however, I am sure that although I was second in command in that business and had already improved the book journal, if it had not been a family business, I, as a woman, would never have been appointed Managing Director. Some male 'expert' from outside would have been selected. Publishing is good to women in that many women occupy high positions, but they hardly ever, all round the world, become managing directors or presidents. To attain that position, they must start their own business.

Also, although I am treated with the greatest respect, admiration, friendship and co-operation by most of the men in the book trade, I still have to fight against my position being trivialised. I am seldom introduced properly and smile patiently through phrases such as 'and this is the lady who knows all about the book trade' and other idiotic descriptions. My name and title are seldom given, and I have now learnt to introduce myself when the preliminary nonsense is over.

But at that time, the glory of 'the lady who knows everything' lay in the future. For six months I did not raise my head from the desk.

I did all the writing and editing for three monthly journals and one annual reference book. The filing was in chaos. Important papers were missing. I worked practically every night and every weekend. But, as I had a full-time person at home to cook meals and do the housework, I enjoyed every moment of re-organising the business. Once something was done, someone else did not either eat it or undo it. My staff, unlike my children, did what I asked them to do.

♦

That there should be something even better in store for me, I would never have believed. I thought that I had beaten the system in finding an area where I was not only doing what I wanted, but actually being paid for it. I continued to feel guilty that I should have sought such a position and not been content with the role of a happy wife and mother. I still accepted the fact that in addition to managing the business, the job of managing two houses and a family was mine.

It never occurred to me that the system was at fault.

I had long believed women were discriminated against and had studied the history of the suffragette movement, using it as a background for my book *Freedom For Priscilla*. But I had read no modern feminist books. So, when women's liberation came to Australia in full blast in 1972–73, and I started reading the literature and attending meetings, it was like a new world.

Always so dumb and slow to learn, I was utterly amazed at what I suddenly discovered. Firstly, I learned about sex role conditioning. I found that I was not peculiar or odd but had simply been forced into one way of life, by society's attitudes, when all my talents and preferences lay in another. There was no good reason why I, simply because I was female, should be suited to or enjoy the caring role of wife and mother. I no longer need feel guilty. I could even expect others in the home to share the cooking and cleaning.

Secondly, I met literally hundreds of women who felt the same as I did. That was the outstanding feature of those early feminist meetings, the exhilaration we all felt at no longer being alone, finding other women with the same feelings, experiences and fears, willing to admit they had been 'had' by the system.

Never one to do anything by halves, I flung myself into the activities of Women's Electoral Lobby, soon being on the co-ordinating committee, editing the Broadsheet, interviewing politicians, appearing on television and radio, helping to write submissions, visiting Canberra. They were heady days. Groups of us would sit up all night, planning and writing. The subject was new, so the impact of our findings was great. We found supportive women of all ages in every profession, in every suburb, in the country, in other states. We realised what could be achieved by working together. We discovered we had power.

The women's movement may not appear as active now, but many of the more obvious reforms were achieved in a relatively short space of time. But the momentum still continues. Committed women are working hard in less spectacular ways, slowly changing both people's minds and the system. It will be a long hard struggle to achieve real equality. Changing the world is always difficult. Many women do not understand our aims, and men have been entrenched in power too long. But, one day, it will come.

As for me, the final metamorphosis was made. I could hold my head high. Not only was I successful, I was not a freak.

There is a song in vogue at the moment, 'This is *my* life'. Every time I hear it on the radio, I feel 'that's me'. I may not have many years left, but they are all mine to enjoy as I like. I can make a mess or a success of them, but the decisions about them will be my own, and I shall be making those decisions with my eyes open.

ORIEL GRAY

Oriel Gray (1920–) comes from an Irish-Australian family, part Catholic, part Protestant. She joined the experimental Sydney New Theatre and later the Communist Party. Her autobiography *Exit Left, Memoirs of a Scarlet Woman* (1985) is divided, like a play, into four acts and describes the stages by which she broke free from father, lovers and comrades to live as a free spirit.

◆ ◆ ◆ ◆

We were all completely immersed in New Theatre. Here were lived, experienced, loved, laughed, fought, argued and then re-lived it all again in the coffee shop across from Circular Quay, with 'the girls' and the sailors as an ever-present chorus line.

There were signs that another depression was on its way. In the theatre there were technical specialists like Frank Swonnell or Reg, and we had our surprising university drop-ins in John Reed, James McAuley and Alan Crawford. But most of the men were children of the thirties, with no tertiary education and no formal training as skilled tradesmen, and women counted for little on the job market.

The Jewish refugees had been trickling into Australia. Party opinion on them was uneasy. They were refugees from fascism and deserving of our sympathy and support. On the other hand, were they the ones with the money and the inclination to pay their way out, while others, notably communists, stayed and fought underground.

If the refugees had got out 'the easy way', it was a hard way for some of them here. They were not welcomed, except among their own people. The average Australian looked on them with the distrust and contempt that was expressed in the term 'reffos'. And there were strong conflicts between Jews and Jews, between the Zionist dream of a Jewish national home, and the socialist concept that the Jew belongs to the country of his origin. The Soviet Union was bitterly opposed to Zionism. Could the Soviet Union, the only bulwark against fascism, be wrong?

Most of us in New Theatre were aware that some kind of a world crisis was on its way. Until it arrived, the theatre continued to provide crises – and a certain amount of humour – of its own. The monthly general meeting was always fruitful ground, especially correspondence. There was the usual letter from the Friends of the Soviet Union demanding payment for the piano (or chairs). A request from a Greek organization for a sketch at their annual ball brought groans. 'They cheer us when we come on, then someone starts playing one of those bloody zibuki things, everyone starts dancing and singing, and no one listens to a word!'

There was a letter from a novelist who would consider writing a play for us, a real Australian play, a very rare commodity. She had written a novel that was practically ignored in her own country, but was well promoted in the Soviet Union. She was invited to tour Russia and came back wanting to tell everyone that the workers' homeland was transfiguring in every respect. At a Waterside Workers' Federation meeting, she was quite carried away. 'And comrades, in the Soviet Union, sexual intercourse is wonderful!' 'It's not too bloody bad here, either, lady,' said a big wharfie politely from the front row.

I do not know how we acquired the set designers Mark and

Michael, known as 'The Brothers Karamazov'. They were two elongated gentlemen, who wore corduroy pants and jackets long before they became fashionable and familiar.

The Russians had an awkward habit of suddenly bringing a style, or an art form, or a morality into the bright light of party approval, and communist organizations throughout the world felt compelled to follow suit. Unfortunately, these innovations could fall into disfavour very quickly. We were so far from the centre of things that an overseas theoretical/cultural journal, or a copy of *The USSR in Construction* might find us numbered among the bourgeois goats.

But as far as we knew at this time, constructionist sets were 'in', and Mark and Michael had designed strange and varied forms of wood, wire, and papier maché which, when fitted together, would give the audience a stunning impression of the basic location for the building of the White Sea canal.

One Saturday afternoon, just before the opening of a Russian play called *Aristocrats*, which made up in length what it lost in translation, Grayce and I came in to find the theatre in turmoil.

For some reason Jack Fegan had threatened to punch Mark or Michael. The opposite one had leapt on him screaming, hammer in hand. Victor had just got everyone calmed down when the Brothers Karamazov launched into a disagreement involving another young man, fortunately unknown and absent. Then, with unnerving rapidity, Mark and Michael joined forces again, damned the theatre as a stifler of creative talent, and swept out, hand in hand.

When the fur and feathers had settled, and someone had delivered a homily on the correctness of the Communist Party in refusing admission to deviates, we realized that no one had any idea of how to assemble the forms to give that stunning impression of the White Sea canal. There was no drawn plan. Mark and Michael had taken the secret with them, if not to their graves, at least to their shared bed-sitter. Charlie Kitchener, our usual set painter, came to the rescue. 'We've got to have some kind of a set, Vic, we open next Monday. It's up near the Arctic Circle or some bloody God-forsaken hole, isn't it? What's wrong with white-washed backdrop and flats, with black pine trees painted on, a lot of pine trees? And we could have pine branches sticking out from the wings. We can pick those up in the Domain or the Gardens.'

I said timidly that those were Norfolk Pines in the Gardens and was rebuffed. But at least they knew I meant well. Not so Leon Sherman. Leon's sense of humour often got in the way of his respect for the movement. Everyone knew that he was not taking the crisis seriously when he suggested we borrow a stuffed Polar bear from the museum.

Jack Fegan came down on the side of the white-wash and pine solution. 'The audience will get the impact', he said, and Jack was too big to argue with.

In the next theoretical/cultural journal we got, we found that constructionist sets were bourgeois, decadent, and out! Naturalism was back, down to the last authentic feather on Chekov's sea gull.

'There you are,' said Leon. 'That stuffed Polar bear would've been just the ideological thing!'

DONALD HORNE

Donald Horne (1921–) served with the AIF 1941–44
and worked as a journalist in England and Australia
before joining the History Department of the
University of New South Wales where he became
Professor. He was appointed Chairman of the Australia
Council in 1984. His well-known *The Lucky Country*
(1964) is the first of many controversial studies of
Australian society. *The Education of Young Donald*
(1967) describes the small-town country society into
which he was born in Muswellbrook, New South
Wales, and his student life in Sydney University.
Confessions of a New Boy (1985) takes him up to his
departure for England in 1950.

◆ ◆ ◆ ◆

◆ *The Education of Young Donald*

In the summer at Muswellbrook, as in other country towns, it was
considered not only cooler but healthier and more manly for boys
to 'sleep out'. My bed was on one of the verandas, beneath a

drawing-room window. This meant that, although I have more conventional memories of sounds that drifted into sleep – of the church clock striking the hours and the quarters, or of the rushing of water in the weir – my immediate and prevailing memory is of quickly thinking the Lord's Prayer and then losing consciousness to the sounds of the card game of bridge. For Thine is the Kingdom. The Power and the Glory. Forever and Ever. Amen. One No Trump. Two Diamonds. Two Hearts. Your lead, partner.

Our house was one of the centres of Muswellbrook's amusement and triviality. It was said of my mother that 'Mrs Horne entertains as much as a doctor's wife' and, while my father took some of his pleasures more seriously, to my mother the pleasures of the late 1920s and early 1930s – bridge, mah-jongg, sing-songs, surprise parties, mini golf, tennis parties, lending libraries, grand balls, poker work, car drives, the talkies, golf tournaments, picnics, swimming, afternoon teas, and late suppers – came together as one big fun fair, open day and night, in which we would wait with eagerness for the next new craze to sweep through the people we knew in Muswellbrook.

What Sydney really meant to us was enjoyment of the natural and the primitive. The demanding bustle of pleasure that occupied my parents in their country town was replaced in the metropolis by the simplicity of sun and water, enjoyed in the bushland on the outskirts of Sydney and on Sydney beaches. It was in Sydney that we beheld the delights of Nature; in the country (so brown and bare that it seemed unnatural) we enjoyed the pleasures of Society. There was a reserve of bush less than a mile's walk from my grandparents' house which was much more pleasant than anything available at Muswellbrook, where the trees were stripped away so that animals could eat dry grass and make money to reduce their owners' overdrafts. Sometimes my father and I would walk there to have a swim and a sunbake, eat our sandwiches, drink our thermos tea, sail my model boat, and have a chat about some such topic as the

Roman conquest of Britain; but the real bushland extension of my grandparents' house was Yowie Bay, an inlet of Port Hacking, then almost deserted, though now a suburb of Sydney, where my grandfather had his 'weekender'. To get to the weekender, we would walk along a sandy bush track and then climb down steep stone steps to the little house that jutted into the bay on stone stilts. We would put the stores in the cupboard and get into the dinghy and row out and fish; or scramble over the boulders picking oysters; or dig around in the mud looking for worms for bait; or, if it was high tide, dive off the veranda into the water. There was a lot of shouting over lunch; in the afternoon we might sit on the veranda and look across the quiet bay and talk until afternoon tea. I would go to sleep to the light of an oil lamp and to the sound of the water lapping around the house; I might listen for a while as my grandfather discussed getting up before dawn to catch the tide. At Yowie we were simple-hearted fisherfolk, taking our milk condensed in cans like true primitives, and ignoring golf handicaps and bridge scores and the other demands of the high-pressure living that was already considered to be one of the great problems of the age.

The motor-car, the most fundamental of all the new crazes, also aided our communion with the natural. Two or three carloads of us, with everybody's children and dogs, would occasionally go for a bush picnic, the men in their cream trousers and blazers and ties and motoring caps, the women in tailored 'suits'. We would go to the National Park, a large bushland reserve south of Port Hacking, or down the Bulli Pass (where somebody's radiator usually boiled over on the steep climb back), or up to the Blue Mountains or the Kurrajong Mountains. At any turn in the road, if a particularly 'beautiful view' revealed itself, we might park for a while and admire it. For lunch we would build a fire of dry leaves, twigs, and small dry branches and grill lamb chops over it on a wire frame until they were black outside, the blacker the better: while we ate the burnt chops, holding them in our hands, a billy of tea simmered on the fire. These black grilled chops were more than a meal: they were an identification with the primitive, and with Australia. If we heard a kookaburra laugh during a picnic we felt even more Australian.

The climax of the year's pleasure was the most traditional. For a week before Christmas Eve my mother would go into the city every day to do her Christmas shopping, while my grandmother prepared for the feasts of the Christmas–New Year festival. She would ice two Christmas cakes, bake dozens of fruit-mince pies, boil three Christmas puddings in the laundry copper, bake two hams, and get ready the dozen or so chickens she had fattened for Christmas: she would chop their heads off, pluck their feathers in the garden, draw their entrails in the kitchen, truss them and stuff them with sage and onion, then roast them in the oven, two at a time. On Christmas Eve we would pack these delicacies into boxes and go off to the house we had rented that year in Cronulla, then a beach resort isolated from the suburbs by bush, but now, like Yowie, part of them. About ten of us would stay in the house; others would drop in for the day during the four weeks we stayed there. We would decorate the house with balloons and paper streamers, then I would put out an empty pillowcase at the end of the bed, with a note to Father Christmas (I did not believe in him, but kept up the pretence for my mother's sake). When I woke up at dawn the pillowcase would be crammed with purchases from the department stores. Instead of the usual mid-morning tea and scones in the kitchen we would all enjoy a glass of port and a slice of fruit cake in the garden before we went down to the beach, sunned ourselves and had our first surf for the season. Boasting immense appetites, we would come back to find that the day's extra guests had arrived, and soon we were seated around the tables, cramming in all we could of our great feast, washing it down with beer. When the last nut was cracked and the remains of the last dried fig were extricated from the last set of artificial teeth we would rest for a while, then go for another stroll down to the beach, and another surf. In the evening, after eating exactly the same meal, we would take down some of the balloons and form sides across the table to play balloon handball. On Boxing Day and until the day after New Year's Day we would go on eating Christmas dinner, supplementing it with fresh fish netted on the beach and sold alive. Then it was all gone, and the bones of the exhausted hams were used to make stock for a delicious split-pea soup, which also lasted for several meals.

For the whole four weeks, unless there was something wrong with the weather, we would go to the beach morning and afternoon. On the beach there was always the feeling of being part of a

friendly encampment; people would drift off into the surf and,
when they came back and dried themselves, describe what had
happened to them; then they would sunbake for a while and drift
off to the surf again. We would discuss the kind of surf it was that
day, what the seaweed, bluebottle, or sunburn problems were, how
the weather looked. Some days my cousin and I spent the whole
time either on the water's edge, building sandcastles and then tun-
nelling water into them so that they fell down, or jumping round in
the surf. There were other days when it was the sun more than the
surf that attracted us, and we would use the surf simply to cool off so
that we could enjoy more sun. We would lie on the beach, our
backs turned up, our cheeks pressed down into the sand, to achieve
the mahogany stain that marked the true White Australian. We
would go crimson quickly, then so quickly brown that the scorched
skin came off in long white strips; we would peel it from each other
with delight, enjoying the gentle tickle and congratulating ourselves on getting out of last year's skin.

It was at Cronulla every summer, in this renewal of our skins,
that we bore witness to a truth that was self-evident to us every day
of the year: that the most important part of human destiny was to
have a good time.

It is hard to convey the sense of special consideration with which an
Australian living in a country town could then regard the large
landholder whose property was developed (even if not by his own
family) before the town itself began to form. Muswellbrook was
particularly concerned with its Old Families, because we saw it as
'land locked'. The large pastoral estates on which the Old Families
lived their remote and unimaginable lives ran right up to the town,
cramming it in, and engulfing it with a feeling of mysterious
presence.

The special consideration we gave them was different from the
city attitudes towards wealth: it was partly a recognition of *priority*
(they got there first) and of the sheer importance and *bigness* of their

holdings. A man whose family had controlled so much land for so long seemed a big man. There was something of the Norman about them: in the original land seizures from the natives, and in the massive indifference of some of them to the townspeople: even in the self-confident territorial identification, as when one gentleman named his son 'Hunter' after the river and its valley, as if claiming for his family a title that covered an area as wide as the English North Country.

Even those members of Old Families who played some part in the town's affairs (perhaps a round of golf, a church attendance, or some charity work) still confounded us because we knew that they could enjoy luxuries and indulge in eccentricities that were then rare indeed. Trips to Europe, for example. Or even trips to Tasmania. They belonged to the social life of Sydney, where they stayed at the Australia Hotel or their clubs, and sometimes raced horses in the Easter and Spring meetings. In Muswellbrook a special hotel was reserved for their purposes. When the daughter of one of the old families engaged in social work in the town her coolness and self-assurance made our mothers feel self-conscious and inadequate.

To cut the Old Families down to size we invented stories about their origins. Even though most of these families were established in the early 'gentry' period of land settlement, we would decide that one family was founded by a tramp who walked into the district carrying his swag, or that the founder of another family won his estate at cards. We tried to destroy their eighteenth-century look (one gave his son the Christian name of 'Squire'); we tried to imagine that these great seigneurs were immediately descended from Texan horse thieves.

In its turn, Muswellbrook, in the manner of country towns, had produced from its 4000 people its own internal structure of social differences, perhaps not significant to the Old Families, who scarcely observed the anthill, but meaningful enough to those who lived inside it. Since enjoying leisure was so important, it was access to the sources of pleasure in Muswellbrook that became one of the significant ways in which those of its citizens who were eating well were able otherwise to distinguish between themselves. Anyone could play tennis, cricket, or football who was good enough for the

district competitions, but there were some forms of enjoyment that
were not available except as privileges or affirmations of status.
From this point of view the most serious events of the year were the
two-day Picnic Race Meeting and the Picnic Races Ball because
almost all of Muswellbrook was excluded from them. (Perhaps
these might be described as an Australian equivalent of an English
point-to-point and a hunt ball. A better parallel might be with the
Irish landowners, or with the more rumbustious English country
gentlemen of the eighteenth century. Old Australian landed families were more like bluff country squires than their English contemporaries.) It was an invitation to the Picnic Races Ball that settled
status. Most of those who went to the ball were the local landholders and their friends from Sydney and from other country districts.
To these were added the members of a merchant family which, with
its department stores in some of the main Hunter Valley towns and
its connection by marriage with an Old Family, gave the town's
social structure a peculiar shape; and by right, or by grace, or by
power of overdraft, there also came the town's professional men
and those, such as the bank managers and the stock and station
agents, who most closely served the interests of the landholders.
There were distinctions within the lesser gentry: for instance, the
leading stock and station agent (who wore an eyeglass) outranked
even the doctors. Whatever most touched the landholders was
most esteemed. Since my father was only a teacher at the govern-
ment school my parents were not invited to the Picnic Races Ball.
'In the West,' my mother would say, as if to suggest that the human
race was not altogether without hope, 'the schoolies *are* invited to
the Picnic Races.'

♦

Cities have to derive a sense of importance from something. Its
cinemas gave Sydney much of its significance. The big 'picture
shows' were its true cathedrals. There were not only Clark Gable
and Jean Harlow and Myrna Loy and William Powell and Jeannette
MacDonald to wonder at; in the most ambitious picture shows

there were copies in marble of famous statues, copies in oils of famous paintings, copies in glass of famous chandeliers, copies in bronze of famous suits of armour, copies in wood of famous styles of furniture, copies in mock stone of famous orders of architecture. There were hundreds of square yards of thick curtains, hundreds of square yards of thick carpet. There were kaleidoscopic lighting effects; a full orchestra would rise from the pit on hydraulic lifts, dressed in clothes that picked up the theme of the music they were about to play; and on the stage whole ballets would perform before the main feature began. Mightiest of all these effects was the Wurlitzer organ, which also rose on a hydraulic lift. Some of its 250 stops played not only the organ but the grand piano, the castanets, the Chinese gong, sleighbells, the xylophone, horse's hooves, the full range of drums, the sandpaper triangle, cathedral chimes, the tambourine, train whistles, the glockenspiel, the thunder sheet, and bird whistles. And beside the big city picture shows were some of the city's most splendid milk bars, exciting to jostle in at interval.

◆

After Christmas Mum and Dad rented a cottage in the Blue Mountains, and while we waited for the Leaving Certificate results to come out we tried to cast ourselves back into the roles we had played five years before when we had last had a holiday together. It was in the Blue Mountains that I was finally able to Think a Thought. Dad and I set off on a day's walking expedition – down a mountain track into the valley and then up another mountain track. For lunch we stopped in a small cave near the end of the downward track. We did not have much to say to each other, so the conditions were good for thought-thinking. When we finished our lunch with a bunch of grapes this reminded me of the grapes Mum and I brought Dad when we first visited him in the mental hospital eighteen months before. He had not even seen them. I then remembered eating grapes with him when I was four, before we went to Muswellbrook. For some reason I had been left at the Kogarah school with him, and I sat in a class of big boys and listened to my father tell them about Julius Caesar's invasion of Britain. Then we sat in the empty classroom while he shared his sandwiches and grapes with me and told me some more about Julius Caesar. Now what was left of him was sitting with me on this bush track, saying nothing and looking along the valley. Since the grapes also reminded me of John Keats, when I looked at the valley I wondered how Keats would have described it. I had no way of describing it. I did not know the names of anything I saw. Australia was an inadequate country, not written about in good literature. As we tidied up and continued our walk I felt bored with Keats and bored with the walk. I thought about hospitals and death. I had not thought much about death. I feared hospitals and pain, not death – the terrifying sharp smells of a hospital, the blood and muck running down its drains. When I had broken my arm at Maitland and they put me in hospital I had seen, as I was leaving the hospital the next morning, a woman patient being wheeled away from the operating theatre, her face white and her mouth open, a patient etherized upon a table. I remembered Pa's face, dead, in its box. I looked at my hands. How could these hands ever rot away into the earth? I tried to imagine dying. 'We just die like dogs,' one of my uncles had said, and I believed him. But I couldn't imagine it. Yet I would die and that would be the end of me. Then I Thought my Thought.

If I didn't believe in God and I didn't believe in life after death why was I always worrying about everything? What did it matter *what* I was? If there was no Good and no Bad why didn't I just be bad if I wanted to? I could be as selfish as I liked, plan everything just to please myself, be unscrupulous, just take what I wanted. What was the point of believing in anything? Everything was meaningless. Why should I act according to beliefs if I didn't believe in them and they got in my way? Beliefs were at lot of bullshit. There was no reason whatsoever why I should act one way or the other. What did *should* mean? Nothing. I was going to die. There was no God to punish me. Nothing meant anything. I could do what I liked. But I would have to be careful. Other people expected you to have beliefs. You should act as if you had them. That would be smart.

You could act as if you believed in honesty and so forth, and all the time you were lying.

I considered these thoughts so important that I kept on repeating them to myself for the rest of the walk, so that I would remember them. Now I really felt optimistic about the future.

◆   *Confessions of a New Boy*

Early in May a truckload of us were singing 'Balls to Mr Winckelstein' on our way from Mosquito Valley to the mobile bath unit. Another truck approached; it was only a narrow bush track – our truck swung to the right.

I was on the right-hand side of the truck and when we swung over – the truck was travelling at about forty miles an hour – my face hit a tree. The tree slashed a cheek, ripped an eyelid, cracked a bone in the eye socket, and threw me to the floor of the truck, where the back of my head struck a pick. Blood splashed the gunners as I tried to throw myself out.

First memory: stunned by pain, I am floating through dark air, held up by gunners' voices saying I have been hit by a tree and am being carried to a medical station on an airstrip. Someone jokes: 'You ought to see the tree!' I feel tired and go back to sleep.

Next memory: I am lying on a stretcher, blind and broken, my skull aching, my body shivering and my mouth vomiting. From somewhere in the blackness a voice speaks. I tell the voice that shivering and vomiting just mean I have 'shock' – I have read about it in a book.

Next memory: through the bandage over my eyes I feel a strong light. Some people discuss the signing of a form. I try to say something. What I am trying to say is that I will sign the form. They put a pen in my hand, hold my hand in place, and despite the bandages I sign the form. Somewhere in the aching rubbish in my brain there is a rustle of anxiety: there is something I mustn't forget. It is lost, in emptiness . . . then there is a prickle of memory. What I mustn't forget is that this is an anecdote.

Last memory: I wake up in private darkness in the ambulance. Blood is clotting my nostrils and wetting my lips. I am going to die.

As I lay in 'B' Ward in the casualty clearing station at Greta, I reconstructed these scenes as simply as if I were painting them as panels in a primitive polyptych honouring the sufferings of a Christian martyr. Drugged, gasping for air, aching, dribbling, I would use the moments when I 'came to' to rehearse details so that I would have something to remember. When someone held a glass up to my face and I could see that the right eye had sunk into purple and yellow pulp, the nose had spread across into the torn flesh of the cheek and the lips had burst into a pink mess, I memorized the colours and added these as something to repeat in my rehearsals. An orderly showed me my blood-stained tunic: it seemed as real as any object in the War Museum. This was the awesome presence of the *authentic*. Part of the story I was telling myself was that when I had first been made to understand that I was in a hospital ward I had thought, 'At least they can't say this is psychosomatic'. This could be the punchline of the anecdote. Several days later, a question from myself as audience: what would I say if some friend commented that it might have been a death wish? In a moment of later clarity I decided I should make this comment myself. It would provide a turn-of-the-knife *dénouement*.

♦

Packer displayed power; his wife displayed glamour. With her mink and diamonds, and a splendid smile on a handsome face, she was a film star in a New York night club. At the end of the week, on the night of the final parade in the Sydney Town Hall when the winner was to be announced (I had already written my story: BONDI GIRL WINS 1947 BEACH GIRL CONTEST), she seemed to be looking at me. Overawed, my imagination jumped: if I were in the position of

Pearl, or Penton (I would not be, of course, since I would, instead, be a novelist) but if I were, and had to deal with these people, I could imagine myself dealing with Packer in great, reverberating arguments – everyone knew this was the only way to deal with a man like that – but how could I feel at ease with a film star, with a perfect smile, wearing mink and diamonds?

After it was all over, and I got back to the office to add a couple of paragraphs to what had already been written, I heard that Packer wanted to congratulate me. There could be no other reason why he had called for me. I went along the forbidden corridor and through an empty ante-room into what, with the books lining its walls, seemed to be a gentleman's study. There Packer sat, behind a desk the size of a dictator's in a movie, with a desk lamp as bright as if we were about to play the third-degree scene.

He began shouting as soon as I reached the door. As I stood in front of his desk the room seemed to shake as if it were a hurricane and I was in the ship's cabin with a mad admiral. *Why had I taken a car to Cessnock?* . . . The car was authorized, and I . . . *Where's the authority?* . . . Well, I had spoken to . . . *I'm telling you there wasn't an authority* . . . What I was trying to say . . . *I don't care what you're trying to say! Why would you want a car? What was wrong with the bus?* . . . There wasn't a spare seat on the bus . . . *Are you too grand to travel by bus?* . . . I said there wasn't a spare seat on the bus . . . *You didn't need a seat! You could have stood up!* . . . Well, I thought there were laws against that . . . *Don't try to be smart with me, Mr Horne! You're sacked!*

There were a few more exchanges, and some repetitions, but when I got back to the flat and began talking about it, this was all I could remember, along with the feeling of fright which came from being in the presence of a man who could kill me with one hand. I stayed awake for a couple of hours – not, as yet, from anxiety about what would happen next; it was a sense of physical shock that kept me awake. It was as if I was back in the army and I had again been hit over the head.

As it happened, when I got to the office the next day, things seemed to have been sorted out. I wasn't quite sure how it had gone, but it was said that Mrs Packer had intervened . . . In any case I had my job back. In fact they had put me on to the features staff . . . When I went to the Features room Mrs Packer was already there; she was explaining it all to me, and smiling . . . She made me a cup of tea . . .

When I woke from this dream it was Saturday morning; I didn't have a job, and on the chair where I had thrown my trousers was what was left of a week's salary.

DICK ROUGHSEY

Dick Roughsey (1924–) was born on one of the
Mornington islands in the Gulf of Carpentaria. The
name 'Roughsey' is the anglicised version of his tribal
name, Goobalathaldin, meaning 'water standing on
end'. After a tribal childhood, he was educated at a
Presbyterian mission, but then returned to his tribe. An
Ansett pilot, Percy Tresize, encouraged him to paint
and he has successfully exhibited bark paintings and
oils. In 1973 he was appointed Chairman of the
Aboriginal Arts Board. The lavishly illustrated *Moon
and Rainbow: the Autobiography of an Aboriginal* (1971)
tells the story of his early life and the legends and
customs of his people.

♦ ♦ ♦ ♦

It was about 1940 and the big war was on when I was still out in the
bush getting my tucker. I was camped with my mates Dan and
Douglas and a few of the old people. Not long before, we had
borrowed a dugout canoe and paddled from island to island until we
reached the mainland. We then walked overland to Burketown to
try and get a job at cattle work. But the police sergeant said there
was no work and put us on the first boat back to the mission.

One morning the three of us sat talking as we watched the old
people go off to hunt fish in the rock-holes at low tide. It was the
wet season and very hard living in the rain, with fish and turtle hard

to catch. We decided to kill a bullock to have a good feed and also get sent away to Palm Island for punishment – and the chance of getting a job afterwards.

We borrowed big knives off the old people, got our spears and tomahawks and set off to track a small mob of cattle we had seen in the area. We tracked the cattle out into the mangroves where they were feeding on green mangrove fruit. There was only one track into the mangroves so Douglas and I climbed into trees above the track while Dan circled around to frighten the cattle back.

Pretty soon the cattle came charging back along the track. Douglas hurled his spear at a big bullock, but it must have hit a rib and the spear skidded off into the mangroves. My spear hit an old cow in the flank, but she kept going and soon smashed the spear against mangroves. We jumped out of the trees and ran off after them.

We caught up with the cattle where they were floundering through a mangrove creek. It had been raining heavily and all the ground was boggy. All the cattle got across except the poor old cow crippled by my spear. She got bogged getting up the bank so we raced over and killed her with a tomahawk. It was hard work dragging her up on the bank. We didn't want the old people to get into trouble over the cow and decided to keep it secret from them. We cut off enough meat for a few good feeds and cooked it among the mangroves.

Later that evening a young boy came over to our camp to play and yarn with us. When he went back to his parents he told them that we must have killed a bullock because we stank of bullock meat. The old men had a meeting and decided they wanted a share of the meat. They were not getting much fish in the bad weather.

Next morning the women and children went off to look for fruit and root foods, while the men pretended to get spears ready for fishing. The men knew the women were afraid of cattle-spearing because they didn't want their menfolk sent away to Palm Island, an offshore island about twenty miles north of Townsville, used as a prison settlement for Aborigines. One of the men spoke to Dan, saying they knew we had killed a bullock and wanted to share the meat. We all got bags and knives and went off to cut up the rest of the cow.

The old men were very happy with all that red meat. Having caught no dugong or turtle for weeks they were hungry for meat. While we were cutting up the cow we lit a fire and roasted the rib-bones over it to eat at once. Soon there wasn't much left of the cow. They even carried away most of the bones. The meat was soon cooking in ground ovens covered over with sand and ti-tree bark.

The men decided to play a joke on the women by pretending there was only fish cooking in the ovens. When the women came back chattering and laughing we were all lying in our shelters pretending to be asleep. The women went round waking their husbands, calling them lazy dogs and asked what sort of fish was cooking in the ovens. The men said they had speared many big fish and told the women to get them out as they would be cooked. But when the women opened the ovens and smelled the meat they were very angry. They wailed and said they would now lose their husbands, who would all be sent away to Palm Island. My mates and I told them that it would be all right as we had speared the cow and wanted to take all the blame. Nobody could resist the lovely smell from the ovens and soon everybody was happy with a bellyful of hot meat.

When we went back to the mission later on, we told everyone we had been killing bullocks. It soon got round to the Superintendent and he came down to the camp to call a meeting and ask who had been spearing bullocks. We owned up straight away and the Superintendent said he would see the Protector of Aborigines and have us sent away to Palm Island. We felt important when all the people started wailing and cutting themselves over us. We didn't care as long as we could get away to Palm Island and then hope for a job with money afterwards.

However, time went by and we heard nothing from the Protector, I think the war was pretty bad then and the Protector had more things to worry about than a few bullocks.

It was about a year later when the mission got a message from the Burketown police, asking for as many young men as possible to come over for work on the cattle stations. Most of the stockmen had gone to the war and now there weren't enough men to keep the beef up to the fighting men. How happy we were to have a job after all those years of sitting idle – a proper job with money and the chance to learn, and to see new things and new places. We rolled our swags and set off in the whaleboat for Burketown.

◆

After the war I got a job on a cattle station just below the Gulf. The owner of that station was a good boss and I had worked for him for a while during the war. I started just before the end of the wet, when the country was still wet and boggy, with water lying everywhere. I didn't know at the time but the Boss had decided to catch his neighbours napping by making a clean sweep of all the calves and cleanskins on their properties while they were still sitting on their verandahs waiting for the country to dry out.

There were five Aborigines, with a white cook and head stockman, in the camp. We all had two horses each and a couple of extra packhorses when we set off to follow a big watercourse away from the homestead. Just before we came to the boundary fence we went down into the bed of the river and rode along through shallow water. The head stockman had wirecutters to deal with the fence – already mended in many places after having been broken by wet season floods.

We put out a scout on each side of the river to ride far and wide to make sure there was no one about. For several days we then mustered along the river and its creeks until we had more than a hundred head of cleanskins, most of them only calves. I knew now that we were not just being helpful to the neighbours – but were doing what is known as poddy-dodging and cattle-duffing.

Beef for our camp came from the best branded bullocks, or a nice fat young cow – the sort of beef you don't kill on the home station. Shooting a branded beast is risky work. The brand is proof of ownership and it is wise to get rid of this quickly in case the owner should come riding along to enquire about the shooting.

My mate Billy was butcher for our camp. He was a dead shot even from horseback. As soon as he had selected and shot a fat beast he would gallop up, jump off and cut the brand and ears off with his knife. He would then get a stick and poke this evidence of owner-ship up the behind of the animal as far as possible. No white man would ever think of searching there. This was far safer than burying it or putting it in a hollow tree. Billy would then slit the hide down the back and peel it off one side. We used to take all the meat off one side, then turn the hide back and turn the beast over to leave the untouched side upwards. Two or three days later – after the crows, dingoes and wild pigs had had their share, you couldn't tell that the beast hadn't died a natural death.

When we had cleaned out that part of the country we drove our small herd back along the riverbed and mended the fence again. We had been careful to leave no trace of our camps and the last showers of the wet season soon washed away our few tracks. After raids on two more neighbouring stations our boss was richer by about 500 head. The neighbours must have thought the dingoes were bad that year.

ROBIN EAKIN

Robin Eakin was born and brought up in Sydney. Her
autobiography *Aunts Up The Cross* (1965) gives a lively
picture of her individualistic doctor father, her
numerous capricious aunts and life in Kings Cross,
Sydney, during the 1930s and the war years.

◆ ◆ ◆ ◆

On his first day home with his new toy, my father indulged in a little
quiet target practice in the surgery, but beyond a ricochetting bullet
which gouged some plaster out of the surgery wall, splintered a glass
case full of instruments and bounced harmlessly out into the light
area, no untoward incidents occurred. Secure in the assumption
that he now knew when it was liable to go off, and when it was
not, he took the gun out with him at night for as long as the situation
lasted, and occasionally fondled it by day as it lay in his desk drawer.
When war broke out, all licences to own firearms were reviewed:
my father took his pistol up to No. 3 Police Station where, over a

cup of tea with the Station boys, he missed the sergeant's leg by inches.

On the afternoon he finally shot himself, my mother was upstairs and as usual entertaining some friends to tea. It was a humid, somnolent day, enervating; and the patient who was sitting by my father's desk cataloguing her woes was one of his regular and more boring hypochrondriacs, whose long list of ailments needed no further response than an occasional murmur of sympathy. Whilst making these reassuring noises, he idly fingered the pistol in the middle drawer of his desk, lying in its accustomed nest of old papers, tobacco pouches, and pipe cleaners. As usual it was loaded, and, as usual, my father hadn't quite got the hang of it.

'I get these terrifying palpitations, Doctor – sometimes when I lie down I think I'm going to choke. And then, suddenly, I'll get a feeling of something awful about to happen – it's my nerves, I suppose. Don't you think I should have something to calm my nerves?'

'Mmmm,' said my father, and pulled the trigger.

The bullet made a deafening report, in the doubly-confined space of the drawer, and of the consulting room. The initial impact of the drawer-bottom probably lightened the blow, which nevertheless neatly blew off part of my father's kneecap. The patient swooned – my father cursed and bellowed – the nurse ran in, first to mop up the blood and call an ambulance into which she assisted my father; then, to revive the patient and put her in a taxi. Upstairs my mother's guests exclaimed at the noise, but my mother assured them, 'Don't worry. The doctor's probably shot himself.'

It was not until some hours later that she learnt that her husband was in hospital, where he stayed for two weeks, the central figure of a good deal of amused attention.

Later that night, I opened the door to two plain-clothes policemen.

'Miss Eakin,' they said, 'you can tell that father of yours that if he doesn't learn to use that gun properly soon, we're going to take it away from him.'

While he was in hospital, the patient who had witnessed the accident recovered sufficiently to ring him for further professional advice. In fact, the hospital switchboard operators were pestered by the wretched woman, and finally agreed to ask the doctor for his opinion. The Sister on duty came one day, 'Mrs. So-and-so is on the telephone. She says to tell you she has that sinking feeling again, and please, what should she do?'

'Tell her,' said my father, 'to strike out for the shore.'

◆

The shortage of alcohol, too, was a spur to invention. My father concocted a sort of house-drink, which had an innocuous taste and a quite spectacular effect. He made it in a huge china punch-bowl, big enough to take a couple of bottles at a time without splashing, or the boredom of measuring, and though its basic ingredient was rum, its component parts varied according to what happened to be available. But whatever the ingredients, the name remained the same, a name to become famous throughout the South West Pacific – 'Bunsby Gaze'.

The original Bunsby Gaze was a racehorse of no particular merit, but whose form my father had been following and in whose performance he had had reason to be disappointed. The first time he mixed the drink he decided that its taste and colour was to be imaginatively compared to the taste of horse's urine – not a very good horse – in fact, Bunsby Gaze. Long after the horse had ceased to race, Bunsby Gazes were still being remembered with nostalgia in the New Guinea jungles.

Sundays became, through the slow building up of habit and wartime commitments, our chief 'at home' day. There were never less than twelve for Sunday lunch and usually twenty or thirty for Sunday supper. My father and I and the hard resident core went to the beach every Sunday morning, while my mother prepared her enormous meals. By evening, the Bunsby Gazes were flowing and when my father thought his audience was in a sufficiently receptive mood he did his imitation. This was of Ronald Colman. It involved no speech or action: the characterisation was simply in my father's concept of the unfortunate man whom he had seen on the screen only once and who appeared to him to have, for a screen idol,

extremely short legs. He also found him singularly lacking in facial
expression. He stuck a burnt match moustache on his face and, hat
and overcoat on, he took up his position kneeling behind the curtains (with which my mother was gradually replacing the doors in as
many rooms as she could get her hands on). I then announced the
act, pulled the curtains, and there knelt my father on Ronald Colman's short legs, glaring at the audience with a fierce and fixed
expression. After one minute he turned and hobbled away. This
regularly reduced people who had seen it week after week to tears of
laughter, so he saw no reason why he should vary the act. After he
shot himself, he could no longer get down on his knees, so that was
the end of Ronald Colman.

VINCENT BUCKLEY

Vincent Buckley (1927–) was born in Victoria,
educated in Melbourne and Cambridge and taught
English at Melbourne University. He is a poet and
critic. His autobiography *Cutting Green Hay* (1983)
gives an account of his Irish Catholic background, his
education and the political and religious cross-currents
in Melbourne in the 1950s and 1960s.

◆ ◆ ◆ ◆

But if folklore was not passed from psyche to psyche, songs were
passed from voice to voice. Both my parents sang or intoned far
more songs than parents normally did or do, and they did so not on
'occasions' or on request or in more-or-less organized company, but
whenever they felt like it. My mother felt like it any time, in any
mood, whether cheerful or depressed, and she always sounded the
same: pure and thoughtful and a little quavery. My father generally
kept his singing for times when he was reasonably content, and thus
his recitals became more infrequent with the years; but whenever
we would go out with the pony and jinker on his rounds as a bush

postman ('ROYAL MAIL' said the jinker, absurdly), he would burst
into song as soon as he got beyond the limits of the town. He would
open with 'The River Shannon', a sentimental emigré song,
snatches of which he would hum or murmur between renditions of
other works: 'The Wild Colonial Boy', 'The Wearing of the
Green', 'Slievenamon', 'The Irish Emigrant's Lament', and a number of American-Irish tunes too similar to particularize. He would
also, however, burst into the lines of Orange faction-songs, of
which I remember 'Derry's Walls' and 'The Boyne Water'. 'Up to
your knees in Irish blood', he would chant:

> Up to your neck in slaughter.
> O didn't we give the Paddies hell
> At the battle of the Boyne water.

It always seemed to me, as a small boy, that he would resort to these
songs when he was more than usually out of sorts with some of his
relations, all of course Paddies; and in any case, although I did not
realize it at the time, he did not know the songs right through.

'Let him go, let him tarry,' my mother would sweetly entune:

> Let him sink or let him swim.
> He doesn't care for me,
> So I don't care for him.

Or she would sing 'A Farmer's Boy' with unvarying nostalgia, as
though it made her think of the girl she was once, a farmer's girl, or
dash off part of a Jacobite song, or 'Weel may the keel row'; and she
taught me a song that I am now teaching my young daughter, and
which I think must be by Percy French:

> O 'twas late he went to breakfast
> And 'twas late he went to bed
> And if you picked up a thermometer
> At least it would be said
> The quicksilver started bubbling
> As they placed it to his head
> And the steam was like a rainbow
> Round McCarthy.

They would both sing 'The Minstrel Boy' and 'God Save Ireland' with gusto; they would recite Paterson, Burns, Steele Rudd without warning, glorying in the way in which these writers stood for the dignity of country workers, and against the bosses ('the heads', as they were called locally). They were certainly ardent Labor supporters; it may be that they were more conscious of and inclined towards Irish nationalism than I had realized, for they seldom spoke of it. Their silence was a kind of rhetoric broken by the counter-rhetoric of their songs. Yet my mother also recited, and sang, Kipling's 'Recessional' as if it were a Christian hymn – as, I suspect, her teacher in the state primary school at Comadai had told her it was.

My own first school was the Catholic primary school in Romsey, run by an Australian order of nuns, the Sisters of St Joseph. They were peculiarly well suited to the task, since they came, by and large, from the same sorts of family as their pupils, even though they had to teach both boys and girls up to the age of thirteen or fourteen; at this age, the pupils sat for the Merit Certificate, which meant the end of formal schooling for most of them. The nuns thought it part of their duty to coach us in football, rounders, athletics and, for one instructive and hilarious period, boxing. The alternative was the local state school, which was next door to my home. There was rivalry between the schools, and some hostility, at least verbal; but disgruntled parents sometimes moved their children from one school to the other, usually on obscure points of honour or justice. Our school was examined by inspectors from both the state and Catholic systems; and there were also legendary officials called truant inspectors, whose authority was resented and evaded by some parents but endorsed by others to the point where it became an internalized ideology. A few parents took it as a point of especial honour that their children had 'never had a day away from school'; it was, in short, a matter of pride both not to have been sick at all and to have been sick yet not to have been incapacitated; the whole business of schooling was thus seen as a system of tests of adequacy, character, obedience – though some, no doubt, thought it an irrelevance.

The school readers were examples of this view of the business; they extolled and encapsulated such views of character. We had the

First Book, the *Fifth Book*, and so on, up to eight: all were standard
primers, and, as I say, they took most country children of the time
(the 1930s of the Great Depression) up to the end of their effective
schooling. We may deduce a definite ideology from these books
which pressed for notions of gradual progress in human affairs, of
natural catastrophes as the occasion for self-testing, of the world at
large (most of it so unimaginably far from Romsey) as a variably
exotic place, of there being adventures at the other end of the
world, of poetry as jaunty songs or narratives which required to be
memorized and learnt from, of the British empire as a vast and
beneficent force, rather like the pattern of God's footsteps, roving
everywhere, or nearly everywhere, and looking after everyone – or
at least all those who were sensible enough to let it. Australia was
British, a new place and occasion for the British virtues, tested as
they were by British institutions, British antiquity and British gal-
lantry. Of course, it was a very different place from the homeland,
which is why it was so lucky that the fertile British had been chosen
to inhabit it. And it was in many ways a hard and hostile place –
Lawson's 'The Drover's Wife' appeared in one of these readers and
was read with much emotion by many country children. By British,
of course, was meant English and certain kinds of Scots: Stevenson
and Scott, for example, made several appearances. There were no
Welsh examples, that I can remember; and no Irish, except the
Tennysonian Allingham. People did hard work, which tested and
improved them, and they might well be poor (as the drover's wife
certainly was), but for the most part the work they did was not dirty
or demeaning, and their lives were not sordid. There were no racial
or social or religious tensions between people; wars were planned
rather than fought, and economics either did not exist or were a
shadowy mystery. The readers, while being more varied and interesting than my account may suggest, tried to join the two conti-
nents, the two homelands, but in the psychological interests of the
founding one.

At the same time, they contained much that was sheer fun, and
one year's reader might have a British bias which would be cor-
rected in the next. The *Third Book* had Stevenson, C. J. Dennis,
The Brothers Grimm, Aesop, Keats ('The Naughty Boy'), Ethel
Turner, James Hogg, Louis Esson, Hans Christian Andersen,

Edward Lear, de la Mare, Roderic Quinn, and many more; the eight-year-old was expected to at least make himself literate. The *Fourth Book* gave a number of Aboriginal legends, of which I remember to this day 'Why the Crow is Black', and of cautionary or exemplary tales ('Lost in the Bush', and 'Simpson and his Donkey', as well as 'The Story of General Gordon'); it also had a decidedly melancholy strain (children in those days were not protected from the awareness of disaster), in 'The Wreck of the Hesperus' and Paterson's 'Over the Range'.

In later books several of Lawson's stories were printed, and the usual Australian authors made their appearance with songs, ballads, vignettes of outback life and cautionary or uplifting tales. But the exotica as well became more frequent: tales from Japan and India, and an increasing number of Scottish entries, the taste generally minor Romantic, as you might expect. I remember the *Fifth Book* well; and from that, or in some subsequent book, I can recall whole sentences which, on checking, I found fairly accurate in my memory: 'Now were all present amazed; and Ulysses said: "Match me this throw, young man, if you can. Then I will cast another quoit farther yet" '; and 'Saved, saved to a man! – saved by the dauntless courage and magnificently heroic devotion of the fishermen of Whitby, who brought their life-boat overland.'

But these heroes of the school readers were mostly, in their various ways, achievers who showed British pluck and endurance, whether they were Christopher Columbus or some small Japanese girl. Perhaps it is all summed up in Tennyson's lines:

> Not once or twice in our rough island story,
> The path of duty was the way to glory.

Though many of us, landlocked Victorians, who on every hot summer day, persecuted by the dusty north wind, longed for the 'cool change', hardly knew what an island was, and could certainly not visualize one with any accuracy.

♦

In any case, the whole of Australia was by this time rotted with the Depression, and nervily aware of wars spreading from remote and brutal places to meet in one Great War. It is impossible to say how deeply the imaginations of Australians were gripped by the previous war, the 'Great War'. The thought of another crept insensately in the humus of economic despair and social disuse. The nation seemed impotent, the country rusted with too hasty use and too early an abandonment. None of us was *used* enough in the right way for the right good. Brain, muscle, feeling, soul, all weakened and languished. Not even the dashing punters, socialites, gentry, publicans and criminals performed with their usual exhibitionist flair. For a child at school it was hard to know what even to hope for. It was clear that you could not stay *there*; life lay elsewhere, if anywhere; your parents knew this and urged on you flight, a careful and honourable escape, and they did it in a way that let you know they saw you as both going and not going. The great reference points of my childhood all have to do with Depression and War, the horrible escape from the horrible imprisonment.

In 1931 I started school, a few months after my father lost his job, and a year or so after, with a pride and hope approximating *hubris*, we moved from the cottage behind the pub up the hill to a house which, God help us, we were buying, with a loan from 'Granddad'. The old car disappeared. For the country as a whole, it was back to horse-and-buggy days. For the working-class male, it was save your burnt matchsticks for the game of crib. They had not flamed very long, anyway.

The decade burned on. Nothing got better, and each month the evidence was brought closer to our door that all of us were living in a slow swirl of poverty and humiliation. Many were worse off than we were, for we had a house, a couple of cows, a horse, and an acre of land – as well as an identity. What we did not have was work, mobility, or the dignity of feeling wanted. But scores of men trudged every month into and through the district, picking like lethargic grasshoppers at the few bits of piecework available, sleeping under the bridge, or in the school shelter sheds, or in the rickety changing sheds down by the football ground. They humped their swags, a far from romantic gesture, and I never heard one of them sing nostalgically to his old black billy, though most of them carried one. Many of them were city workers who knew nothing of country work. One day, just as the potato digging season was starting, a young man knocked at our door: could he have some hot water, and might he and his family pitch their tent under the largest pine tree inside our bumpy acre? His family? Yes, his wife and baby were with him. Tent? We went to inspect it, and even I, at the age of seven or eight, could see that such a hessian makeshift would never do. If we cleaned out our lumber-room, would they use that? They wouldn't, thank you; but the wife and baby did spend much of each day in the house, talking to my mother.

The man himself was desperate. He had no work and no money, had had no work for some time, and didn't know how to go about asking farmers for it. As it turned out, he didn't know how to do it when he got it, either. For my father took him around, introduced him, got him work, and worked beside him, digging potatoes – in damp weather, surely one of the hardest jobs in the world. My father, in any case, would force fork through mud strongly and often enough to get his dozen bags a day, at 1s 6d the bag. His new mate could manage only three, and the last of those had to be finished off by my father; the new man's whole body wracked with breathlessness and his hands raw from the fork-handle. It was too much for him; after a fortnight or so, he moved on, carrying his liabilities, of which the tent itself was cumbrous enough to constitute a reason for never going anywhere. And the wife and baby, wherever they went, and whatever hospitality they got, cannot be expected to have arrived at any conversation warmer and sweeter than my mother's.

◆

It was set stockily at the end of a small street behind the Catholic Cathedral: a piece of the city which did not feel like a city, a stern yet civilized block of buildings in what felt like parkland; and, indeed, if the bulk of the cathedral and its tatty 'palace' loomed over it on one side, and a school and a hospital confronted it on another, on a third the Fitzroy Gardens glided and bent away to its own cool green planted centre. Nothing could more surely remind you that Melbourne was, in a way, a small-town city. The school was a small-town city school, though cathedral and hospital were of the due proportions.

I was small, too, and on my first day was made to realize how close I would have to live with these buildings and their 300 pupils. The school was a square; the students were in navy blue, the masters (most of them priests) in black cassocks or soutanes. On the fourth side of the square the latrines abutted on the handball courts, two of them, gloomy grey with heavy wire netting above; the cricket 'nets' under the walls of the cathedral residence (that palace), were of heavy wire, too, and the 'turf' was asphalt. It was a blue-black environment, with some colour variation provided by the darkened grey of concrete. I knew no one, except my brother, who knew no one but me; yet he had to defend me from the manic assaults of another boy who seemed to resent that, small as I was, he was smaller still, and who would not remain knocked down. No brother could protect me from my first caning, which also occurred on my first day, and also involved, as flogger, an unusually small person, a priest who, in his shapeless soutane, thought I was mocking him. I had never heard of algebra, and did not appreciate what sort of game I was being invited to play in learning it. So I was flogged for asking what 'equals' means in the first equation we were given. The priest flogged and flogged away in an incompetent fury, his soutane whirling in unrhythmic movements as he tried to align hand and strap; and the class, many of them old-timers, but some clever scholarship boys like me, groaned with disbelief and fear as Fr G. hauled me around for the next cut. How many of them would have liked to ask what 'equals' means?

There was to be no love here. But there was geniality, a great deal of it. The whole ethos was one of genial casualness, an odd mixture of formality (the priests were to be called 'Sir', and we were addressed, probably for the first time in our lives, by our surnames) and joshing intimacy. Boys joked freely with masters in the yard, sometimes played handball or kicked the football with them; and the favourites slyly tied up soutane sleeves as they had done in the time of Stephen Decalus, and the masters pretended anger, as they had done then. All was communal; the keynote was reassurance;

everything was under control, so the masters had ensured, and if everyone co-operated, it would remain so. Even competition, in the classroom or the public examination hall or on the playing-field, had an amateur, throwaway air. Pretensions to greatness were not to be encouraged, since greatness was not in the offing in any future we could promise ourselves. Small and cramped, the school was not used to being the best at anything, so it would become expert at being itself, and pride could then be invested in the very smallness and unimportance.

KEVIN GILBERT

Kevin Gilbert (1933–) was born in New South Wales
of mixed Aboriginal, English and Irish descent.
Orphaned at the age of seven and poorly educated, he
worked as a casual labourer until he was given a life
sentence in 1957 on a charge of murder. He served
fourteen and a half years, during which time he began
to write. He is now poet, playwright, painter,
community worker and political activist. This brief
autobiography comes from *Living Black* (1977), a book
in which Gilbert edits and records the life-stories of
many Aboriginals as well as his own.

♦ ♦ ♦ ♦

A lot of people are going to disclaim what I say. They are going to
say that I am a stirrer, a sensationalist, a jailbird, anything but face
what they represent, what they have done and what they allow to
continue in this nation. So, this time, I am going to tell you who I
am, why I am that way and how society has moulded me.

I am a non-tribal Aboriginal; one of the Wiradjuri people. My
blood links extend into the Kamilaroi people. My father was white,
English-Irish; my mother, Aboriginal-Irish. A mixture like that
becomes an interesting family cocktail. Sometimes it becomes a
family catastrophe.

I was born on the banks of the Lachlan River at Condobolin in New South Wales. I was blacker than my brothers and sisters, but my mother said this was on account of her finding the other kids under the gumtree leaves and me in an old hollow burnt log. My father got four acres of land on Goobang Creek and did a bit of market gardening, droving, butchering, you name it. Those were the years of the Depression.

I loved the garden, the irrigation channel, watching the water-rats swimming and the water-birds feeding in the rushes, so I didn't mind being alone. I was the youngest of a family of eight and the others were all at school. My days were rounded off by the two-mile walk my mother and I often took to visit her brother and his wife and all those lovely little black relatives of mine on the Condobolin Aboriginal Reserve.

In those early years only certain things stood out to suggest that we were different from whites. When we occasionally attended the local picture shows the area we had to sit in was roped off from the white area. Some shops we just never went into. Some whites we just never spoke to. Some buses were just for Aboriginals on sports days.

We mostly drove everywhere in horse-drawn buggies or caravans. Every year we'd go across to the Riverina district to Leeton in New South Wales to pick peas and grapes. They were days of crossing the red sand ridges of the Mallee country, chasing rabbits, watching huge red kangaroos watching us, mallee-hen hunting, and looking for bower-bird nests and emu eggs. Always searching for game, helping to keep something in the larder; seeing our group swim the rivers to reach a sheep or cattle station to buy fresh meat or flour or tea. And when there was no money, swimming it anyway and hoping that there was an old battler, an old shearing cook who'd fill your sugar-bag with tucker. At Leeton, the very poor seasonal workers and the Aboriginals used to camp on Wattle Hill where there was piped water, toilets and a shower block.

I was seven, desperately in love with some sexy little gin from the tent next door, and stealing and eating sweet big grapes and peaches when suddenly my parents died. As horrifyingly sudden as that. And there were screams and wailing and people rushing . . . The people in Leeton formed a committee and rented a house for us in Willow Street. It was the nicest house I'd ever lived in and the biggest. The local policeman stuffed it because he used to hide in our backyard to keep an eye on what was happening and my older brothers and sisters swore at him, reporting him to the town. We moved out to an old ramshackle, fallen down house at Fibro Swamp.

I got my first job ever, working in the vineyard. The job consisted of pulling wire ropes which were attached to bells and gongs throughout the vineyard to scare the stinking English starlings away from the currant and sultana grapes. I knew they were rotten English starlings that some pommy mug brought out to Australia because my boss told me so. I had the Devil's own delight in waiting for those bludging little birds to settle on the grapevines then letting all hell break out with the clanging of gongs and bells. I took the greatest delight in seeing them almost fly out of their feathers, and if there was actually a feather floating behind them . . . Anyhow, my boss paid me eight shillings a week, or at least he promised to pay me eight shillings a week. I reckoned I was worth twice that much so I told him I wanted a whole pound a week and he sacked me.

My brothers joined the army. My young brother was fifteen and he put his age up and went into the ninth divvy, then the commando section. He did the rough spots in New Guinea. The jungles he fought in were very much like the jungle of twisted trees and bullrushes at Fibro Swamp, only, over here, instead of Japanese soldiers, we had the legendary bunyip, the giant water snake, the little people and the hairy youree – the huge shaggy man-like creature that the whites call 'yowie'.

We had our other wars here too. To eat we had to steal: fruit, vegetables, sheep, and grapes and tomatoes which were much too nice to be called 'fruit' or 'vegetables'. At school we were down on two counts. We were black and orphans. We used to fight like hell and it was nothing to see fourteen or fifteen white kids stoning us and shouting names at us. When we caught the little bastards on their own we sat them down on top of Bathurst burr bushes by way of apology. Of course their parents were outraged and so were the police. They gave us 'one more last chance' and, being hungry, knowing we'd have to drive our sulkies out to the Murrumbidgee River to catch some fish, we stole beans and tomatoes and turnips and stashed them in the sulky.

My thirteen-year-old sister and I swam across an irrigation channel to steal grapes. One day we had just filled the four-gallon bucket when the owner's hand came through the bush and grabbed me. My sister took off. He yelled, 'Come back here or I won't let your little brother go.' Now my brothers were pretty smart and they told me not only what some nasty man might try to do to girls but also how best I could discourage it. I wheeled my body around and kicked him in the nuts. It put him in hospital and me and my sister into the police cell and then into an orphanage.

I found out a little more about white society in there. They were big, fat, heavy gutted people in there: shouting, bullying, pigging. And I kept running away, trying to find my way back to the bush. Finally, my seventeen-year-old sister who was newly married and pregnant took us back to the bush. We went back to living in humpies, living on the fringes of town or, at times, living on a vineyard property in sheds. I recall the pain of being poor: peering into shop windows and being glared at by white shopkeepers; picking up cigarette ends from along the roadway; gathering old scraps of hessian or kerosene tins and cutting them open to make roofing iron and hut walls; getting scraps of clothing or shoes from the rubbish tips; and positively drooling over the sweets and food container packets that the whites had thrown away. I remember watching my heavily pregnant sister laboriously climb the ladders to the top of the apple trees, a great calico bag swung on leather around her neck, to earn a few bob so we could eat and go to school. I remember seeing her in the fog-shrouded morning get up to go into the forest to cut the limbs of fallen pine trees for the sawmills, crying with the pain of her cracked and blistered hands and peeing on the blisters to toughen them so she could work harder. She got one shilling and threepence a tree. She's still out there, raising kids, working voluntarily with our own people, quietly helping where she can.

I left school and lived on Aboriginal reserves, in fringe settlements on the edge of towns, scrounging for old copper and brass, hunting rabbits to live, waiting for the seasonal work to come again.

I saw the misery, the hunger, the awful poverty of our people around me. With no education, no trade training, no employment prospects, I realized my only chance was to become a contractor or the manager of a sheep or cattle station.

Then I married a European girl. We had two children. There were fights and poverty and jealousy. It ultimately led to a brawl in the middle of the night alongside some country road. I was pissed, she was tired and despairing and grabbed a rifle . . . the jury in the country town of Dubbo called it murder. Five defence witnesses weren't called, and me, an Abo in a hick country town – what was more natural than to receive a sentence of penal servitude for life?

Bathurst jail. Prisoners, squashed, sullen, marching in long grey files, removed from care or dignity, answering to their new names, 'eighty-six', 'one-o-four', 'three fifty-one', the grey mess of a meal, the slamming of the great metal cell doors, the bullying and debasing of prisoners, the guards who used their positions to abuse and prey on the prisoners. On visiting days you peered at your family from behind a steel mesh. I remember seeing my perky little son, my beautifully tanned daughter with her mother's eyes and hair and a nose just like mine, God help her, and the pain of thinking, why did it happen, how could it happen, what went wrong and nothing will ever make life right again. And the guards snarling, 'Righto, time's up, get to your cell,' and outside the visiting box, 'Move. Faster than that . . . quick march!' And the jab in the kidneys as you went past just to show they were 'tougher' than you.

The years of attempting to appeal or escape, and solitary confinement, bread and water, batons, fists, kicks.

The memory of the humour of Aboriginals – clustering together with them in the prison yards, telling stories of our people, mimicking the guards, seeing them working as a group in the meanest prison jobs – never a trade or kitchen job for blacks. 'Lump as many of the black bastards as you can in one cell. They're happier that way anyway.'

Maitland jail. Overcontrol, greater suppression of the prisoners' rights, more bullying of prisoners, and poisonous food slowly built tensions to riot proportions throughout the jails. I wrote a sixteen-page indictment of the vices of the guards and prison treatment and an eight-page outline of my case to try and get it re-examined. The screws found it and didn't like the idea. I got some more solitary and bread and water and a trip to Grafton jail.

Grafton. 'So you're a smart black bastard are ya? Well, we know how to handle black bastards up here – get your clothes off!' You strip your clothes off. 'Turn around, bend over!' They look intently up your arse. Some of them look for so long I'm sure they're queer. 'Straighten up!' They look into your mouth, your hair, your ears then belt you across the mouth with the baton, jab you in the kidneys. One screw steps back when he's a bit winded to let another have a go – four or five beating, pulling, twisting at you at once.

There were no newspapers, no radio, no talking to other prisoners except the three or four who worked with you in a little brick shed. You had to keep your eyes down when other intractable prisoners walked past to go into their workshop. You got so you actually laughed when the 'local' short term prisoners who were on softer treatment came up to the dreaded intractable yards to fill the water jugs or sweep the yard and quivered with fear at the guards. You got to questioning yourself when one of these 'sweepers' came across to fill a bucket of water. When curiosity got the better of him, he looked directly at us intractables, only to be knocked to the ground and kicked by the guard who screamed abuse at him for his audacity – the prisoner squirmed on the ground squealing with pain and fear. We laughed, 'Ya weak bastard.' We were being transformed into products of the system.

White society in this country hasn't changed all that much since the colonists first landed and began flogging the convicts. Remember your history books when an incident like that occurred and the Aboriginals who came up recoiled in horror, screaming frantically and throwing sticks at the soldiers and the flogger? Remember do you? It hasn't changed much. And no, you haven't grown in stature to match this country yet. You are still the alien, the outsider and only when you embrace the whole of this country, every sacred living thing upon it and in it and around it, will you grow and survive, because only those who love the land and love justice will ultimately hold the land.

CHESTER EAGLE

Chester Eagle (1933–) was born in Bendigo, Victoria,
and educated in Melbourne. A teacher, lecturer and
occasional reviewer, he has written several novels and
two autobiographies. This extract comes from *Mapping
the Paddocks* (1985) in which the young boy's
experience is partly shaped by his admiration for Don
Bradman.

♦ ♦ ♦ ♦

I asked Father if I would see Bradman bat. He said it depended on
how long the war lasted. If we didn't beat the Huns and the Japs
pretty soon he'd be too old to play again. He'd been invalided out of
the army, and it might take a while for cricket to get started after the
war. The good news was that it was England's turn to tour Australia, so if the great man did play another season, it would be in our
country; Father said he'd take me to see him. He was already on our
mantelpiece – a square photo, rounded at the corners, with a stylish,
printed autograph. And he could, in a rudimentary way, be seen in
action in tiny booklets of photos which you flicked with your

thumb so that the pictures replaced each other in rapid succession, showing a jerky but at least a moving image of Bradman executing the cover drive and, his specialty, the late cut.

Another approximation of reality was described to me by Father. Once the cable connections had been made with England, it was possible to send telegrammatic messages encoding the action of an over (six balls, in England) at Lords, the Oval, Old Trafford, Leeds or Manchester. Australian commentators, with a judicious admixture of pen tapped on table, or coconut shell, reconstructed the play for local listeners as if it were happening before their eyes. Father admired this illusion. We were very far away, but we were as good as the Poms. Bradman proved it.

When he was a boy, he'd thrown cricket balls at a single stump to improve his fielding. If his throw missed, he had further to chase. I did the same on a dusty plot beyond the kitchen fence. My wicket was a kerosene tin stacked on another kerosene tin. I rarely succeeded in hitting it, and wondered what made Bradman different. The ball was hard to find in the stubble on the other side of my pitch from the peppertrees, the dunny, and the pile of trunks and fence posts which was our woodheap. This was where chooks had their heads chopped off, and it regularly reminded Father to tell me of swaggies who, after offering to cut a pile of firewood, took their money and departed before the cheated housewife discovered that the carefully stacked pile of logs was hollow.

That was their illusion. Ours, after years of depression, was that the postwar world could be bright. This was an item of faith. On a cold September morning, Mother dressed me by the fire. 'We're at war with Germany,' she said; I knew the news was momentous but rode to school as on any other day, aware that though everything was familiar, some change had begun, too big for me to understand.

Years passed. An aerodrome was built in the next town. Troop trains thundered north. Newspapers showed arrows pressing bulges in the front lines of Egypt, Russia, France. American soldiers threw coins to admiring children in the streets of my dusty town. Irrigation came, and electricity. We got a fridge. My brother neared eighteen, and wanted to be a tail gunner; one afternoon, five years from the morning when she'd told me about the war, Mother came home from Finley, put the shopping basket in the kitchen and leaned her head on the refrigerator which gave us ice cream, now, in summer. She was crying. I stared. 'Travers wants to be a tail gunner,' she said, 'and I've just heard what happens to them. Tail gunners are killed more often than anyone else in the plane. They're such a mess they can't even get them out of the seat!'

I didn't want my brother killed, but to think about that required a different sort of imagination from the games I played in the dugout. My mother's distress was much more immediate. The war was a limitless horror.

Time passed. The Germans were defeated. The papers ran articles on the fitness of Bradman and the likelihood of his return. The Japs remained to be defeated. The Americans were pounding them with fleets of bombers, but they hadn't given in.

Then, when I was twelve, came the news. An atom bomb had been dropped on Hiroshima. No surrender had been received, but the Americans were waiting.

A city had been destroyed. I'd been to Melbourne, I knew what a city was, and a city had been destroyed. I walked to the window of our diningroom and stared down the avenue of peppertrees. The enormity of what had been done was beyond all words. Despite my fantasies of spies and destruction, I knew it was too much. War, made respectable by popular songs and newspaper articles, had gone too far. The tide needed to be reversed. I cannot remember my parents' reaction, nor neighbours' comments when they called, only the realization that the world had been taken past the point where it could get back. The war, which would soon end, would be leaving us high and dry above the waters that had produced Hammond, Larwood, Voce, Maurice Leyland, Eddie Paynter, Stan McCabe, Archie Jackson, Clarrie Grimmett and Victor Richardson. They were as dead as . . . no, the days that had produced them were as dead . . . as the dead of Hiroshima.

And a couple of days later we were able to say, as dead as the dead of Nagasaki.

Peace. Generals signed treaties with ceremonial pens. An Australian services team began to do battle with the Poms. The world was trying to resume. There were more articles about Bradman's health. He was fit, he was unfit. His back. His age. His form. Could he repeat in his late thirties the deeds of his youth? Could a champion whose zenith had been the double summer, English and Australian, of nineteen-thirty, shine in the summer of forty-six forty-seven?

He played, and Father took me to Melbourne. He'd made 187 in Brisbane, though the English writers said he was out at 21. The Englishmen lost by an innings. 234 in Sydney. The great man was more sedate than he'd been prewar, the papers said, but he was still the master. I awaited his magic. When a small man in an Australian blazer entered the arena with another figure in Marylebone Cricket Club colours (Father told me that prewar English amateurs used a different gate from the professionals), I found Hammond, light on his feet despite his weight, more noticeable than the Don. After crowd speculation as to who had won the toss, the Australian openers appeared. For the first time I heard the hush attending the first ball of a test. It was almost an hour before Bradman came to the wicket. He was padded, now, gloved, carrying a bat, and wearing the baggy green cap which was more natural, for me, than the stiff, jockey cap of England. To my surprise, Father, along with thousands of others, stood to clap. I had never dreamed that my shrewd, disbelieving Father was capable of hero worship, and I realized that someone he passionately believed in was making his way to the centre. Bradman walked more slowly as he approached the pitch. He took block, straightened, tugged his cap, acknowledged the applause, then bent over his bat. Bradman was where he belonged.

DAVID MALOUF

David Malouf (1934–) was born in Brisbane of
Lebanese and English parents. After graduating from
Queensland University he taught English in England
and at Sydney University. He has written novels,
poetry, and the libretto of the opera *Voss*. The
autobiographical novel *Johnno* (1975) uses two strongly
contrasting characters, like Johnston's *My Brother Jack*.
The autobiography *12 Edmondstone Street* (1985) deals
with his childhood, family and home in Brisbane, and
life as an expatriate writer in Italy.

◆ ◆ ◆ ◆

◆ *Johnno*

In winter Scarborough was just a fishing village at the end of the
line. In summer it was a vast encampment. In the early years of the
war, while hostilities were still confined to Europe, and the Royal

Navy, not to speak of Singapore, stood firmly between us and any threat of invasion, we had a caravan at Scarborough and would drive down on Friday evenings in our '27 Hup. There was a regular colony of campers on the strip of grass behind the beach and a whole gang of kids who played Donkey on the long wet sands when the tide was out or Cowboys and Indians in 'The Trees'. Johnno was one of them, and he had been a tearaway even then. One of those wiry, barefoot state-school kids that my mother preferred me not to play with and my father, I suppose, wanted me to be like.

Johnno was what my mother called bad company. 'Show me your company,' she would recite largely, 'and I'll tell you what you are.'

I didn't frankly know what I was and I preferred not to think of Johnno as 'my company', he wouldn't have had me anyway. But I lined up waiting to be called when they picked teams for Red Rover or Rounders, and slunk off quietly when it became obvious that I would be last. I tagged along when they went out on the dunes with a flashlight to find soldiers and their girls, catcalling along with the rest till someone appeared fumbling with his flybuttons and gave us money to get lost. The Americans arrived early in '42, and we went on frenchie hunts along the cliffs or round the Skating Rink at Redcliffe. You could find as many in a single afternoon these days as the white horses we counted, galloping about in sunstruck paddocks, as we drove down in the car; and I didn't let on that till recently I had thought they were some sort of fungus, hanging shiny and white from the twigs. But I never really belonged to the gangs. I was happiest at home under the tentflaps, reading my favourite Dumas and dreaming myself back into that marvellous Olden Days when people wore satin and spoke French and when everything that happened was History. I was very strong on history. Not the terrible history of our own misplaced continent, with Burke and Wills staggering off across the desert or Leichhardt coming to the end of a dotted line somewhere west of Quilpie – but the history that was recounted in the books I bought at Old Neds in Melbourne Street, huge closely printed Victorian volumes that told the story of the Fair Rosamund and the Wars of the Roses, with diagrams of the Plantaganet family branching out across two pages in marriages and remarriages more interesting than our own family's decent and regular line-up of uncles and aunts, and vastly more demanding of my schoolboy memory than the first four governors.

Australia was familiar and boring. Now was just days, and events in *The Courier-Mail* – even when those events were the Second World War. History was The Past. I had just missed out on it. There was nothing in our own little lives that was worth recording, nothing to distinguish one day of splashing about in the heavy, warm water inside the reef from the next. Only the appearance once of a turtle, stranded at the bottom of one of the red-soil cliffs. And an afternoon of panic, after Singapore had fallen at last and invasion wasn't at all improbable, when we saw what we thought was a Japanese sub lurking in the shallows – though it turned out later to be a petrol tank jettisoned from a passing plane. In the evening the lamp had to be pumped. In the morning there was water to be fetched, in a kerosene tin, from the tank at the top of the hill. Between there were just days. Nothing extraordinary happened.

♦

The rituals by which my own life was regulated it never occurred to me to doubt. They were so utterly reasonable. When I came in from school I changed out of my good things into a sweater and shorts; hung my uniform in the closet by the bed, put my socks in the washbasket, my shoes in the cleaning cabinet, and was allowed on the back verandah (but never never in the kitchen or any other part of the house itself) either a wedge of Cassie's date slice or two anzacs, with a tumbler of malted milk and an apple to clean my teeth. I didn't shout indoors; I never said 'she' (She was the cat's mother); and I never swore. If asked to do a message for a neighbour I never refused of course, but I never accepted payment either, no matter how strongly encouraged; not even an ice-cream out of the change. I ate my vegetables, even horrible silverbeet, without complaint; always washed my hands after the lavatory and never called a shilling a 'bob'. All these rules and regulations, I was convinced, not only trained you in the best behaviour, they also taught you discipline, and discipline was character-building. Like never taking the day off school unless you were really ill ('Come on now,' my mother would say brightly at the first sign of a complaint, 'we're not Catholics today, we're Christian Scientists – and there's nothing the matter with us!'). Or skipping the dentist. Or the silverbeet. Doing what you didn't like doing gave you moral backbone, as silverbeet gave you muscle and all that drilling at the dentist's gave you perfect teeth. Moral backbone was what prevented people, when they grew up, from drinking and gambling and getting into debt. Children who lacked discipline grew up spineless and had false teeth.

I don't know when all this came to seem to me anything less than the gospel truth. Or what part Johnno, with his wildness and not the sign of a filling, had to do with my growing scepticism, my defection from the dogma that if what you *didn't* like doing was good for you what you *did* like doing was not.

When I think of myself at thirteen I see a neat, darkly serious, well-brought-up little figure with a straight tie knotted in the conventional manner (my father abominated the Windsor knot), clean nails that I was prevented from biting with bitter aloes, a clear left-hand parting, shirts that Cassie insisted on starching till they were so stiff I could barely move in them, and the air of someone who is too well pleased with himself to be true. I wasn't true, of course. I had too many secrets. One of them was a sense of humour (though I had found as yet no good use for it) and the other was the shrewd suspicion, based on irrefutable personal evidence, that there was more going on under people's clean, well-brushed clothes than the building of muscle by silverbeet. I had begun, secretly, to believe some things and disbelieve others, and I was overwhelmed by the discovery that I had a choice. I was still strong enough on Mister Menzies, Commonwealth Savings Bonds, Stromberg Carlson radiograms, and something I had picked up from Band of Hope meetings on the beach at Scarborough, that even a slave is free under the British flag. But I had lost all faith in Santa Claus (years ago), the power of peroxide in the treatment of warts, was beginning to be shaky about the Catholic Church, and had freed myself, by frequent scientific experimentation, of the absurd notion that touching myself 'down there' would make it fall off – though I couldn't entirely discount the possibility, at some later date, of going blind.

♦

I had fallen heavily in my last year for a Somerville House girl called Roseanne Staples, who wore nylon stockings that shifted their lights like mother of pearl and was a G.P.S. diving champion. All one Wednesday at Moss's, and again the next, we danced dreamily under the rafters and I took her afterwards for mint juleps or malteds at the Pig 'n Whistle, a milk bar at the top of town that had been a favourite pick-up place for American soldiers and retained something of its wartime glamour and notoriety. It was regarded as daring and I was out to impress. When the waitress, who looked as if she might remember the place in the old days, slid our milk-shakes down the glass-topped counter, she winked in the direction of the innocent Roseanne and whispered: 'There y'are love. That'll put lead in yer pencil.' I could hardly wait for the week to pass. But on the third Wednesday, as we went whirling across the floor in what seemed to be a most accomplished manner, Roseanne, with a casualness that astonishes me even today, it was so low-keyed, so undramatic, pronounced the words that put an end to our affair, pfft! just like that, and changed the course of my life. Looking straight over my shoulder, in the most neutral tones: 'If there's one thing I can't stand,' said Roseanne Staples, slowly, 'it's boys who don't pivot.'

I was thunderstruck. The pivot – that little sidestep and pass at the corner of the floor that I had never quite got the knack of, it seemed so silly, hardly worth worrying about. I smiled wanly and guided her through the rest of the set, closing my eyes and swallowing hard as we approached the corners and wishing Moss's was triangular. Four corners was suddenly more than I could bear. Back safe among the boys I waited for something less subtle, like a Gipsy Tap.

So much then for the test of manhood. There were things they hadn't warned us of, pitfalls in the corners of rooms, girls who would expect you to pivot and perform God knows what prodigies. There was also the Cold War, the Cobalt Bomb, pre-marital intercourse, the death of God – it was a battlefield, as the headmaster had warned us, and I thought with envy of all those old boys whose names were picked out in gold on the honour-boards, lying safe in some corner of a foreign field that would be forever Wynnum or Coorparoo. Ours was to be a quiet generation. It was the little tests that would break us (not forgetting the wives and mothers) and there was no one to help us through.

♦ *12 Edmondstone Street*

My father felt it. As we walked away he was deeply silent. Our moment together was over. What was it that touched him? Was he thinking of a night, three years before, when the Commonwealth Police had arrested his father as an enemy alien?

My grandfather came to Brisbane from Lebanon in the 1880s; though in those days of course, when Australia was still unfederated, a parcel of rival states, Lebanon had no existence except in the mind of a few patriots. It was part of greater Syria; itself then a province of the great, sick Empire of the Turks. My grandfather had fled his homeland in the wake of a decade of massacres. Like other Lebanese Christians, he had sorrowfully turned his back on the Old Country and started life all over again in the New World.

His choice of Australia was an arbitrary one. No one knows why he made it. He might equally have gone to Boston or to Sao Paolo in Brazil. But the choice, once made, was binding. My father and the rest of us were Australians now. That was that. After Federation, in the purely notional view of these things that was practised by the immigration authorities, greater Syria (as opposed to Egypt and Turkey proper) was declared white – but only the Christian inhabitants of it, a set of official decisions, in the matter of boundary and distinction, that it was better not to question. My father's right to be an Australian, like any Scotsman's for example, was guaran-

teed by this purely notional view – that is, officially. The rest he had
to establish for himself; most often with his fists. But my grandfather, by failing to get himself naturalised, remained an alien. At
first a Syrian, later a Lebanese. And when Lebanon, as a depen-
dency of France, declared for Vichy rather than the Free French, he
became an enemy as well.

He was too old, at more than eighty, to be much concerned by
any of this, and did not understand perhaps how a political decision
made on the other side of the world had changed his status, after so
long, on this one. He took the bag my aunts packed for him and
went. It was my father who was, in his quiet way – what? – shaken,
angered, disillusioned?

The authorities – that is, the decent local representatives – soon
recognised the absurdity of the thing and my grandfather was released: on personal grounds. My father never told us how he had
managed it, or what happened, what he *felt*, when he went to fetch
his father home. If it changed anything for him, the colour of his
own history for example, he did not reveal it. It was just another of
the things he kept to himself and buried. Like the language. He
must, I understood later, have grown up speaking Arabic as well as
he spoke Australian; his parents spoke little else. But I never heard
him utter a word of it or give any indication that he understood. It
went on as a whole layer of his experience, of his understanding and
feeling for things, of alternative being, that could never be expressed. It too was part of the shyness between us.

CHARLES PERKINS

Charles Nelson Perkins (1936–) was born in Alice
Springs, went to school in Adelaide and took a degree
at Sydney University. He has held senior posts in the
Department of Aboriginal Affairs and has been very
active in promoting the interests of Aborigines.
A Bastard Like Me (1975) is an autobiography with an
angry message.

◆ ◆ ◆ ◆

I was born into that divided atmosphere and lived in it until I was
about ten. We moved into Alice Springs after leaving the settlement
at the telegraph station. We lived in a hut in Alice Springs. It was a
mud hut with straw on the top. It was the ugliest little building in
Alice. We stayed there for only a short period of time. They moved
us out because no Aborigines were allowed to live in Alice Springs.
We were moved to a place they call Rainbow Town where all the
Aboriginal people were living. All the skin colours gave Rainbow
Town its name. The shacks were called the Cottages and the town
was built especially for Aborigines, about a mile outside of Alice

Springs. It is all demolished now and new housing is up there.

We had to stay there. We were not allowed in Alice Springs after dark, only for the pictures on Saturday night, the same old pattern. That rule has relaxed a little over the years because there are so many of us. We have become economically viable, to use a European phrase. But before this the idea was simple: 'Keep the streets clean of Aborigines!' That was the way we had to live – as scum, the unwanted.

I was ten when I became fully conscious, for the first time, that we were separate, cut off physically and socially from the rest of the town, and back on the reserve. We were just not allowed in town unless it was for a specific reason. The older people were taken in for work and brought out again. School was on the reserve itself. It was optional if you went or not.

The only thing that I can remember about school is that it was pretty crude and rude. The teachers were always fighting with the students. I can remember many occasions when a white teacher was chased around the room by some burly Aboriginal bloke for one reason or another. I don't suppose the teachers lasted very long after an experience like that. I don't think the children were inclined to learn anything anyhow.

We were segregated in this way and we took our orders from the police. They controlled our lives. They were kind or hard on us as they saw fit. The white bosses on the reserve were not too bad really, but they had limited vision and operated a very restricted system.

I more or less went along with it all. I was still a child. Nevertheless, I always had the feeling that there was a gap, something missing in me. I think a lot of part-Aborigines feel that there is something wrong, something missing in them, and that the pieces are not fitting into place. I have always felt this all my life and it has probably been the thing that has stimulated me to be dissatisfied with most things.

Right through my life I have never been really satisfied with anything. Everything to me has been not as I think it should be. I think this has been a good thing in some ways. It has made me attempt to achieve things that other Aboriginal people would normally consider unobtainable. I was motivated by the feeling that something was wrong in my early life. I often thought, for example, 'Why should that old lady, my black grandmother, be across the fence and not talk to me? Why can't I talk to her? Why can't she be with us? Why isn't she living with us?' I was not able to find the answers at that time, but these things kept bugging me right through my life.

Even when I was sent down to Adelaide for my schooling, there was something in my mind telling me, 'It's not right.' I think this has been the great tragedy in my life, apart from a few other things, that I developed a resentment about. Also, the thing that has been missing from my life and made me feel an incomplete person, is the fact of not having that normal family association that I should have had. I think if I had had that, it would have made me perhaps a better man in many ways, a more complete man. I think I would have been able to operate better. I would have had more confidence in society and less bitterness.

MARY ROSE LIVERANI

Mary Rose Liverani (1939–) was born in Glasgow and
came to Australia aged thirteen when her family
migrated to Wollongong, New South Wales. *The
Winter Sparrows: Growing Up in Scotland and Australia*
(1975) recounts her experiences in the Glasgow slums
and her life in Australia until she left school. It is a
classic in migrant literature.

◆ ◆ ◆ ◆

This dreary beginning at Gullawobblong High, and the situations I
encountered that day, the problems inherent in them, set me to the
task of evolving a whole set of new responses in the search for
which I was forced to ask myself, what will I be? whereas those
around me kept quizzing, what will you do when you leave
school?

First, there was the confrontation with a new kind of dialogue.

'Sorry about interrupting you, Mrs Mahon,' the Deputy said,
drawing me behind him into the classroom. 'I've got a new wee

girlie for you. A lass from Glasgow.' He turned to the faces above the desks. 'Good morning, one bee.'

His name, it seemed, was Mr Whittle, and the name must be used when saluting him. Miss and Sir were no longer acceptable titles. If you said: excuse me, Miss, you would hear giggles and if the lady were married she would react indignantly: MRS Brown, if you please.

'This is Mary Lavery. She's from Scotland.' Evidently he felt it necessary to locate Glasgow. 'She's probably feeling very strange.' This was an effort of imagination I wasn't often to encounter at school. The Deputy squeezed my arm. 'How long have you been out, lass?'

'A week, sir.'

'Uh huh. Well, you'll find this class a particularly nice lot of boys and girls who'll be only too pleased to help you settle in. You'll be an Aussie before you can say Robert Burns.' This statement contained a number of horrific assumptions that weren't immediately apparent to me, though it didn't take too long to work them out.

First, niceness is a virtue preceding all others. To be nice is better than being stimulating, or analytical, or witty. You must always say 'How are you', or 'how are you going,' nicely, but without expecting an answer. If some fool starts to tell you how he is, keep smiling but walk off and leave him with his jaw dropping, or keep smiling and stare at his right ear lobe. Then he will dry up and smile nicely, asking you how you are.

Second, people always want to settle, like old hulks settling into the mud. People don't crave drama or excitement or uncertainty. Make sure they set hard.

Third, people always want to be Australian.

If you aren't you can get by with a particular note of apology. 'I'm not yet, but I'm doing my best.'

The Deputy, his warm welcome at an end, spied me out a seat and directed me to it.

'There you are. There's a seat beside Wendy. She's a bit of a yakker, so don't let yourself be tempted.'

The girl he was portraying giggled and cooed:

'Oh, Mr Whittle, that's defamation of character. I'm as dumb as a mummy.'

All the class laughed at this, and the Deputy smiled benignly.

'Well, there's someone awfully like you, sitting in your seat, who never takes a breath.'

He looked across at the teacher, for support.

'Isn't that right, Mrs Mahon?'

It was, evidently. I sat down amid the confusion of laughter and noisy chat that erupted suddenly in the room, and the Deputy left. Another rule: seek out humour in the banal or you will be isolated from the fellowship of laughter.

'That will do, one bee.' The teacher was tightening her mouth. Little lines sprouted from her top lip. The Deputy had gone, leaving not one reverberation of his wit. 'We must get this prose finished or there will be no time for revision before the exams.'

During the lesson, Wendy began a non-stop monologue to which I responded with nods of the head. So you're Scottish. I'm English, from Kent. We came out in 1950. Have you done French? She's a real drip, Mrs Mahon. Always tired. All the teachers are, except Mr Whittle. He teaches maths. I'm going to a private school next year. Mum and Dad think this school's too rough. We have sport every Wednesday. That's today. It's compulsory. Do you like sport? You can choose between swimming, softball and tennis. I play tennis. Of course you wouldn't have your costume here. Swimmers, the Australians call them. So you'll probably have to play softball. How did you do at school in Scotland? Are you any good at French?

I was trying to remember the word for mourning. I'd seen it somewhere.

'Oh, all right,' I whispered. Was she never going to shut up? *Le deuil*, that was it. This passage was from *Jean Christophe*.

'Right, class, get on with it.' Mrs Mahon dropped her chalk into the groove under the board and moved sideways to her desk. 'If you don't get it finished before the bell goes, you can finish it for homework.'

'Aw geez, you're tough,' someone groaned.

Colloquial language and familiarity of tone are permissible when speaking to the teacher. A formal mode of approach will only make him ill at ease and he will avoid your eye. He might even think you are being insolent. You are not to exalt him. He doesn't think he is worth it. To obey him will be enough. It will establish the difference between you.

I couldn't remember the French for some words, so I left blanks and concentrated on the verb endings. When I lifted my head, I saw the teacher watching me. Blast. I've caught her eye. Now she's coming to examine my work. She's got a queer hair style. Flat to the head. I really hate that, especially when it's grey. Dreary. And those loose little curls all round the bottom. Pin curls, not very well formed, and straight bits poking out. Wonder why she wears such a low-necked dress when her skin's all shrivelled at the front?

The teacher wrote in the missing words for me and dangled her pen above each verb like a divining rod, seeking out the wrong inflections. Apparently satisfied there were none, she ticked the passage and initialled it. Then, in an embarrassingly loud voice that got the attention of the class, she said: 'Very good, girlie. I can see we won't have any problems with you.'

You don't see much then, do you?

Wendy stiffened beside me. Her whisper, despite its softness, was faintly disapproving.

'Are you a brain or something?'

It sounded like: Are you a Catholic?

Careful. 'Heavens, no. I've read some of the book that passage is from.'

'What! In French?'

Her whisper vanished in a squeak.

'Well, actually, our teacher read it to us.'

How is she taking it?

'Aw, you were lucky, then?'

Ah that was it. Luck, luck. I grinned with relief. 'Yes, I was, wasn't I?'

◆

That first night, however, problems other than the absence of sewerage dominated our conversation. As Susan had pointed out, we had no beds, except for the big brass and iron frame left by the previous tenant. So, after tea, which was laid out on a wooden board meant to cover the laundry sinks, we piled all our coats and blankets together and slept on the floors, excited by the novelty of the situation. Where on earth were we to get beds and chairs? There weren't enough blankets to go round when we had to use some to lie on. We didn't even have the hire purchase deposit, for new beds would cost a fortune.

'Damned lucky it's summer,' I heard my mother growling at my father. He was wandering around in an aimless sort of way, at a loss to know what to do. About five o'clock, the second afternoon, there was a knock at our front door and we all rushed to open it. My mother squeezed to the front and we split up on both sides of her to examine the woman standing there. She was just finishing off a cigarette, drawing avidly at the last of the dout before flicking it onto the verandah and screwing her heel into it. We waited for about five minutes while she coughed, holding her head between her hands. Her hair was yellow and frizzy.

'Yes?' my mother asked, finally, when the coughing stopped.

The woman's voice was deep, and rusty, crackling like static.

'G'day. Doreen Glim's me name. Live across the street. Heard from your little fella you're a bit short of beds. Just remembered I've got one under the house. Used to be me and Fred's before we got our new suite. It's no good to us. Might do till you get something better.'

She waited expectantly, a faint smile fretting her reddish pancake makeup with infinities of hairline cracks. Her eyes, half closed but missing nothing, looked behind us. Before my mother could answer, she went on:

'If your husband's home, maybe he and Fred can carry it over – after dark.'

Pride and necessity fought each other across my mother's face. She was furious and glad. After a minute's thought, she nodded her head and held the door open wide.

'Come in, Mrs Glim.'

'Doreen.'

'It's true we havenae any beds. We've only just moved across from the migrant hostel. Who was it told ye, did ye say?'

'Me. Ah did, Mammy,' Jackie spoke up proudly. 'Ah told all the kids we were sleeping on the floor. They said they were going tae ask their mothers if they could too.'

He was going to get a slap afterwards, blabbing our affairs outside. Susan pinched his arm as soon as the woman had gone.

'You're a right big mouth!'

His slap was postponed till later, however, for there was another knock at the door. Another neighbour. With another bed. And a table. And chairs. And a wardrobe. All evening long. And curtains. Some of the kids who had been watching us from the fence slunk in behind their parents and eyed us cagily before casting their beadies into the far-flung corners of our fibro realm. And not even hiding what they were doing. Talk about ignorant! We stared back at them, wooden faced, blocking off their vision where it was practicable.

When they had all gone, the house was full of dust and aglitter with alien cobwebs, the floorboards black from tramping feet. We were to sleep on the floor again that night, my mother decided, until she scrubbed the furniture down with lysol. She was terrified of bugs. Someone had given us a huge whitewood table. We covered it with newspaper and had our dinner from it, sitting on fruit boxes.

'Well, ye cannae say they've no' decent people.' That was my father. 'There's no' too many that'll come tae your door like that tae gie ye things. They've got big hearts, Australians.'

My mother agreed with him. 'Aye, they're good people.'

We sat round the table with our heads bowed, silently offering gratitude for our kind neighbours. They were hospitable too. The next night, Mrs Glim appeared again, devouring her cigarette, her eyes slitted against the smoke.

'C'mon over and have a drink with me and Fred. Go on,' she pressed, as she saw my mother getting ready to refuse. 'It'll do you good. And me and Fred are glad o' the company.'

So my mother and father went and returned about an hour later.

'What did ye do, Mammy?' I asked her. 'What did ye talk aboot?'

'Och, we had a couple o' glasses o' beer. Ah cannae mind what we talked aboot, tae tell ye the truth. They've got two girls aboot your ages and the man's a contract miner.'

That night, after setting the table for supper, I went outside onto the front path. It was nine o'clock. I looked up at the sky, speechless with admiration for its sumptuosity, a rich black fabric shot through with flashing ice. What I liked best about the stars was their distance. They were far out of touch. In Scotland, the sky pressed down upon you like a coolie hat, restricting your vision. I held my head up until I got a crick in my neck and then I glanced up and down the street. It was completely silent. Not a light was on in any house.

I went back inside, to Margaret, who was pouring tea in the kitchen.

'People go tae bed here, awfully early. There's nobody up in the street.'

'They cannae have much tae say to each other,' she said. And added, after a moment's reflection: 'Maybe their dreams are exciting and they rush tae them as soon as they can.'

People continued to be helpful and pleasant. They brought forks, spades, scissors and scythes so that we could cut down the paspalum and plant vegetables. We got blisters from wielding the scythes. My mother looked down on my father one afternoon, when he was bent over, his face purple with exertion. He needed a special scythe for he was left-handed.

'That's the right implement ye've got in your hand,' she called to him. 'A' ye need now is a hammer.'

My father just grinned.

'Never misses an opportunity, does she?'

The neighbours supervised our work with friendly approval, expressing appreciation as my father, in his stolid and unhurried way, turned over sod after sod, building the earth up in a series of burial plots, so it seemed. It's more than the abos ever did. Bunch o' no hopers they were. Drinking all the time. Never even mowed the lawn. Would you like a few tomato plants, morning glories, a bit of pig face? Here, have a few plums. Each morning for weeks and weeks, while conflict at the pit continually tapped my father's pay packet, a bucket of vegetables was deposited on our side of the fence by our pensioner neighbour. It wasn't always easy to thank him. He seemed to work in his garden when we were elsewhere. On the rare occasions that we managed to catch him, he listened sweetly to our professions of gratitude and smiled over our shoulders, nodding his head slightly.

'Uh huh.'

'They're such nice people,' my mother kept saying. You had to balk at that fact. There was no going past it or around it. Yet I didn't like them. I was ill at ease and resentful that I had to owe them gratitude. It was too much effort, the strain of smiling constantly, of agreeing all the time, anxiously agreeing, of saying: really? Is that so? Or, good gracious, imagine that, or I can hardly believe it. But they were so vulnerable nothing could induce you to tackle them. It would be offensive to question them, to imply you thought they were fools, or, at best, that their arguments were invalid. Some instinct warned us to pander to them and our jaws ached permanently from grinning. In the beginning, apart from the old pensioner, it was difficult to differentiate one from the other, for their speeches were all formulaic, and the set phrases were punctuated with niggling little irruptions of laughter that made you drop your eyes. It took time to work out that words should be discarded as identity markers.

CLIVE JAMES

Clive James (1939–) was born and educated in Sydney.
He edited *Honi Soit*, the Sydney University newspaper
and worked briefly for the *Sydney Morning Herald*
before completing a second degree at Cambridge and
achieving enormous success as a journalist, critic, and
TV personality. He has published two volumes of
autobiography: *Unreliable Memoirs* (1980) which covers
his Australian years and *Falling Towards England*
(1985).

♦ ♦ ♦ ♦

I was born in 1939. The other big event of that year was the out-
break of the Second World War, but for the moment that did not
affect me. Sydney in those days had all of its present attractions and
few of the drawbacks. You can see it glittering in the background of
the few photographs in which my father and I are together. Stocky
was the word for me. Handsome was the word for him. Without
firing a shot, the Japanese succeeded in extricating him from my
clutches. Although a man of humble birth and restricted education,
he was smart enough to see that there would be war in the Pacific.
Believing that Australia should be ready, he joined up. That was

how he came to be in Malaya at the crucial moment. He was at Parit Sulong bridge on the day when a lot of senior officers at last found out what their troops had guessed long before – that the Japanese army was better led and better equipped than anything we had to pit against it. After the battle my father walked all the way south to Singapore and arrived just in time for the surrender. If he had waited to be conscripted, he might have been sent to the Western Desert and spent a relatively happy few months fighting the kind of Germans whose essential decency was later to be portrayed on the screen by James Mason and Marlon Brando. As it was, he drew the short straw.

This isn't the place to tell the story of my mother and father – a story which was by no means over, even though they never saw one another again. I could get a lot of mileage out of describing how the good-looking young mechanic wooed and won the pretty girl who left school at fourteen and worked as an upholsterer at General Motors Holden. How the Depression kept them so poor that they had to wait years to get married and have me. How fate was cruel to both of them beyond measure. But it would be untrue to them. It was thirty years or more before I even began to consider what my parents must have meant to each other. Before that I hardly gave them a thought, except as vague occurrences on the outskirts of a solipsistic universe. I can't remember my father at all. I can remember my mother only through a child's eyes. I don't know which fact is the sadder.

Anyway, my mother let our little house in Kogarah and we went to stay with my Aunt Dot in Jannali, another half hour down the Illawarra line. This move was made on the advice of my father, who assumed that the centre of Sydney would be flattened by Japanese bombs about two hours after the whistle blew. The assumption proved to be ill-founded, but the side effects were beneficial, since Jannali was a perfect spot to grow up in. There were only a dozen or so streets in the whole area. Only one of them was paved. The railway line ran through a cutting somewhere in the middle. Everything else was bush.

♦

After school and at weekends boys came from all over the district to race on the Sunbeam Avenue footpaths. There would be twenty or thirty carts, two-thirds of them with ball-races. The noise was indescribable. It sounded like the Battle of Britain going on in somebody's bathroom. There would be about half an hour's racing before the police came. Residents often took the law into their own hands, hosing the grim-faced riders as they went shrieking by. Sunbeam Avenue ran parallel to Margaret Street but it started higher and lasted longer. Carts racing down the footpaths on the far side had a straight run of about a quarter of a mile all the way to the park. Emitting shock-waves of sound, the ball-race carts would attain such speeds that it was impossible for the rider to get off. All he could do was to crash reasonably gently when he got to the end. Carts racing down the footpath on the near side could go only half as far, although very nearly as fast, before being faced with a right-angle turn into Irene Street. Here a pram-wheeled cart like mine could demonstrate its sole advantage. The traction of the rubber tyres made it possible to negotiate the corner in some style. I developed a histrionic lean-over of the body and slide of the back wheels which got me around the corner unscathed, leaving black smoking trails of burnt rubber. Mastery of this trick saved me from being relegated to the ranks of the little kids, than which there was no worse fate. I had come to depend on being thought of as a big kid. Luckily only the outstanding ball-race drivers could match my fancy turn into Irene Street. Others slid straight on with a yelp of metal and a shower of sparks, braining themselves on the asphalt road. One driver scalped himself under a bread van.

The Irene Street corner was made doubly perilous by Mrs Branthwaite's poppies. Mrs Branthwaite inhabited the house on the corner. She was a known witch whom we often persecuted after dark by throwing gravel on her roof. It was widely believed she poisoned cats. Certainly she was a great ringer-up of the police. In retrospect I can see that she could hardly be blamed for this, but her behaviour seemed at the time like irrational hatred of children. She was a renowned gardener. Her front yard was like the cover of a seed catalogue. Extending her empire, she had flower beds even on her two front strips, one on the Sunbeam Avenue side and the other on the Irene Street side – i.e., on both outside edges of the famous corner. The flower beds held the area's best collection of poppies. She had been known to phone the police if even one of these was illicitly picked.

At the time I am talking about, Mrs Branthwaite's poppies were all in bloom. It was essential to make the turn without hurting a single hair of a poppy's head, otherwise the old lady would probably drop the telephone and come out shooting. Usually, when the poppies were in bloom, nobody dared make the turn. I did – not out of courage, but because in my ponderous cart there was no real danger of going wrong. The daredevil leanings-over and the dramatic skids were just icing on the cake.

I should have left it at that, but got ambitious. One Saturday afternoon when there was a particularly large turn-out, I got sick of watching the ball-race carts howling to glory down the far side. I organised the slower carts like my own into a train. Every cart except mine was deprived of its front axle and loosely bolted to the cart in front. The whole assembly was about a dozen carts long, with a big box cart at the back. This back cart I dubbed the chuck-wagon, using terminology I had picked up from the Hopalong Cassidy serial at the pictures. I was the only one alone on his cart. Behind me there were two or even three to every cart until you got to the chuck-wagon, which was crammed full of little kids, some of them so small that they were holding toy koalas and sucking dummies.

From its very first run down the far side, my super-cart was a triumph. Even the adults who had been hosing us called their families out to marvel as we went steaming by. On the supercart's next run there was still more to admire, since even the top-flight ball-race riders had demanded to have their vehicles built into it, thereby heightening its tone, swelling its passenger list, and multiplying its already impressive output of decibels. Once again I should have left well alone. The thing was already famous. It had everything but a dining car. Why did I ever suggest that we should transfer it to the near side and try the Irene Street turn?

With so much inertia the super-cart started slowly, but it accelerated like a piano falling out of a window. Long before we reached the turn I realised that there had been a serious miscalculation. The miscalculation was all mine, of course. Sir Isaac Newton would have got it right. It was too late to do anything except pray. Leaning into the turn, I skidded my own cart safely around in the usual way. The next few segments followed me, but with each segment describing an arc of slightly larger radius than the one in front. First gradually, then with stunning finality, the monster lashed its enormous tail.

The air was full of flying ball-bearings, bits of wood, big kids, little kids, koalas and dummies. Most disastrously of all, it was also full of poppy petals. Not a bloom escaped the scythe. Those of us who could still run scattered to the winds, dragging our wounded with us. The police spent hours visiting all the parents in the district, warning them that the billycart era was definitely over. It was a police car that took Mrs Branthwaite away. There was no point waiting for the ambulance. She could walk all right. It was just that she couldn't talk. She stared straight ahead, her mouth slightly open.

♦

In retrospect it seems incredible even to me that I had come so far and remained so ignorant. It was not just that I was nowhere compared with an English sixth-former or an American prep school graduate. I was nowhere compared even with my fellow Hurstville alumni who had gone to Sydney High. When I met Elstub on the train he was reading *The Age of Anxiety* and I was reading *Diving to Adventure*. Knowing nothing, I scarcely suspected what I was missing. Barely realising what a university was, I looked forward to it as something vague on an indeterminate horizon. The immediate task was to survive as an office boy in the L. J. Hooker organisation, my first proper job. In my senior high school years I had tried several different jobs during the school holidays. The most disastrous was as a shop assistant in Coles, where I rapidly discovered that I was incapable of dealing with impatient customers without becoming flustered. Merely to discover that the anodised aluminium tray I was supposed to wrap was wider than the wrapping paper was enough to set me darting about distractedly in search of wider paper or a narrower anodised aluminium tray. In just such a frenzy I ran into a display stand on which were carefully arranged hundreds of cut glass bowls, dishes and plates. The stuff proved to be amazingly durable, which raised questions about the composition of the glass. Instead of shattering, it bounced. But it bounced everywhere, and before the last piece had stopped rolling I was on my way home. I had a similar job in Herb Horsfield's Hobby House, but rather than sell wind-up toys to wind-up customers I retreated into the toilet and read *The Caine Mutiny*. When Herb finally realised that he was making no sales at all when I was in charge he reluctantly opened discussions about terms of separation. He quite liked me, which was foolish of him in the circumstances.

♦

Between second and third years I tried to recoup my position in the parental eye by getting a job in the long vacation. I was accepted as a trainee bus conductor. The buses were green Leyland diesels operating out of Tempe depot. The easy routes went overland to places like Bexley and Drummoyne. The difficult routes went through the city. I found the job fiercely demanding even on a short route with a total of about two dozen passengers. I pulled the wrong tickets, forgot the change, and wrote up my log at the end of each trip in a way that drew hollow laughter from the inspectors. The inspectors were called Kellies, after Ned Kelly, and were likely to swoop at any time. A conductor with twenty years' service could be dismissed if a Kelly caught him accepting money without pulling a ticket. If a hurrying passenger pressed the fare into your hand as he leapt out of the back door, it was wise to tear a ticket and throw it out after him. There might be a plain-clothes Kelly following in an un-marked car.

Days of fatigue and panic taught me all over again that I am very bad at what I am not good at. We worked a split shift with four hours off in the middle of the day. Effectively this meant that we were on the job twelve hours a day, since there was nothing else to do with the four hours off except hang around the depot. I got so tired I used to sleep the whole four hours on a bench in the billiard room. Once I conked out with a lighted Rothmans in my hand. I dreamed of a bushfire burning down Jannali school with Miss Turnbull still inside it. I woke to face a cloud of smoke. The whole front of my shirt had burned away. The billiard room was full of conductors and drivers who had been placing bets on when I would wake up. The white nylon singlet I had been wearing under the shirt was scorched the colour of strong tea.

I lasted about three weeks all told, which meant that I hardly got past probation. The routes through town were more than the mind could stand even in the off-peak hours. In peak hours the scene was Dantesque. All the buses from our depot and every other depot would be crawling nose to tail through town while the entire working population of Sydney fought to get aboard. It was hot that summer: 100° Fahrenheit every day. Inside the bus it was 30° hotter still. Hammering up Pitt Street in the solid traffic at about ten miles an hour, the bus was like the Black Hole of Calcutta on wheels. It was so jammed inside that my feet weren't touching the floor. I couldn't blink the sweat out of my eyes. There was no hope of collecting any fares. At each stop it was all I could do to reach the bell-push that signalled the driver to close the automatic doors and get going. I had no way of telling whether anybody had managed to get off or on. My one object was to get that bus up Pitt Street. Passengers fainted and just hung there – there was nowhere for them to fall. The air tasted as if it had just been squirted out of the safety valve of a pressure cooker full of cabbage.

In those circumstances I was scarcely to blame. I didn't even know where we were, but I guessed we were at the stop just before Market Street. I pressed the bell, the doors puffed closed, and the bus surged forward. There were shouts and yells from down the back, but I thought they were the angry cries of passengers who had not got on. Too slowly I realised that they were emanating from within the bus. The back set of automatic doors had closed around an old lady's neck as she was getting on. Her head, wearing a black veiled hat decorated with wax fruit, was inside the bus. The rest of her, carrying a shopping bag with each hand, was outside. I knew none of this at the time. When I at last cottoned on to the fact that something untoward was happening and signalled the driver to stop, he crashed to a halt and opened the automatic doors, whereupon the woman dropped to the road. She was very nice about it. Perhaps the experience had temporarily dislocated her mind. Anyway, she apologised to me for causing so much trouble. Unfortunately the car just behind turned out to be full of Kellies. Since it would have made headlines if a university student had been thrown off the buses for half-guillotining a woman of advanced years, I was given the opportunity to leave quietly. Once again this failed to coincide with my own plans only in the sense that I had already resigned. In fact I had made my decision at about the same time as the old lady hit the ground.

BARBARA HANRAHAN

Barbara Hanrahan (1939–) was born in Adelaide
where, her father having died when she was barely a
year old, she lived in an all-female house with her
mother, grandmother and mongoloid great-aunt. She
studied art in Adelaide and London and is a painter
and printmaker. *The Scent of Eucalyptus* (1973) evokes
her Adelaide childhood, while *Kewpie Doll* (1984)
focuses on her life as art student. Described by her
publishers as novels, both are clearly autobiographical.

◆ ◆ ◆ ◆

◆ *The Scent of Eucalyptus*

(The journey to the lavatory is perilous. We approach it cautiously –
in pairs: my grandmother and great-aunt, my mother and I.)
   My mother lighted our way with matches; marking our path with

a sooty trail. She seemed unaware that the shrivelled ends betrayed us, winced as I nudged her; burned her fingers. In the pool of shadow by the shed still charred from the fire, already long ago, I saw my enemy: pigtailed Chinaman – silent one who pounces. Creepy-creepy. I held my breath – tiptoed to confuse; counted the encroaching trees to calm the pigeon in my chest: furry-fingered fig, green-gloved peach, apricot and orange, quince with blotting-paper stars.

We were there.

The lavatory was different in the day-time. In the hide-and-seek summer we cried 'barleys' and collapsed on the seat in turn – heart pounding, eyes sparkling – pumping out the pee and shit as fast as we could; longing to be gone – to creep through the soursobs, breathe in the crackling blueness of the sky. Carol told Elvio, the Italian boy, to come in too – there was nothing to see but her skirt. When we were thirsty, and the tap was too far, we pulled the chain and drank from cupped hands. We had books we hid on the cistern shelf.

At night it was cosy inside: the door latched, the Chinaman vanquished, my mother close, spicy smell. There was no light-switch but the dark was friendly. I lifted the wooden lid – one last ritual to go through: listened for the mole; he was there, but he was cunning. Once I felt his moist snout up my bottom; once, through the open door, I saw a bird – an albatross, a snow goose. I made a poem.

At night the lavatory became a confessional booth, an altar to the past. My mother told me about my father. She could not see me as she puffed at the cigarette Nan did not like her to smoke in the house. I began to cry.

◆

I am a city child. At night I am lulled to sleep by the owl-hoot of last trains; see the cold lights of planes stub the stars. By day I am bound by the fickle winks of amber, green, and red at corners; walk to school over earth I cannot see beneath a concrete crust.

I see the earth spinning like an aniseed ball in space – covered with a brittle casing of mortar; hammered by a ceaseless rain of cigarette packets, sweet papers, chewing-gum, dog shit, and gobs of yellow phlegm. This is my nightmare – when the noise of cars crowds out the nightjar; when I am strangled by telegraph wires, smothered by the gas-works' stench.

Yet there are rainbow patches in my concrete quilt. And at night in my sleepout, perched between the cement verandah and the chocolate earth, I hear the train whistles blend with the cries of cats; and sleep to the scent of stocks and lilies nurtured by the moon. I wake to a chorus of roosters, and the derisive hoot of an unlikely kookaburra; and the eye of the sun mocks the tinsel memory of the traffic lights.

I am a city child. I am bound by a tram-line to the city minutes away; to the parklands and clock-towers, the chimneys and flag-poles; to the Beehive Corner and Balfour's.

But the city is an island surrounded by hills and sea. And one day I cross the road, and stare at Hook the bootmaker's from the other side, and see that the silver ribbons stretch in another direction too.

They nibble, as surely as Nan's sewing-machine, through the cement – away from the city, towards the sea and the sand and the tired mothers I see returning with red-faced children; towards the Gulf of St Vincent that laps the boot that kicks at Kangaroo Island in the atlas; towards the blue that is the Indian Ocean, edged with the names of seaside towns that sound of England and poetry: Semaphore and Tennyson, Grange and Henley, Glenelg and Brighton, Seacliff and Marino Rocks.

And then I was on the tram, and it sailed down the Beach Road towards the Plaza Picture Theatre, collecting passengers at every stop. We left St Ives behind, and raced market-gardens blooming with cabbages and crouching figures, jungles of bamboo and lanes of beans, roadside stalls where Italian women with faces like the Madonna and handkerchiefs round their heads sold gladioli and tomatoes, red-brick houses waiting to blaze with Virginia creeper, and the Kooyonga Golf Links where retired executives meditated over bright green grass. Then the tram lurched and stumbled over a bridge, and I saw the river coiled beneath us; watched it – smaller, thread oily marshlands. And then the tram went faster, the back-yards pressed closer, and we peered unashamedly at asbestos bun-galows and ragged gardens choked with alyssum, lobelia, and orange marigolds – tufted French ones and frilly pompon giants. And we surveyed coldly, rotting bicycles and wash-tubs hidden on roof-tops, fowl-houses improvised from bedsteads, limp clothes-lines strung with bathing suits.

Suddenly I caught my breath, leaned forward – and sure enough, caught a glimpse of leaping blue. And lost it behind a hill of tamar-isks. Then, as we rounded another hill, before us appeared a basin-ful of sea, brimming and lurching a pale rim. As the tram surged down Seaview Road, the blueness was everywhere, and so bright that my eyes pricked with pins – I looked away. Then we stopped with a shudder; got off at Main Street, and there were people all about – chattering and gleaming like satiny monkeys, smelling of salt and ice-cream and sun-tan oil.

◆

Yet when the red-brick path is pricked with rain, when the asters are tipped with mildew, and the flower-beds sleep, all my life changes. As the chrysanthemums lurch, their petals stained with mud, my mother tells me she is to marry the man with the mous-tache and the R.S.L. badge who is her friend. As the last leaves fall from the trees, she tells me that we will leave the house in Rose Street. My mother and Nan and Reece and I will live with the man in a new house in a new suburb. And the chrysanthemums are sullied, the earth is hard, rain falls on iron.

Once the words were said, they radiated through the house. They resounded in the passage, hung in corners, sunk into the verandah, floated in sullen puddles on the lawn. Everything was changed. The house belonged to others. The spring that budded already in fruit-trees, the bulbs that waited in the earth, would flourish for them.

And because the garden shrank from me, I shunned it – went only to pluck a root from here, a branch from there; to dig for chrysanthemum and agapanthus, iris and rose. The old wild world was no more. The garden contracted to pot-plants on a sill: four geraniums – white and salmon, pink and rose; scraps of green that were forget-me-not and noon-flower; twigs that held promise of privet hedge and fuchsia. There was no other garden – just trees I used to climb, a clothes-line, a path that led to a lavatory.

We took down curtains and painted walls, coaxed tables from corners, found pencils and sixpences and handkerchiefs lost for years. And strangers plucked at furniture, robbed the specimen shelf, sheathed with newspaper. Charles Ebenezer came down from the wall, the harvest festival dinner-set made islands on a floor.

We lit a fire under the quince – it recalled that other fire that ushered the baker's death. Sparks wreathed the tree – there were no tart fruits, no blotting-paper stars. My grandmother's skin smelt of ash. (And I will dream of quince-trees and fire twenty years later, when iceflowers bloom at the window in a white city pelted by whiteness all night long.)

What we did not burn was thrown in the well. The fairies who stared disappeared with rusted tin and three marble nymphs that sank dully.

On the last day, when I ventured once more into the garden that was not a garden, death was all about: as a mouse – its paws drawn stiffly, its fur damp with rain; at my foot, as a one-winged blowfly stumbled; beside the plant I would not see blossom at its next seventh year; rotting leaves, abandoned snail-shells, a bone.

♦ *Kewpie Doll*

The room was full of stones. Creamy limestone slabs with a texture like velvet, and a cold cheesy smell.

I was sitting in the Printmaking Room at the Art School making a lithograph. I had escaped to a world of my own. All the insect-bite worries fell off me. Nothing counted but my hand with the crayon making marks on the stone. My teacher was a man with silver hair and an accent that clicked at the back of his throat. He meant an outside world oceans away. French chalk fell like snow, there was a polleny drift of resin, a gum-arabic layer that turned the chalky stone as polished as bone. The lovers were captured under a sticky gum veil and there were paper flags to flap with to hasten drying. The pastel ghosts from the Twenties faded away; the modern girls doing Fine Art were meaningless.

I pulled down the handle, the stone went under the press . . . and I peeled the paper off to see my image reversed. I held all the shadowy crayon lines and the crisp lines of the pen on a piece of paper in my hand. Then I inked up again with the roller – not one print, but several . . . all the time keeping the stone damp. The creamy limestone surface was so sensitive, it seemed a living thing. Night swooped over the old building; Miss Dixon was teaching Needlework down the corridor, but in the Printmaking Room I found a new world. I felt Van Gogh and Beardsley were with me. My loneliness petered away. I walked accompanied by my people. It didn't matter that all were ready to doubt me, to see me as just the quiet girl who came from daytime teaching in her sheath frock.

Etching meant the teacher bringing the sheeny grey piece of zinc from the storeroom. I polished till all the greyness turned silver; I placed the zinc on the hot-plate for the smells to begin. There were golden toffee scents as the wax ground melted and I spread it with a roller over the piece of zinc. When the metal was cool again, I drew on it with a sharp-pointed needle. The needle skimmed over the layer of wax, exposing the metal. I drew at the small table by the hot-plate; my hair hid my face in a bell. I was hidden, become just fingers on an etching-needle, drawing out more friends. When the drawing was finished, I put the plate in a tray of acid. Little bubbles rose that I brushed away with a feather. The acid bit the lines of my drawing into the plate. It was a Brothers Grimm process, an occupation for Hansel and Gretel or the Babes in the Wood. Then inking up: forcing printing ink into deep-bitten lines, and then I lay the plate on the bed of the press and carefully placed a piece of damp paper on top of it. Miss Ethel Barringer had chosen the press for the Art School – she was an artist who'd died years ago, as she stooped to pick a blue flower, and I imagined that the cloche-hatted ghosts of the Twenties girls were smiling, turning the handle of the etching press with me. The still moment when the plate was through – even quieter as I folded back the etching blankets; as I peeled away the paper marked with the black spidery lines of an etching. Back to front, inconvenient, devious. No one was about, so I could admire for a moment. Then I quickly hid my pleasure, and started inking the plate for the next print.

I made woodcuts. Faces stared out. Springtime lovers to start with, then women in torment. As well, I gouged out earth mothers with moths in their hair and witchetty grub necklaces; big robust women bowered in leaves.

My grandmother had sewn me a black Italian cloth printing apron. I took it off at the end of the class. There was no time to wash my hands, I covered them with white cotton gloves and walked fast down the Terrace to catch the five to nine train – so tired, but a cosy buzz of happiness inside me; the prints hidden away in a cardboard folder I carried beneath my arm. I walked under the spreading branches of trees, down a leafy green alley. The trees seemed choked with birds; there was a mad singing, and Adelaide was a fantasy in the night.

INDEX OF TOPICS

◆ ◆ ◆ ◆

ACKNOWLEDGEMENTS

◆ ◆ ◆ ◆

The editors and publisher are grateful to the following for the permission to reproduce copyright material:

Angus & Robertson Publishers for Henry Lawson, 'A Fragment of Autobiography' from *Henry Lawson Autobiography and Other Writings*; Mary Gilmore, *Old Days: Old Ways* (1934); Miles Franklin, *My Brilliant Career* (1901), *My Career Goes Bung*, (1946), *Childhood at Brindabella*, (1963).

Jonathan Cape for Patrick White, *Flaws in the Glass* (1981).

Chatto & Windus for David Malouf, *12 Edmondstone Street* (1985); Barbara Hanrahan, *Scent of Eucalyptus* (1973), *Kewpie Doll* (1984).

William Collins for George Johnston, *My Brother Jack* (1964), *Clean Straw for Nothing* (1969); Alexander Chisholm, *The Joy of the Earth* (1969); Xavier Herbert, *Disturbing Element* (1976).

Curtis Brown for Martin Boyd, *Day of My Delight* (Lansdowne 1965).

Clem Christesen for *The Island* (in progress).

Robin Dalton for Robin Eakin, *Aunts up the Cross* (Anthony Blond) 1965).

Faber & Faber for Hal Porter, *Watcher on the Cast Iron Balcony* (1963).

Hamish Hamilton for Graham McInnes, *The Road to Gundagai* (1965), *Humping my Bluey* (1966), *Goodbye Melbourne Town* (1968).

Dorothy Hewett for 'Autobiographically Speaking'.

David Higham and Associates for Keith Hancock, *Country and Calling* (Faber 1954); Stella Bowen, *Drawn from Life* (Collins 1941).

Longman Cheshire for Alan Marshall, *I Can Jump Puddles* (1955), *This is the Grass* (1962), *In Mine Own Heart* (1963).

The Macmillan Company of Australia for Joseph Jenkins, *Diary of a Welsh Swagman* abridged and annotated by William Evans (1975); Judah Waten, *Alien Son* (Angus & Robertson 1952); Roland Robinson, *The Drift of Things* (1973); Kylie Tennant, *The Missing Heir* (1968).

McPhee Gribble Publishers for Chester Eagle, *Mapping the Paddocks* (1985).

The National Library of Australia for John Shaw Neilson, *The Autobiography of John Shaw Neilson* (1978).

Thomas Nelson Australia for Mary Rose Liverani, *Winter Sparrows* (1975).

Joyce Nicholson for 'Destination Uncertain' from *The Half Open Door* (Hale & Iremonger 1982).

Penguin Books Australia for Oriel Gray, *Exit Left* (1985); Bernard Smith, *The Boy Adeodatus* (1984); A. B. Facey, *A Fortunate Life* (Fremantle Art Centre Press 1981); Jack Lindsay, *Life Rarely Tells* (Bodley Head 1958); Joan Lindsay, *Time Without Clocks* (Cheshire 1962); Donald Horne, *The Education of Young Donald* (Angus & Robertson 1967), *Confessions of a New Boy* (Viking 1985); Vincent Buckley, *Cutting Green Hay* (1983); Kevin Gilbert, *Living Black* (1977); Kathleen Fitzpatrick *Solid Bluestone Foundations* (Macmillan 1983).

Elsie Roughsey for Dick Roughsey, *Moon & Rainbow* (Reed 1971).

A. D. Peters & Co Ltd for Clive James, *Unreliable Memoirs* (Jonathan Cape 1980).

Rigby Publishers for Charles Perkins, *A Bastard Like Me* (Ure Smith 1975).

University of Queensland Press for David Malouf, *Johnno* (1975); Hal Porter, *The Paper Chase* (1980).

Australian Autobiography from Penguin

The Boy Adeodatus
The portrait of a lucky young bastard

Bernard Smith

Those who know Bernard Smith, scholar and interpreter of the visual arts, will rightly expect his autobiography to be unconventional. No one can fail to find it extraordinarily moving.

This is the story of an illegitimate son and of the mother who decided to keep rather than destroy him. It is the story, too, of a foster mother who loved children, and of her extended family. Begun in homage to both mothers, the book also become the story of a son's search for the sexual vitality of his lost father.

Highly acclaimed by critics, this extraordinary and moving autobiography recreates vividly the atmosphere of a Sydney suburb around World War I, and subtly explores the changing times and values of his childhood and youth.

'a unique book among Australian autobiographies . . . an autobiography to linger over, to sip, to savour'   Ed Campion, *Bulletin*

'a moving work of art and intellect . . . a celebraton of his childhood, youth and early manhood and the marvellous families with whom he grew up . . . A work of high literary and stylistic achievement'
Peter Ward, *Australian*

'As autobiography, as social history, as Australian art history and as literature, *The Boy Adeodatus* is an important aesthetic event'
Adelaide Advertiser

The Education of Young Donald

Donald Horne

The classic autobiography of a well-known Australian, *The Education of Young Donald* is both the personal story of one man in the twenties and thirties and the story of an entire generation.

'*The Education of Young Donald* is altogether a box of delights . . . and as a series of pictures of a period and a generation, it is admirable. Read it.'   *Australian Book Review*

'*The Education of Young Donald* may well be read for the light it casts on Australia in the reluctant years before the "take off" long after *The Lucky Country* is forgotten'   H. G. Kippax

Exit Left
Memoirs of a Scarlet Woman

Oriel Gray

In *Exit Left* Oriel Gray, playwright, bohemian and free spirit, tells with wry affection of learning to survive without the emotional and political lifelines of her father, lovers and comrades in the unsettled thirties and forties. Her memories evoke the songs that were sung, the jokes that were told, the colours that were worn that season, and all the trifles of her times that now seem significant.

Oriel Gray grew up in Sydney and, as a young romantic, plunged in the passionate and stormy world of New Theatre and the Communist Party. Her revolutionary zeal, however, was sometimes compromised by a tendency to fall in love. She horrified her socialist father by innocently falling for a foreign fascist military officer, and later shocked the party by setting up house with her sister's wayward husband.

'We lived, experienced, laughed, loved, fought, argued, and then lived it all over again.'

Living Black

Kevin Gilbert

'Aboriginal Australia underwent a rape of the soul so profound that the blight continues in the minds of most blacks today.'

Kevin Gilbert has talked with his people and taped their story – in the bush, in small country towns, and in the black ghettos of Sydney and Melbourne.

'What emerges is a damning indictment of the white man for his despicable discrimination, his injustice and intolerance, his ignorance and, above all, his failure to recognize the Aboriginal as a fellow human being — a human being as old as time and an affinity with his land that the white man will never understand.' *Herald*

'A frank and compelling social document which exposes themes and issues important in the everyday lives of Aboriginal Australians. Its criticisms and lessons should not be ignored.' Neville Perkins *Australian*